Alte Brücke (Old Bridge; p211), Heidelberg

GERMANY MEET OUR WRITERS

Andrea Schulte-Peevers
@aschultepeevers

Andrea has written for Lonely Planet for over a quarter century and authored or contributed to well over 100 titles.

Barbara Woolsey
@xo.babxi

Barbara is a travel journalist and guidebook author who has lived in Germany since 2013. She writes about culture, food and lifestyle. When not working for Lonely Planet, find her DJing in Berlin's best clubs.

Contents

Best Experiences 6
Calendar 18
Trip Builder 26
7 Things to Know
About Germany................36
Read, Listen, Watch
& Follow 38

Berlin 40
Trip Builder 42
Practicalities..................... 44
Only in Berlin 46
Capital of Art 48
Berlin After Dark 50
Berlin's Nazi Legacy......... 52
Treasure Island 54
History's Greatest Hits 56
Berlin Wall Demystified ... 59
Listings 64

Day Trip to Potsdam 66

The Baltic Coast & Islands 70
Trip Builder 72
Practicalities......................73
Epically Medieval...............74
Modern German
History 78
Great Outdoors 80
German Riviera 82
Listings 84

Hamburg 86
Trip Builder 88
Practicalities..................... 89
Hidden Gems 90

Ride the Night 94
Audiovisual & Arty 96
Speicherstadt
& HafenCity 98
Listings 100

Central Germany 102
Trip Builder 104
Practicalities....................106
Discover Goethe's
Weimar.............................108
Explore a Storied
Small Town 110
Explore Erfurt's
Historical Legacy............. 112
The Trail of the
Brothers Grimm 116
Follow the Bauhaus Trail...118
Listings 120

Saxony 122
Trip Builder 124
Practicalities....................125
A Gulp of Baroque
in Dresden 126
Riparian Bliss 130
Paint Your Hike 132
Sounds Like Leipzig 134
Mountains of
Abundance 136
Venture into the
German Far East 139
Listings 140

Munich 142
Trip Builder 144
Practicalities....................145
Beer in Munich 146

The Wittelsbachs'
Royal Palaces 150
The Art Scene..................152
The 1972 Olympiapark....156
Listings 158

Bavaria 160
Trip Builder 162
Practicalities....................164
Discover a Beautiful
Altstadt 166
Enjoy Magical
Bamberg...........................168
A Riverside City 170
Füssen's World
Heritage Sites.................. 172
Northern
Romantic Road................178
Southern
Romantic Road................ 181
Listings 184

Freiburg & the Black Forest 186
Trip Builder 188
Practicalities................... 190
Eat at Freiburg's
Münster Market 192
Snowshoe Through
the Black Forest 194
Bake a
Black Forest Cake 196
Race Downhill
on a Toboggan.................198
Gorgeous Gorge Hikes....200
Cycle Around
Lake Constance 204
Listings 208

Above Erfurter Dom (p113), Erfurt

Weekend in Heidelberg	210

Practicalities	236
Arriving	238
Getting Around	240
Safe Travel	242
Money	243
Responsible Travel	244
Accommodation	246
Essentials	248
Language	250

ESSAYS
The Green City	60
Munich's Oktoberfest	148
Mad King Ludwig II	176
The History of the Cuckoo Clock	206
Sibling Rivalry on the Rhine	230

Cologne & the Rhineland	214
Trip Builder	216
Practicalities	217
Cologne Cool	218
Champagne & Altbier	222
Charlemagne's Aachen	224
Cruising into Dragonland	226
Ruhr Reloaded	228
Listings	234

VISUAL GUIDES
Berlin Icons	62
Bavarian Icons	182
German Beer Primer	232

FAIRY-TALE TOWNS

Romantische Strasse (Romantic Road)
Length: 460km
Number of official stops: 29
Official website: romantischestrasse.de

Märchenstrasse (Fairy Tale Road)
Length: 600km
Number of official stops: 50
Official website: deutsche-maerchenstrasse.com

▬ There's something about small-town Germany that lends itself to stories: the half-timbered buildings, the cobblestone squares, the mists that fill medieval lanes on a winter's evening. And then there are the touchstones of how we imagine stories: the Romantic Road, *Grimms' Fairy Tales* and storybook castles. Germany has all of this and so much more.

→ THE BROTHERS GRIMM

Jacob and Wilhelm Grimm were born in Hanau in the early 19th century. They lived in Kassel and collected (and wrote) folktales in their spare time.

Left Quedlinburg (p110) **Right** Statue of the Brothers Grimm, Hanau (p117) **Below** Schloss Neuschwanstein (p173)

THE GRIMM FAIRY TALES

Grimms' Fairy Tales included 'Hansel & Gretel', 'Little Red Riding Hood', 'Cinderella', 'Sleeping Beauty', 'Rapunzel', 'Snow White & the Seven Dwarves' and 'Puss in Boots'.

↑ LUDWIG II & NEUSCHWANSTEIN

King Ludwig II (r 1864–86) was responsible for many of the more extravagant and magical castles and palaces across Bavaria, including the greatest fairy-tale castle of all, Neuschwanstein.

Best Fairy-Tale Experiences

▶ Dream of magic at Schloss Neuschwanstein. (p173)

▶ Travel the postcard-perfect villages of the Romantic Road; linger above all in Rothenburg ob der Tauber. (p178)

▶ Follow the Brothers Grimm along the Märchenstrasse (Fairy Tale Road). (p116)

▶ Climb to the hilltop castle and wander the medieval streets in Quedlinburg. (p110)

▶ Discover the medieval charm of northern Hanseatic towns, such as Stralsund. (p75)

Western Europe's three longest rivers – Danube (2850km), Rhine (1236km) and Elbe (1091km) – pass through Germany.

The Danube rises in Furtwangen im Schwarzwald, in the Black Forest, and flows through 10 countries en route to the Black Sea. Germany has 16 national parks.

NATURAL GERMANY

It may be best known for its charming villages and happening cities, but Germany has an abundance of wild spaces. From the Black Forest in the south to Europe's great rivers and fantastic national parks, Germany is ideally placed to get you out into nature.

Best Natural Experiences

▶ Explore Jasmund National Park, its chalk cliffs an inspiration for many German artists. (p79)

▶ Take a boat trip from Regensburg along the river to the dramatic Danube Gorge, complete with its own monastery. (p170)

▶ Cruise the Rhine south of Cologne through a world of vineyards, castles and pretty towns. (p226)

▶ Take a boat trip down the Elbe River in Saxony, with boats setting out from Dresden. (p130)

ANCIENT HISTORY

You don't have to look too far in Germany to hear the echoes of the distant past. That's because its stories are written in the country's architecture and museums, and in the structures and legacies left behind by the cultural giants who strode the German (and world) stage.

★ THE HANSEATIC LEAGUE

The 13th-century Hanseatic League was a trading alliance of city states with more than 150 members. It was northern Europe's most powerful economic entity.

Best History Experiences

▶ Explore Weimar, forever associated with Johann Wolfgang von Goethe. (p108)

▶ Marvel at the historic riches of Martin Luther's Erfurt. (p112)

▶ Listen to Johann Sebastian Bach's music at Thomaskirche in Leipzig. (p134)

▶ Learn about the Hanseatic League in Lübeck. (p75)

▶ Trace the legacy of Charlemagne in Aachen. (p224)

↙ GOETHE'S WEIMAR

As well as being the preeminent figure of German literature and philosophy, Johann Wolfgang von Goethe (1749–1832) served as a town planner, architect, social reformer and scientist.

This page: Top Lübeck (p75)
Bottom Weimar (p108)
Opposite page: Regensburg (p170)

ALTSTADT ARCHITECTURE

It's not just small-town Germany that excels when it comes to soaring medieval architecture. German rulers down through the centuries have used their cityscapes as statements of power and intent. Sometimes this meant a cathedral for the ages. Elsewhere it was a landmark opera house or the visionary portfolio of Bauhaus architecture. Visiting such sites is like encountering a version of German history written in stone.

Cologne
A signature cathedral

Kölner Dom is, quite simply, one of Europe's finest cathedrals. Whether you climb the 533 steps to the top for superlative views, or admire the gilded interior with its sacred relics, the cathedral dominates the city's skyline as a beacon of architectural heft and significance.

🚆 1hr from Frankfurt am Main
▶ p218

Heidelberg
A luminous university town

Some places just have a special magic and Heidelberg is just such a place. Whether thronging with life and visitors in summer, or turned golden when bathed in misty winter floodlights, Heidelberg is filled with architectural gems, including a castle, the Alte Brücke (Old Bridge) and just about everything in the Altstadt.

🚆 1¼hr from Frankfurt am Main
▶ p210

FROM LEFT: G215/SHUTTERSTOCK, FLORIN CNEJEVICI/SHUTTERSTOCK, © SPSG/REINHARDT & SOMMER, ROLF G WACKENBERG/SHUTTERSTOCK

Potsdam
A pretty palace
In Potsdam, the Schloss Sanssouci (another World Heritage Site) is a former palace retreat of Frederick the Great. Like some gilded architectural fantasy, it's an exquisite (and extensive) palace surrounded by extravagant gardens and it makes for an unmissable day trip from Berlin, just 25km away.

🚆 *35min from Berlin*
▶ p66

Dessau-Rosslau
Bauhaus beauty
Few architectural styles have changed our lives quite like Bauhaus, the influence of which ripples down through every aspect of modern life. With a philosophy that a building's form should enhance its function, Bauhaus most adorns Weimar and Dessau-Rosslau; the latter is home to the genre's finest works.

🚗 *5¼hr from Heidelberg*
▶ p118

Bamberg
An iconic image
Few buildings evoke an entire region quite like Bamberg's superb Altes Rathaus. Straddling the river, this half-timbered treasure combines quaint beauty with an important (and very German) historical story. It was built as part of the struggle between church and secular authorities.

🚆 *35min from Nuremberg*
▶ p168

Regensburg
UNESCO-recognised splendour
Few cities in Germany can match the uniform magnificence of Regensburg. Rising from the banks of the Danube, it's an extraordinary place where you can walk past ornate palaces and glorious churches, then take a boat trip to an astonishing riverside mausoleum.

🚆 *1½hr from Munich*
▶ p170

20TH-CENTURY
ECHOES

For better or worse, Germany was at the heart of many of the 20th century's most important historical moments, from WWII to the fall of the Berlin Wall. The significance of such moments still resonates deeply in this thoughtful country through monuments, museums and in the reinvention of a country from devastated pariah state to a forward-thinking, pro-European leader.

→ THE BERLIN WALL

The Berlin Wall divided Berlin for just over 28 years, from 13 August 1961 to 9 November 1989.

Left St Nikolai Church (p93), Hamburg **Right** Berlin Wall (p40) **Below** Topography of Terror (p52), Berlin

THE BOMBING OF DRESDEN

The bombing of Dresden over three nights (13–15 February 1945) dropped nearly 3000 tonnes of bombs on the city, killing at least 25,000 people, and possibly 10 times that.

↑ BERLIN MUSEUMS & MEMORIALS

Berlin's Nazi past is evident at sights such as the Topography of Terror, Holocaust Memorial and Sachsenhausen concentration camp.

Best 20th-Century Historical Experiences

▶ Relive Berlin's role as history's protagonist at the Reichstag, Brandenburg Gate and remnants of the Berlin Wall. (p40)

▶ Tread lightly through the haunting ruins of St Nikolai Church, a symbol of Hamburg's devastation during WWII. (p93)

▶ Visit Travemünde and Rügen, elegant early-20th-century beach resorts for Europe's rich and famous. (p78)

▶ Get to know Dresden, a baroque city whose reinvention and reconstruction post-WWII is perhaps the most remarkable. (p126)

Germany has an estimated 1300 breweries.

There are 13 officially designated wine-growing regions in Germany, with around 11,000 wineries.

Around six million visitors attend Munich's Oktoberfest, with 35 beer tents dispensing up to seven million litres of beer.

Best Culinary Experiences

▶ Enjoy Franconian regional wines and cooking across Bavaria, including in Nuremberg. (p166)

▶ Bake your very own Black Forest Cake at Cafe Zimmerman in Todtmoos, deep in the Black Forest. (p196)

▶ Indulge your inner foodie at Freiburg's Münster market, with a stirring cathedral backdrop to regional dishes masquerading as street food. (p192)

▶ Play the rivalry between Cologne and Düsseldorf to your advantage by comparing two of Germany's best beer traditions. (p230)

▶ Attend Munich's Oktoberfest by all means, but the city's beer traditions transcend just one festival! (p146)

THE GERMAN **TABLE**

Germany has built its culinary reputation around tradition and excellence, and foodie travellers will find much to entice and even determine their path through the country. From centuries-old beer traditions to respected wine regions, and from old-school taverns serving local specialities to temples to modern innovation, Germany has it all.

OUTDOOR ACTIVITIES

Germany's wild places are ripe for exploration, from winter activities in the south to wandering through national parks and other protected areas. Ski resorts are never far away, and snowshoeing, tobogganing, hiking and cycling are all ways to get out and appreciate the country's picturesque landscapes.

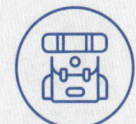

Best Active Experiences

▶ Hike Wutach and Ravenna gorges and the trails of the Black Forest in Germany's southwest. (p200)

▶ Circumnavigate Lake Constance, Europe's third-largest, on a bicycle. (p204)

▶ Follow the 116km Malerweg (Painters' Trail) through the Elbe Valley of Saxony. (p132)

▶ Hike through Saxony's fascinating Ore Mountains. (p136)

▶ Take Germany's longest toboggan in Todtnau. (p198)

★ **WHEN TO SKI**

The German ski season (which is also when you can go snowshoeing or tobogganing) runs from December to March.

← **WHEN TO HIKE**

The best hiking months are May to September, though it can depend on the year – some years, trails don't open until well into June.

This page: Top The Malerweg (Painters' Trail; p132)
Bottom Ore Mountains (p136)
Opposite page: Münster market (p192), Freiburg

MODERN GERMAN LIFE

Germany's history is a powerful lure for travellers, but even though the backdrop may date back centuries, this is a modern, dynamic country with cities to match. Nights hum with activity, and the nation's cultural life similarly sparks off in all manner of creative directions. It can be an intoxicating place.

Düsseldorf
The Ruhr reimagined

It's not the sort of place that people know much about, but Düsseldorf is so much fun, with its very own beer and hundreds of Altstadt bars in which to enjoy it, plus a Frank Gehry–reimagined harbourfront, a cutting-edge art scene and a multicultural demographic mix that adds so much to the city.

🚆 1¼hr from Frankfurt am Main
▶ p222

Cologne
German culture and architecture

We have a solution to the age-old Düsseldorf–Cologne competition: visit both. With its own beer, museums dedicated to subjects as diverse as chocolate and the Romans, a world-class art gallery and a sculpture garden for cocktails, this is one city that captures the joy of being in Germany.

🚆 1hr from Frankfurt am Main
▶ p218

FROM LEFT: JORG GREUEL /GETTY IMAGES, CKTRAVELS.COM/SHUTTERSTOCK, IRINA WS/SHUTTERSTOCK, STEWART MARSDEN/GETTY IMAGES

German Riviera
Baltic resorts
Coastal Mecklenburg-Western Pomerania, where Germany's Baltic coast bumps into Poland, is the country's Riviera and has been a summer playground for locals for more than a century. Highlights among many include the car-free joys of riding a horse-dawn carriage around Hiddensee Island and swimming and sunning on Usedom Island.

🚢 *2½hr from Stralsund*
▶ p82

Hamburg
Germany in microcosm
It's impossible not to fall in love with Hamburg. The city is almost like all of Germany in one place, from stylish and cool (Elbphilharmonie and Speicherstadt) to risqué and kitsch (Reeperbahn) and gritty and authentic (St Pauli), while being filled with historic treasures (the Rathaus and Deichstrasse).

🚆 *1hr 10min from Hanover*
▶ p86

Berlin
Europe's coolest city?
Berlin has long been one of Europe's most happening cities, but where trends come and go elsewhere, Berlin leads and moves with the times, always at the forefront of artistic, cultural and culinary trends and with a full board of festivals. And its nights never seem to end.

🚆 *2½hr from Hamburg*
▶ p40

Nuremberg
Christmas market and old town
With its expansive and lively old town, Nuremberg is one of Germany's most engaging cities, but it becomes utterly irresistible from late November when its world's-best *Weihnachtsmarkt* (Christmas market) takes over the Altstadt. The food, the atmosphere, the architectural backdrop – there really is no better place to be at Christmas.

🚆 *1hr from Munich*
▶ p166

0 — 100 km
0 — 50 miles

The best bet for a blue-sky holiday in Germany isn't in midsummer but in May, June and September.

Demand for accommodation peaks during July and August. View tours and overnight adventures in advance at lonelyplanet.com.

↗ **Summer Pride**
Pride festivals, whether smaller local gatherings or drawing a million or more people in Berlin and Cologne, celebrate LGBTIQ+ communities with parades, parties and protests.

Come June, life moves outdoors as the summer solstice means the sun doesn't set until around 9.30pm.

JUNE — Average daytime max: 22°C — Days of rainfall: 14.3 (Berlin) — **JULY**

Germany in SUMMER

FROM LEFT: FILMBILDFABRIK/SHUTTERSTOCK, R.CLASSEN/SHUTTERSTOCK
PICTURE ALLIANCE/GETTY, PICTURE ALLIANCE/GETTY IMAGES
BOTTOM: D BUSQUETS/SHUTTERSTOCK

↓ Samba Festival

A vibrant celebration of music and dance, the Samba Festival transforms tranquil Coburg into a pulsating 'Little Rio'.

▶ Coburg

▶ samba-festival.de

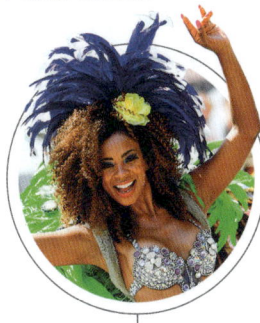

→ Schleswig-Holstein Musik Festival

During the Schleswig-Holstein Musik Festival, listen to live classical, jazz, pop and electronic music in castles, churches, warehouses and animal barns.

▶ shmf.de

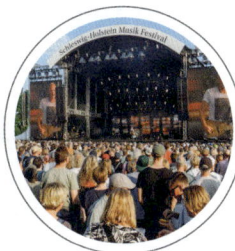

July and August often bring heatwaves, which can trigger sudden and intense thunderstorms, especially in the afternoons and evenings.

Average daytime max: 22°C
Days of rainfall: 13.9

AUGUST

Average daytime max: 24°C
Days of rainfall: 13.4

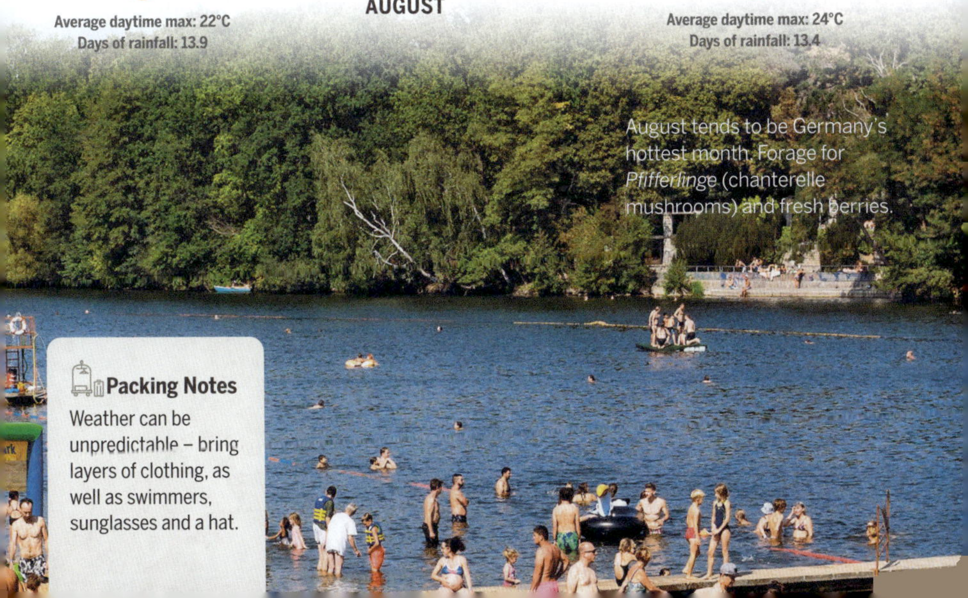

August tends to be Germany's hottest month. Forage for *Pfifferlinge* (chanterelle mushrooms) and fresh berries.

Packing Notes

Weather can be unpredictable – bring layers of clothing, as well as swimmers, sunglasses and a hat.

↘ Oktoberfest

This most famous of German celebrations actually begins in late September most years. Munich comes alive.
▶ Munich
▶ oktoberfest.de
▶ p148

↓ Reeperbahnfestival

Live music of every imaginable genre cranks up at St Pauli venues (from nightclubs to churches) at Hamburg's biggest bash.
▶ Hamburg
▶ reeperbahnfestival.com

The main travel season is over, making September the perfect month for travelling without the summer crowds.

September is a fabulous month, with milder weather – it's often sunny but not too hot.

SEPTEMBER

Average daytime max: 19°C
Days of rainfall: 13

OCTOBER

Germany in AUTUMN

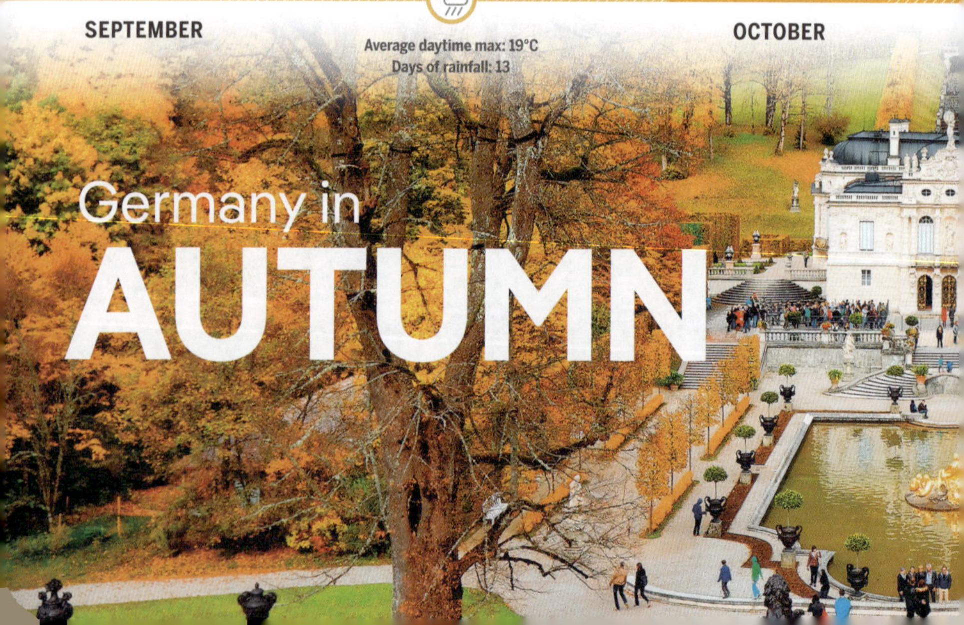

↘ Cannstatter Volksfest

Stuttgart's Cannstatter Wasen lifts the spirits with oompah bands, carnival rides and fireworks.
▶ Stuttgart
▶ cannstatter-volksfest.de

↗ Wine Festivals

Keep your ear to the ground as wine regions often celebrate the grape harvest with much merriment in autumn.

As the weather cools, the leaves start to change colour in forest areas around the end of September.

FROM LEFT: FOOTTOO/SHUTTERSTOCK, PICTURE ALLIANCE/GETTY IMAGES, ATCHACAPTURE/SHUTTERSTOCK, MO PHOTOGRAPHY BERLIN/SHUTTERSTOCK
BOTTOM: AARONCHENPS2/SHUTTERSTOCK, BUILDING SHOWN COURTESY OF THE BAVARIAN PALACE ADMINISTRATION, WWW.SCHLOESSER.BAYERN.DE

GERMANY PLAN BY SEASON

Average daytime max: 13°C
Days of rainfall: 12

NOVEMBER

Average daytime max: 6°C
Days of rainfall: 14.3

November is a quiet month as the weather cools and rain is never far away. But there are few queues at tourist sights.

🧳 Packing Notes

Rain is always possible: a waterproof coat and sturdy shoes are a good idea for all-weather sightseeing.

Snowfall typically occurs from December to March, but milder winters are increasingly the norm, even in the Alps.

↙ Christmas Markets

Mulled wine, spicy gingerbread and shimmering ornaments are staples of German Christmas markets. Nuremberg's Christkindlesmarkt is especially famous.

▶ Nuremberg
▶ p167

Unpredictable winters have an effect on skiing and many resorts now rely on artificial snow, despite high cost and environmental concerns. Pray for snow.

December–January is a mini high season, but by mid-January it's mostly Germans who are travelling; ski resorts are full.

DECEMBER

Average daytime max: 2°C
Days of rainfall: 15.8

JANUARY

Germany in
WINTER

→ Berlinale Film Festival

One of the world's most prestigious film festivals, the Berlinale Film Festival runs for two weeks of screenings and glamour parties.
▶ Berlin
▶ berlinale.de

↓ Carnival

Carnival is celebrated with costumed street partying and parades. The biggest parties are in Düsseldorf, Cologne, Mainz, the Black Forest and Munich.

Short and cold days make this a good time to make in-depth explorations of museums, churches and hearty winter cooking.

FEBRUARY

Average daytime max: 1°C
Days of rainfall: 14.6

Average daytime max: 3°C
Days of rainfall: 12.3

One of Germany's coldest months, February is good for skiing and quiet attractions, although it can feel like high season in the Alps.

Packing Notes

Winters can get fiercely cold, so pack gloves, a hat, a heavy coat and boots.

By March, days get longer, temperatures warm ever so slightly and the first signs of spring are in the air.

↓ The Föhn

Be ready for the Föhn, a warm, dry down-slope alpine wind in Bavaria that sparks quick temperature swings.

March is also when fresh herring hits the menus in coastal regions; dishes with *Bärlauch* (wild garlic) are all the rage.

↓ Easter

Easter is second only to Christmas when it comes to German celebrations; many towns (including Nuremberg) put on large Easter markets.

MARCH

Average daytime max: 7°C
Days of rainfall: 12.3

APRIL

Germany in
SPRING

FROM LEFT: KARL-JOSEF HILDENBRAND/GETTY IMAGES, PHOTOCREW1/SHUTTERSTOCK, PICTURE ALLIANCE/GETTY IMAGES, MO PHOTOGRAPHY BERLIN/SHUTTERSTOCK, PICTURE ALLIANCE/GETTY IMAGES BOTTOM: BRULIA/SHUTTERSTOCK

Bach Festival

Experience baroque brilliance at the Thüringer Bachwochen, where music echoes through centuries-old churches and castles in Bach's home region.

▶ thueringer-bachwochen.de

▶ p114

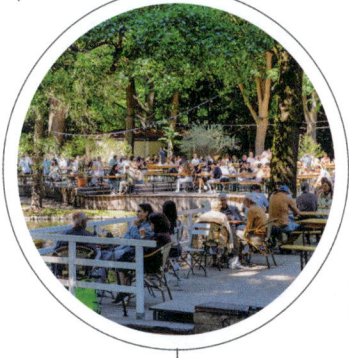

↘ Walpurgisnacht

Young and old dress up as witches and warlocks for the Witches' Sabbath festival (30 April) in the Harz; it's a great time to be in Quedlinburg.

▶ Quedlinburg

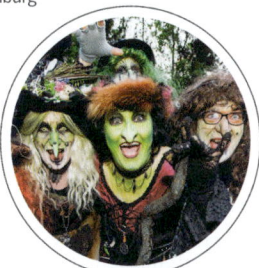

May is not quite summer, but it can be even better: nice weather, crowds are yet to arrive and beer gardens hum.

Average daytime max: 13°C
Days of rainfall: 13.1

MAY

Average daytime max: 19°C
Days of rainfall: 14

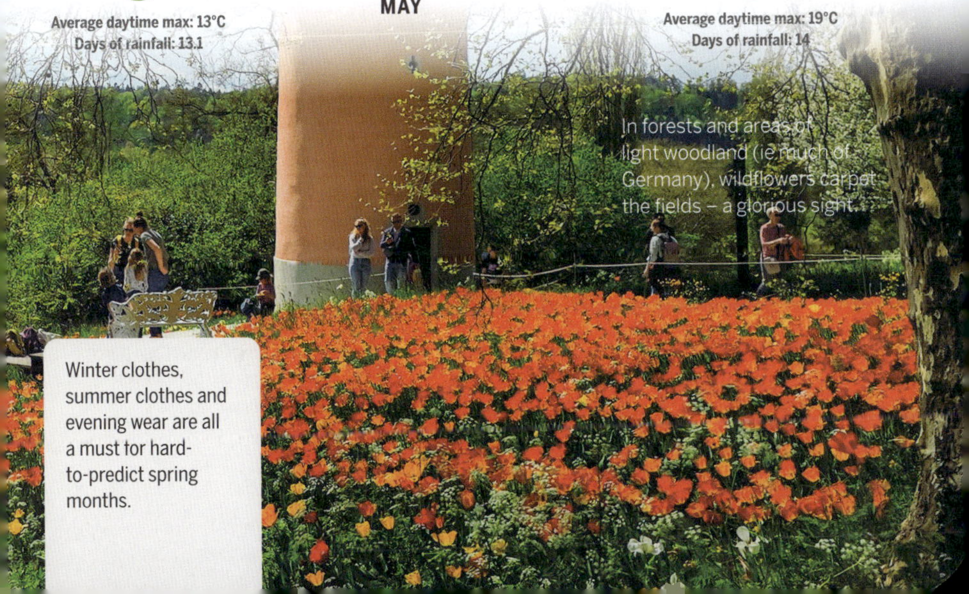

In forests and areas of light woodland (ie much of Germany), wildflowers carpet the fields – a glorious sight.

Winter clothes, summer clothes and evening wear are all a must for hard-to-predict spring months.

BIG-CITY GERMANY
Trip Builder

TAKE YOUR PICK OF MUST-SEES AND HIDDEN GEMS

Germany's cities are exciting places to visit, and a trip in which you spend time in just a handful will leave you with so many lasting memories of this remarkable country. Begin in Hamburg, end in Munich and have a whole lot of fun along the way.

🗺 Trip Notes

Hub towns Hamburg, Berlin

How long Allow 10 days to two weeks

Getting around Travelling between the cities by train makes sense, avoiding traffic snarls and parking problems. All cities have excellent public transport.

Tips Ask at each city's tourist office about discount cards – most cities have them and they offer discounted entry to attractions and public transport, often with a free guided tour thrown in.

Düsseldorf
Flying under the radar, Düsseldorf is one cool city. It's a city that knows how to have a good time, especially with its very own beer, as well as all manner of museums and galleries.

🚆 6½hr from Dresden

Cologne
Come to see the cathedral – one of Germany's finest – by all means, but art, architecture, local beer, a buzzing Carnival and much more will keep you here longer.

🚆 1hr from Düsseldorf

FROM LEFT: PHOTOFIRES/SHUTTERSTOCK, R.CLASSEN/SHUTTERSTOCK, BLAKE HORN FOR LONELY PLANET, TATIANA DIUVBANOVA/SHUTTERSTOCK

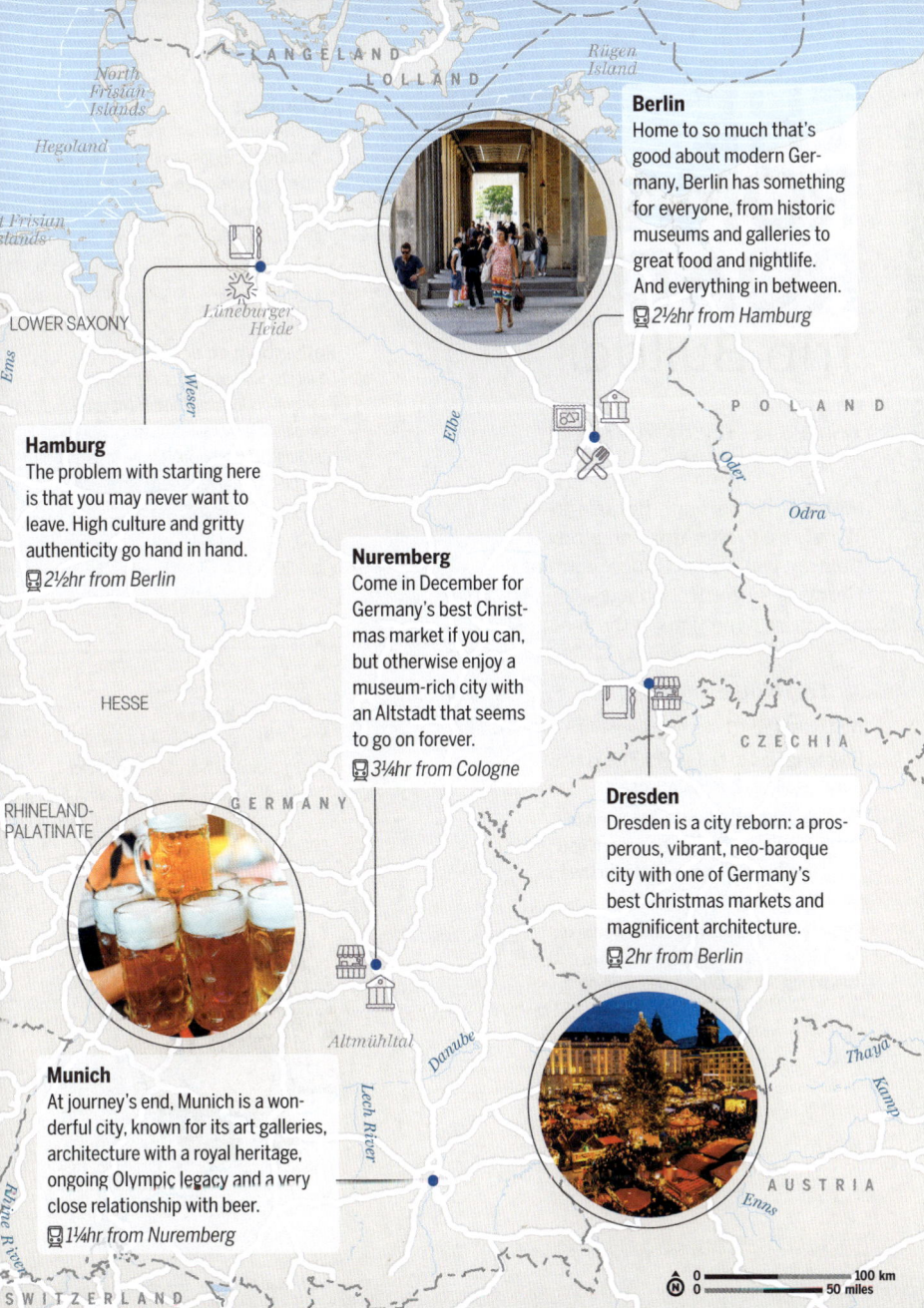

Berlin
Home to so much that's good about modern Germany, Berlin has something for everyone, from historic museums and galleries to great food and nightlife. And everything in between.
🚆 2½hr from Hamburg

Hamburg
The problem with starting here is that you may never want to leave. High culture and gritty authenticity go hand in hand.
🚆 2½hr from Berlin

Nuremberg
Come in December for Germany's best Christmas market if you can, but otherwise enjoy a museum-rich city with an Altstadt that seems to go on forever.
🚆 3¼hr from Cologne

Dresden
Dresden is a city reborn: a prosperous, vibrant, neo-baroque city with one of Germany's best Christmas markets and magnificent architecture.
🚆 2hr from Berlin

Munich
At journey's end, Munich is a wonderful city, known for its art galleries, architecture with a royal heritage, ongoing Olympic legacy and a very close relationship with beer.
🚆 1¼hr from Nuremberg

THE ROMANTIC ROAD
Trip Builder

TAKE YOUR PICK OF MUST-SEES AND HIDDEN GEMS

Drive through Bavaria from Würzburg to the Alps and along the way you'll pass a succession of Germany's prettiest villages. This is no tourist hype. This is the real deal.

Trip Notes

Hub towns Würzburg, Augsburg

How long One to two weeks. This is slow travel – take as long as you can.

Getting around Although a version of this is possible by public transport, you really need your own wheels to do the full 460km.

Tips Try to avoid visiting Rothenburg ob der Tauber on a weekend – the town and its parking areas can get overwhelmed.

Würzburg
In the centre of a major wine-producing region and known for its culinary excellence, Würzburg has a fabulous fortress and fine museums.
🚆 *2hr from Munich*

Rothenburg ob der Tauber
Of all the Romantic Road's towns, Rothenburg ob der Tauber most resembles a fairy tale, awash in medieval buildings along cobblestone streets and encircled by ancient defensive walls.
🚗 *50min from Würzburg*

Nördlingen
The almost circular small town of Nördlingen is a tangle of old, old streets, with a massive church rising above it all – climb to the top for extraordinary views.
🚗 *35min from Dinkelsbühl*

Dinkelsbühl
Smaller and much quieter than Rothenburg, Dinkelsbühl is another medieval gem with a landmark late-Gothic church, all clustered behind high walls with watchtowers looking out over pretty Bavarian countryside.
🚗 *35min from Rothenburg ob der Tauber*

Harburg
More a castle than a town, Harburg is like a film set, so closely does it resemble a child's evocation of a castle. It's so big, the Romantic Road passes *underneath*.
🚗 *25min from Nördlingen*

Donauwörth
The Danube and the Romantic Road come together, and part of the old town sits right on the river. Park outside the city centre and walk with wonder.
🚗 *15min from Harburg*

Landsberg am Lech
One of the least-known towns along the Romantic Road, pretty Landsberg is a worthy stop with all the necessary ingredients – old churches, old-fashioned walls and postcard-ready streets.
🚗 *35min from Augsburg*

Augsburg
One of the oldest cities in Germany and the Romantic Road's largest, Augsburg has an ancient core peppered with spires and buildings that date back to the Middle Ages.
🚗 *40min from Donauwörth*

THE GERMAN HEARTLAND
Trip Builder

TAKE YOUR PICK OF MUST-SEES AND HIDDEN GEMS

The geographic heart of the country is also its cultural heartland, an area where history, architecture and other cultural touchstones have come together through the centuries. It's like trying to take in all of Germany in one concentrated dose.

🗺 Trip Notes

Hub towns Regensburg, Weimar, Dresden
How long Allow one week to 10 days
Getting around You could do this route on public transport but it will take longer; rent your own wheels and go at your own speed.
Tips Save the car for intercity travel: drive to the heart of each town, park your vehicle and explore on foot.

FROM LEFT: MASOODASLAMI.DE/SHUTTERSTOCK, MATT MUNRO/LONELY PLANET, TRABANTOS/SHUTTERSTOCK, BUILDING SHOWN COURTESY OF THE BAVARIAN PALACE ADMINISTRATION, WWW.SCHLOESSER.BAYERN.DE, ETTMER PHOTOGRAPHY/SHUTTERSTOCK

Kassel
Brought alive by its connection to the master storytellers, the Brothers Grimm, Kassel has a Grimm-themed festival and a world-class archive of Europe's favourite stories.
🚗 2½hr from Bamberg

Erfurt
One of the loveliest old cities in what was once East Germany, Erfurt has heritage squares, a 14th-century covered stone bridge and twin cathedrals.
🚗 2hr from Kassel

Quedlinburg
A Romanesque church, a Renaissance palace and half-timbered medieval facades seemingly at every turn – the village of Quedlinburg has attractions far out of proportion to its small size.

🚗 *2hr from Weimar*

Leipzig
Among the most dynamic cities in the former East Germany, Leipzig is perhaps best known as the one-time home of Johann Sebastian Bach. He composed many of his masterpieces (and played the organ) here.

🚗 *1½hr from Dresden*

Weimar
It's difficult to overstate the importance of Weimar in German history: without it, there may have been no Enlightenment. Goethe made Weimar his own, and Bauhaus architecture also left its mark.

🚗 *30min from Erfurt*

Regensburg
There are few more beautiful old towns than the World Heritage–listed core of Regensburg. Within reach of the city on the Danube is Walhalla, an astonishing homage to Germanic greatness.

🚗 *1¾hr from Munich*

Bamberg
Showpiece architecture, one of Germany's most celebrated beers and a wonderfully intact old town littered with old-world architecture, both sacred and secular… Bamberg is one of the most charming small cities in Germany.

🚗 *1¾hr from Regensburg*

THE BALTIC NORTH
Trip Builder

TAKE YOUR PICK OF MUST-SEES AND HIDDEN GEMS

More accustomed to German tourists than foreigners, Germany's Baltic coastline often surprises those who make it this far north. This is a little-known realm of medieval cities and stately resort towns running all the way to the Polish border.

🗺 Trip Notes

Hub towns Lübeck, Stralsund

How long In a week you can cover this route without rushing, but it'll take longer if you decide to lie on a beach.

Getting around Public transport for smaller towns is sporadic, and on weekends the frequency of departures drops for everywhere else.

Tips Depending on your style of travel, renting a car and exploring on your own may be a cheaper option than going on guided tours.

FROM LEFT: MP_FOTO/SHUTTERSTOCK, ANDREW MAYOVSKYY/SHUTTERSTOCK, FOOTTOO/SHUTTERSTOCK, ANDREW MAYOVSKYY/SHUTTERSTOCK

Flensburg
Begin a short walk from Denmark in Flensburg, a lively port town with a long old town and lots of waterfront places to eat and drink.
🚗 2¾hr from Hamburg

Lübeck
The one-time heart of the prosperous Hanseatic League of trading city states, Lübeck combines numerous echoes of that period with lovely squares, markets and feel-good streets.
🚗 2¼hr from Flensburg

Travemünde
Like a German Nice, Travemünde once drew all manner of celebrities and cultural luminaries. Stately hotels, wellness retreats and fine-dining tearooms suggest they still know how to look after visitors.
🚗 *35min from Lübeck*

Jasmund National Park
Art has always taken inspiration from life in Jasmund National Park on the island of Rügen. The German master painter, Caspar David Friedrich, immortalised the park's Königsstuhl white chalk cliffs.
🚗 *1hr from Stralsund*

Stralsund
It's easy to lose yourself in Stralsund's streets, which seem little changed in centuries – its churches, squares and other public spaces are classic *Backsteingotik* (red-brick Gothic gabled architecture).
🚗 *1½hr from Wismar*

Greifswald
Arrayed in part around a cute harbour, Greifswald survived WWII unscathed and it's long been a favourite of painters (Friedrich again) for its charming *Backsteingotik*.
🚗 *80 min from Jasmund National Park*

Wismar
If Wismar looks familiar, it may be because it has frequently been a star of the silver screen. In real life, this World Heritage–listed old town has gabled roofscapes and an intriguing history.
🚗 *1hr from Travemünde*

ACROSS THE SOUTH
Trip Builder

TAKE YOUR PICK OF MUST-SEES AND HIDDEN GEMS

At either end of this trip, you'll visit one of Germany's most popular attractions. In between, you'll leave the tourist crowds behind and discover a side to Germany that many tourists bypass, enjoying a delightful combination of historic towns and fresh air with big horizons as you go.

🗺️ Trip Notes

Hub towns Munich, Stuttgart

How long Allow one week

Getting around You'll probably get a better deal and have more choice of car rental if you pick your car up in Munich or, better still, Munich airport, as you can avoid driving into Munich.

Tips It's possible (and much more pleasurable) to avoid the autobahns altogether and drive each leg on backroads.

FROM LEFT: FRANCESCO BONINO/SHUTTERSTOCK, STEVE BARZE/SHUTTERSTOCK, S.BORISOV/SHUTTERSTOCK, FEELTHEDRONE/SHUTTERSTOCK

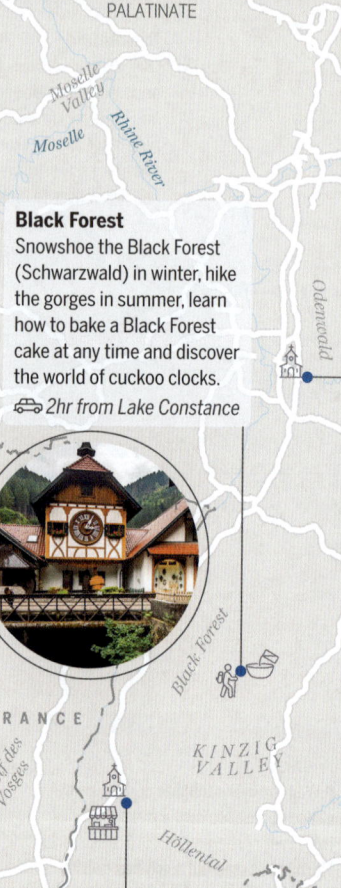

Black Forest
Snowshoe the Black Forest (Schwarzwald) in winter, hike the gorges in summer, learn how to bake a Black Forest cake at any time and discover the world of cuckoo clocks.
🚗 *2hr from Lake Constance*

Freiburg
Enjoy the quiet provincial atmosphere of Freiburg, one of southern Germany's more appealing small cities, with a fine cathedral. Sample local cuisine in the Münster market.
🚗 *1hr from Black Forest*

Heidelberg

Baroque Heidelberg deserves as much time as you can spare. A riverside location, a ruined castle, an ancient university, an intimate Altstadt, buzzing streets – what's not to like?

🚗 2hr from Freiburg

Lake Constance

Germany's largest lake is a scenic world of agreeable lakeside towns and alpine views. Rent a bicycle and cycle the lakeshore as far as your legs will carry you.

🚗 2hr from Wieskirche

Wieskirche

If you're a lover of the baroque, the pilgrimage church of Wieskirche has a vivid interior of ornate gold decoration and frescoes. It's not to be missed.

🚗 30min from Füssen

Füssen

Füssen is a pretty little town with a series of big drawcards on its doorstep. One of Europe's most celebrated castles, Neuschwanstein (pictured), sits against a backdrop of splendid alpine scenery.

🚗 1¾hr from Munich

7 Things to Know About
GERMANY

INSIDER TIPS TO HIT THE GROUND RUNNING

1 Beer Is Life

They take beer seriously in Germany; at last count there were more than 1300 breweries and this number is growing all the time. All are subject to one of the world's oldest food regulations, the 1516 Reinheitsgebot (Beer Purity Law), which allows only water, barley and hops in the brewing process. To avoid disappointment, be aware that Munich's Oktoberfest always begins in September.

▶ Learn more about German beer on p232.

2 A Sausage Isn't a Sausage

As for beer, so too for sausages, which may just be Europe's most underrated street food. There are strict rules and traditions surrounding sausages and almost every region seems to have its own variety. At last count, there were more than 1500 different types in Germany. There's Berlin's famous currywurst. Or Nuremberg's light-spiced, smaller, thinner Nürnberger Rostbratwurst. Or the Coburger, Bavaria's longest sausage.

▶ See more about food on p14.

3 Smoking

Germans smoke more than perhaps you might expect (20% of the adult population) and public smoking rules differ from state to state; they're often less strict than in other European countries.

▶ See more on p249.

4 Summerloch

The *Summerloch* (summer hole) is when schoolchildren have six weeks off in summer and the whole country seems to be out of the office.

▶ See more about Germany in summer on p18.

5 Cash or Card?

There aren't many places in Germany now where you can't pay with a card, but cash remains more widespread than you might expect (and more so than elsewhere in Europe). In many places, including cafes and pubs, cash is very often the preferred mode of payment; set aside some smaller bills for tips and emergencies.

▶ See more about money on p241.

6 Public Nudity

Germans are passionate believers in *Freikörperkultur* (FKK), or free body culture. This proudly unselfconscious cultural tradition embraces nudity as natural, not naughty, and it's as much a part of the German cultural identity as enjoying a crisp Pilsner and a *Currywurst* in a beer garden. FKK isn't about exhibitionism. It's a lifestyle choice, one that believes in being free to embrace your body without shame or stigma. It also puts the benefits of allowing nature direct contact with the body as an important facet of body health.

None of this means, of course, that you can simply strip off in public whenever the urge takes you. Many parks, lakes and spas, such as Munich's central English Garden, have dedicated FKK zones where anyone is welcome to get nude without any legal ramifications. However, the movement also encourages nude hiking, cycling, camping and sports, often organised by FKK *Verbände* (clubs).

▶ See more about etiquette on p248.

7 Speed Limits

Yes, it's true – there are no speed limits on about 70% of German autobahns (freeways), though 130km/h is recommended. However fast you decide to go, be aware that other drivers may be going very fast – stay out of the fast lane unless you're overtaking.

▶ See more on p240.

FROM LEFT: LEMONO/SHUTTERSTOCK, ONLY_UP/SHUTTERSTOCK, YEVHENIIA LYTVYNOVYCH/SHUTTERSTOCK, RUFAZILLU/SHUTTERSTOCK, GRAPHIX DESIGN/SHUTTERSTOCK, THE8MONKEY/SHUTTERSTOCK.

Read, Listen, Watch & Follow

 READ

Grimms' Fairy Tales (Jacob & Wilhelm Grimm; 1812) Classic of European storytelling: read the originals before watching on Disney.

The Bridge of the Golden Horn (Emine Sevgi Özdamar; 1988) Themes of migration and identity in 1970s West Berlin.

Stasiland (Anna Funder; 2004) The Stasi's vast spying apparatus, as seen by both victims and perpetrators.

The Projectionists (Clemens Meyer; 2024) Compelling characters masterfully offset against the backdrop of an unravelling Europe.

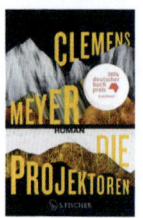

 LISTEN

Symphony No 9 (Beethoven; 1824) An exuberant composition incorporating Schiller's 'Ode to Joy'. Or pick anything by Handel, Brahms…

Mutter (Rammstein; 2001) This genre-busting album showcases the diverse talents of an iconic band with thought-provoking lyrics.

Geschichte ist Gegenwart: The New Germany (Katja Hoyer and Oliver Moody; 2022–25) Podcast with insights into culture, society and politics.

Germany: Memories of a Nation (Neil MacGregor; 2014) Podcast exploring six centuries of German history, using figures from art, literature and politics.

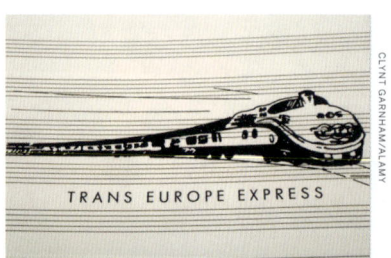

Trans-Europe Express (Kraftwerk; 1977; pictured above) One of four Kraftwerk albums to make *Rolling Stone*'s list of Germany's all-time-best 50 albums.

WATCH

All Quiet on the Western Front (Edward Berger; 2022) German soldiers during WWI.

The Lives of the Others (Florian Henckel von Donnersmarck; 2006; pictured bottom right) A Stasi agent questions surveillance and his role in it.

Run Lola Run (Tom Tykwer; 1998) Stylish, fast-paced thriller with killer techno soundtrack capturing Berlin's late-90s energy.

Unorthodox (Maria Schrader; 2020) A young Hasidic woman escapes from Brooklyn and is spiritually reborn in Berlin.

Dying (Mattias Glasner; 2024) Multi-award-winning epic of dysfunctional family life.

FOLLOW

Ausländer (auslanderblog.com) Travel news and destination tips.

The Local (thelocal.com/category/germany-news) What's happening.

Deutsche Welle (dw.com) News and human interest.

I Am Expat (iamexpat.de) German social-interest site with latest news.

Der Spiegel (spiegel.de) Respected news and analysis.

BERLIN

HISTORY | CULTURE | NIGHTLIFE

RESEARCHED BY ANDREA SCHULTE-PEEVERS

- **Trip Builder** (p42)
- **Practicalities** (p44)
- **Only in Berlin** (p46)
- **Capital of Art** (p48)
- **Berlin After Dark** (p50)
- **Berlin's Nazi Legacy** (p52)
- **Treasure Island** (p54)
- **History's Greatest Hits** (p56)
- **Berlin Wall Demystified** (p59)
- **The Green City** (p60)
- **Berlin Icons** (p62)
- **Listings** (p64)

BERLIN
Trip Builder

Berlin delivers a kaleidoscope of experiences, from world-class art and poignant history to wild nightlife, quirky hangouts and vast green escapes, all wrapped in the city's trademark blend of grit, creativity and anything-goes energy.

Step into Berlin Wall drama at the **Gedenkstätte Berliner Mauer** (p58)
🚶 1min from S-Bahn Nordbahnhof

Glide past historic Berlin icons on a **Spree River cruise boat** (p55)
🚶 5min from Museumsinsel U-Bahn

Hunt down your favourite artefact among the treasures of **Museum Island** (p54)
🚶 2min from U-Bahn Museumsinsel

Confront Nazi history in chilling detail at the **Topography of Terror** (p52) exhibit
🚶 6min from Potsdamer Platz station

Scarf a doner kebab, then test your nightlife stamina on a **bar-hop around Kreuzberg** (p50)
🚶 Right at Kottbusser Tor U-Bahn station

PRENZLAUER BERG

ALT-HOHENSCHÖNHAUSEN

Belt your heart out at Bearpit Karaoke in **Mauerpark** (p58)
🚶 8min from U-Bahn Eberswalder Strasse

Track down the famous 'kiss' mural at the **East Side Gallery** (p58)
🚶 2min from bus 300 stop Berlin, East Side Gallery

FENNPFUHL

FRIEDRICHSHAIN

LICHTENBERG

Cool off on a hot day with a cocktail and a dip in the **Badeschiff** (p65)
🚶 10min from S-Bahn Treptower Park

Engelbecken

RUMMELSBURG

Urbanhafen   Landwehrkanal

Vor dem Schlesischen Tor

FRIEDRICHSFELDE

ALT-TREPTOW

Cycle down the smooth runways of **Tempelhofer Feld** (p46)
🚶 10min from Boddinstrasse U-Bahn

NEUKÖLLN

Explore trippy, light-filled installations at **Dark Matter** (p47)
🚶 5min from tram stop Gustav-Holzmann-Strasse

Spree River

PLANTERWALD

PREVIOUS SPREAD: BELUSUAB/SHUTTERSTOCK
FROM LEFT: SYLVAIN SONNET/GETTY IMAGES, TURTIX/SHUTTERSTOCK,
MARK READ/LONELY PLANET, FDR STOCK/SHUTTERSTOCK

Practicalities

ARRIVING

Berlin Brandenburg Airport Berlin's primary gateway is connected to the city (14 to 35 minutes) by FEX Airport Express and RE20, RB24 and RB32 trains several times an hour. Buy an ABC tariff (€5) ticket at vending machines on level E0 of Terminal 1. Taxis and ride-hailing services cost €50 to €80.

Berlin Hauptbahnhof Central train station, served by S-Bahn, U-Bahn, buses and trams for onward travel. Taxis and ride-hailing services pick up on Europaplatz.

HOW MUCH FOR A

Currywurst
€3.50

Half-litre beer
€4–6

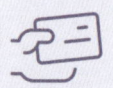

Public transport 24-hour pass
€11.20

GETTING AROUND

U-Bahn (subway, U1, U2 etc) The quickest way to travel. Runs from 4am until about 12.30am, with all-night services on Friday, Saturday and public holidays.

S-Bahn (suburban train, S1, S2 etc) Same hours as the U-Bahn, but runs less frequently and makes fewer stops – useful for longer distances.

Bus and tram Slower but great for cheap sightseeing, especially lines 100, 200 and 300. Night buses run half-hourly between 12.30am and 4.30am.

WHEN TO GO

JAN–MAR
Cold, dark, but blissfully crowd-free, with culture in full swing.

APR–JUN
Mild and often sunny – beer gardens buzz and festivals fill the streets.

JUL–SEP
Warm to hot and perfect for outdoor anything, with the odd thunderstorm.

OCT–DEC
Autumn foliage and Christmas markets brighten darkening days.

EATING & DRINKING

Don't leave town without gobbling a *Currywurst*, Berlin's cult snack: fried sausage, vegan or classic, drenched in curry-dusted, spiced tomato sauce.

Invented in Berlin in 1971 by Turkish immigrants, the Berlin-style doner kebab combines spit-roasted meat, salad and garlicky yoghurt in a pita.

Best currywurst Curry 36 (served till 5am).
Best market hall Markthalle Neun (p64).

WHERE TO STAY

Pick an area near where you plan to spend the most time to avoid a lot of travelling.

CONNECT & FIND YOUR WAY

Wi-fi Coverage is good and most cafes and public venues have free (though often password-protected) wi-fi.

Navigation Most neighbourhoods are compact enough to explore on foot or by bicycle. To travel between them, use public transport.

Neighbourhood	Pros/Cons
Charlottenburg	Wide range for all budgets and a solid restaurant scene. Far from key sights and nightlife.
Mitte	Walk to most blockbuster sights. Touristy, expensive and quiet after dark.
Kreuzberg	Party 'hood with lively bar and food scene. Few sights and gritty streets.
Friedrichshain	Bubbling nightlife, cool Cold War–era sights and offbeat attractions. Transport difficult in some areas.
Hackescher Markt area	Trendy hipster quarter near sights, with standout shopping and restaurants. Pricey, busy and touristy; no parking.

MUSEUMSPASS

The **Museumspass Berlin** *(visitberlin.de/de/museumspass-berlin)* allows admission to the permanent exhibits of about 30 museums for three consecutive days. Available online and at participating museums.

MONEY

Credit card use has grown significantly, but there are still many places that accept cash only. Discounts on transport, shopping, attractions and entertainment are widely available for seniors, children and students.

01 Only in **BERLIN**

BUNKERS | PARKS | SPIES

Few cities do offbeat better than Berlin, a place that bursts with creativity, where thinking outside the box is second nature and conventions are often tossed aside. Once you've checked off the blockbuster sights, peel back a few layers to discover a smorgasbord of places and experiences that are truly unique to the German capital.

How to

When to go Book ahead for the Stasi prison, Sammlung Boros and the Trabi Safari. Tempelhofer Feld buzzes on sunny weekends but exudes a quiet, melancholy charm in the off-season.

Getting around All places are U-Bahn-accessible, except the Stasi prison – take tram M5 to Freienwalder Strasse, then walk 15 minutes.

Airport tours Explore Tempelhof Airport's legendary history on two-hour tours departing from the visitor centre at Platz der Luftbrücke.

Adventure playground One of Berlin's most magical places is **Tempelhofer Feld**, a huge next-gen urban park reclaimed from the airfield made famous by the 1948–49 Berlin Airlift. Cycle down the old runways, swing dance between veggie beds, watch the sunset with beer in hand, or sink your shot in an arty mini-golf course built from scavenged materials.

Dystopian treasure chest Check out red-hot contemporary art at **Sammlung Boros** in the concrete maze of a Nazi-era air-raid shelter that later moonlighted as a Soviet POW camp, a tropical-fruit warehouse and a fetish techno club. Tours sell out fast, so snag a ticket early.

Cells, secrets and fear Go behind bars at the Stasi's most notorious prison, now the **Gedenkstätte Berlin-Hohenschönhausen**, where more than 11,000 suspected regime opponents were

locked up between 1951 and 1989. Book ahead for a gut-punch 90-minute tour through cells, interrogation rooms and, if you're lucky, stories from a former inmate.

Ti(n)ny car, big legacy
Ever fancied cruising around Berlin in an East German relic? The **Trabi Safari** hands you the keys to a classic Trabant, affectionately called Trabi. After a quick how-to on the quirky two-stroke engine and steering-wheel gear stick, you'll be rolling through the city in a convoy. You can self-drive or ride shotgun while your guide crackles over the radio, pointing out key sights such as the Brandenburg Gate, East Side Gallery and Checkpoint Charlie.

Above Tempelhofer Feld

02 Capital of ART

WORLD-CLASS ART | INNOVATIVE GALLERIES | ECLECTIC PIECES

Art aficionados will find their compass on perpetual spin in Berlin. With hundreds of galleries, world-class collections and as many as 20,000 working artists, the city has staked out a spot on the global art map. From cutting-edge contemporary shows in converted factories to blockbuster visiting exhibitions, the local scene thrives on diversity, experimentation and a fearless embrace of new ideas.

How to

When to go Most museums are closed on Monday, but stay open late one night, usually Thursday.

Ticket tips Book tickets online to avoid long waits and guarantee admission, especially on weekends and for blockbuster exhibits.

What's on Find a daily updated calendar and interactive map listing current shows at 150 top galleries at *berliner-galerien.de*.

Top left Neue Nationalgalerie
Bottom left Haus Schwarzenberg

Culture immersion Near Potsdamer Platz, the **Kulturforum** museum cluster was built after WWII as West Berlin's modern cousin to Museum Island. If you're tight on time, hit up the **Neue Nationalgalerie** first: this knock-out collection of 20th-century Western art sits in a stunning glass-and-steel temple by Mies van der Rohe. Nearby, the **Gemäldegalerie** shows off an epic Old Masters lineup, including a Rembrandt room and gems by Cranach, Vermeer and Canaletto. Both spots keep things fresh by hosting headline-grabbing temporary shows. Other Kulturforum museums are more niche, focusing on arts and crafts, musical instruments, prints and drawings.

Art train Stroll into **Hamburger Bahnhof**, a neoclassical train terminal turned contemporary-art giant. Its sprawling halls pulse with post-1960s icons – think Warhol, Beuys, Kiefer – plus post-reunification Berlin art and an entire hall with Beuys' mind-bending installations. In summer, its garden comes alive with free DJ parties.

Urban canvas Street art has practically gone mainstream in Berlin, where you can pop into the free **Urban Nation** museum for a primer on styles and protagonists. Out in the field, the **RAW Gelände** in Friedrichshain, the **East Side Gallery**, the facades of eastern Kreuzberg, **Haus Schwarzenberg** in Mitte and the **Teufelsberg** ex-spy station are the most fertile hunting grounds, both for classic stars such as Blu and Shepard Fairey and next-gen aerosol artists. **Alternative Berlin Tours** offers street-art tours.

More Arty Hubs Around Town

Auguststrasse, Berlin's first post-Wall art artery, still rocks the scene with heavy hitters like **KW Institute for Contemporary Art** and **Galerie Eigen + Art**. Another hot strip is upper Potsdamer Strasse, especially the **Mercator Höfe**, a courtyard filled with blue-chip galleries like Max Hetzler, Esther Schipper and Thomas Schulte.

For a unique vibe, drop by **Tankstelle Galerie**, a midcentury petrol station turned sleek art space shared by Galerie Judin and Pace Gallery, complete with a garden, café and bookshop.

For photography lovers, **C/O Berlin** in Charlottenburg is an essential stop, while Fotografiska in Mitte pushes boundaries with thought-provoking shows on gender, identity and queerness.

03 Berlin After DARK

HEDONISM | DIVERSITY | BEATS

In Berlin, you're rarely more than a short stroll from the next bar. The edgier, grittier haunts are packed into Kreuzberg, Friedrichshain and Neukölln, where the music's loud, the lights are low and clubs such as Berghain keep the party going 24/7. Charlottenburg, Mitte and Prenzlauer Berg play it cooler – more 'let's have another glass of wine' than 'let's lose three days'.

How to

When to go Day-to-night parties are on the rise, but most clubs don't open until midnight; some go nonstop from Friday to Monday morning.

Dress code Forget the all-black myth – styles vary by club and type of party. Best advice: create your own look and wear it with confidence.

Booze and smoke Lighter and alcohol-free drinks are increasingly popping up on bar menus, even in the grittiest spots. While not legal, smoking is often tolerated.

Top left Kreuzberg
Bottom left Trinkteufel

Party central More gritty than pretty, the bars and cafes around Kottbusser Tor and along Oranienstrasse pump out high-octane nighttime action. From punky dives such as **Trinkteufel** to candlelit cocktail lairs like **Würgeengel**, plus bar-club hybrids such as **Paloma** and **Monarch Bar**, this area is built for bar-hopping marathons. As elsewhere in town, *Spätis* (late-night convenience stores) now often double as budget-friendly, beer-fuelled hangouts.

Next-gen clubbing Berlin's nightlife may be a little bruised from the pandemic and gentrification, but don't worry: the beat is still strong as a new generation of party-makers reshapes the scene. Alongside sweaty techno temples such as Berghain and **Tresor**, there's Afrobeat nights, Arab electronic beats, daytime disco, sex-positive parties and queer-led collectives in spaces old and new, from **SO36** to **Maaya**, plus outdoor raves in fields and abandoned warehouses. **Resident Advisor** (ra.co) has the latest intel and lineups.

Rainbow parties Berlin's queer scene is as big and bold as the city itself. The historic gay quarter around **Nollendorfplatz** caters for every taste, from casual cocktails to full-on fetish feasts. **Neukölln** is a rapidly growing, super-diverse hot spot with an arty and alternative vibe, while **Friedrichshain**'s buzzing club scene attracts a younger, mixed crowd. Grab a free copy of *Siegessäule* magazine (also online: *siegessaeule.de*) for dates and current topics.

 Best Clubs for Getting Lost in the Beat

In good weather, **Club der Visionäre** is a dreamy day-to-night party spot with cold beer, crispy pizza and electro beats in a willow-fringed canal-side boat shed.

Small but buzzy **Paloma** lures with old-school charm, a great sound system and top local DJs spinning house and disco.

Berlin's most famous sex-positive fetish playground, **KitKatClub** has multiple floors, a swimming pool, long lines, a tough door and a dress code.

Brave hours-long lines and the city's toughest door for a chance to party at **Berghain**, the hedonistic techno cathedral inside a power station.

Head to **Sisyphos**, an indoor outdoor party village with a festival feeling, for nonstop summer-weekend shenanigans.

04 Berlin's Nazi **LEGACY**

HISTORY | REMEMBRANCE | RESILIENCE

Berlin carries the weight of its past as Nazi Germany's capital in memorials, museums and original buildings scattered across its cityscape. These places confront the realities of dictatorship, war and persecution with unflinching honesty. Visiting them feels less like sightseeing and more about standing where history happened and reflecting on the shadows these sites cast on today's world.

How to

When to go Visit Topography of Terror after 5pm for smaller crowds. Sachsenhausen closes on Mondays from mid-October to mid-March.

Getting there For Sachsenhausen, take the S1 or a regional train to Oranienburg station. From there, bus 804 runs hourly to the camp, or it's a 2km walk.

Be respectful As tempting as social-media shots may be, remember that the Holocaust Memorial is a space for reflection, not a photo backdrop.

Anatomy of oppression

On the grounds where the Gestapo and SS once orchestrated their unspeakable reign of terror, the **Topography of Terror** pulls you into the Nazi regime's inner workings. The sobering exhibition introduces Hitler's most trusted circle and the methods they used to seize and maintain power through decrees, fear and calculated brutality. To prevent information overload, download the one-hour audio tour to your phone or borrow a free audioguide.

Field of silence

Germany's central **Holocaust Memorial** is a haunting maze of 2711 concrete slabs rising like sarcophagi over a rolling field. It may seem austere, but if you let it, you can sense the weight of suffering and loss as you make your way through. Deepen the experience in the underground exhibit, which includes the

Room of Names, where victims' lifespans are projected on walls while a solemn voice reads their brief biographies.

Gates of evil A quick trip north of Berlin, **Sachsenhausen concentration camp** held over 200,000 prisoners between 1936 and 1945. Today it's a memorial site, and the scale of suffering hits home as you walk past its roll-call square, barracks and the grim Station Z execution site. Exhibits detail forced labour, starvation, disease and mass killings. The quiet here feels heavy – a place where history is tangible and the demand to remember is palpable.

In the Footsteps of History

Get shivers standing in the very room where Nazi leaders planned the 'Final Solution', now part of the **Gedenkstätte Haus der Wannsee-Konferenz**.

Stand in the room where Nazi Germany's unconditional surrender ended WWII in Europe, at the **Museum Berlin-Karlshorst**, which preserves the memory of that day and the suffering leading up to it.

The **bunker** where Adolf Hitler committed suicide is now a car park, marked only by an information panel on the bunker network, construction-details data and the site's post-WWII history.

The **Gedenkstätte Deutscher Widerstand** tells the stories of those brave souls who risked or lost their lives by actively resisting the Nazi regime from within Germany.

Above Holocaust Memorial

05 Treasure ISLAND

ANTIQUITIES | ART | RIVER

Flirt with an Egyptian queen or size up a Neanderthal skull before drifting into Monet's dreamy landscapes. Welcome to Museumsinsel (Museum Island), Berlin's renowned museum ensemble packed with millennia of fascinating art, artefacts and sculpture from Europe and beyond. Even with the famous Pergamonmuseum closed for renovation, a few hours spent here feel like a first-class trip through time and human achievement.

How to

When to go If you want a quieter experience, visit on weekday mornings, after 3pm, or anytime in winter.

Deeper dive Make use of the excellent free multilingual audioguides and focus on no more than two museums in a single day.

Ticket to savings The Museumsinsel Ticket offers same-day admission to all four museums plus the Pergamonmuseum – Das Panorama.

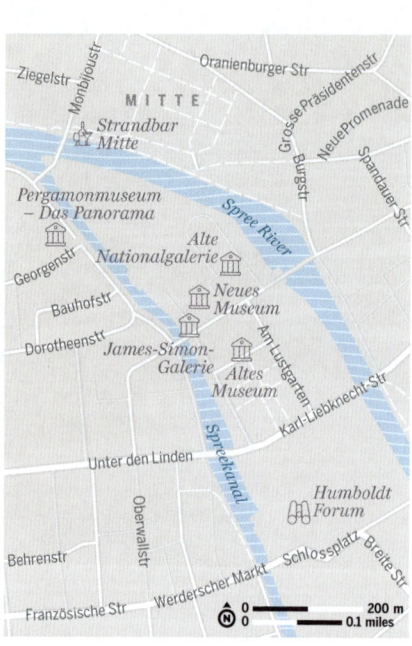

Ancient treasures By all means, fall in love with eternally gorgeous Queen Nefertiti and the Egyptian collection at the **Neues Museum**, but don't skip its prehistoric wing. Standouts include a wizardly Bronze Age golden conehead in room 305 and a 700,000-year-old Paleolithic stone axe (the museum's oldest object) in room 308.

Stairway to art Sashay up the double staircase fronting the **Alte Nationalgalerie**, a showcase of 19th-century European art. Get lost in Caspar David Friedrich's moody landscapes, cheerful French Impressionist canvases and Schadow's tender marble sculpture of two princesses.

Pergamon imagined No question: it's a bummer the Pergamonmuseum is closed, but you can still glimpse its grandeur at **Pergamonmuseum – Das Panorama**, a stunning 360-degree photorealistic circular painting

depicting the ancient city of Pergamon in 129 CE. In the foyer, get up close with 80 pieces from the museum's collection, including a colossal head of Heracles.

Historic cruise Kick back on an open-deck Spree **riverboat**, gliding past Museum Island, grand old buildings and the government district, perhaps sipping a traditional Berliner Weisse – a local beer laced with woodruff or raspberry syrup.

Dancing under the stars
The majestic facade of the Bode-Museum shimmers in the Spree, fairy lights flicker overhead and the vibe is pure Berlin charm at the nightly dance sessions – tango, swing, Latin – at **Strandbar Mitte** riverside beer garden.

Other Museum Island Stars

Top billing among the Greek, Roman and Etruscan antiquities in the **Altes Museum** – the first to open on Museum Island in 1830 – belongs to the **Praying Boy**, sculpted in Rhodes around 300 BCE.

The sleek **James-Simon-Galerie** is the gateway to Museum Island and houses the central ticket office, lockers, toilets, a gift shop and a canalside cafe.

The massive **granite basin** outside the Altes Museum is 7m in diameter, was carved on site from a single slab back in the 1820s and weighs over 70 tonnes.

Head to the rooftop terrace (with cafe-restaurant) of the **Humboldt Forum** for the best view of Museum Island.

Above Alte Nationalgalerie

06 HISTORY'S
Greatest Hits

LANDMARKS | VIEWS | GRAND BUILDINGS

Mitte stitches many of Berlin's trophy sights into a compact quilt. From the Reichstag to the TV Tower, via Unter den Linden's Prussian landmarks, it's politics, pageantry and centuries of history on this 2.5km walk.

Trip Notes

Getting around Start your walk at either end. When you're done, the U5 subway will quickly whisk you back to where you started.

When to go Time-slot tickets to the Reichstag dome are free but must be prebooked at *bundestag.de,* so plan your tour accordingly – and don't forget photo ID.

Haute sausage Feeling flush? Pop into the Hotel Adlon to splurge on Berlin's most expensive *Currywurst,* sprinkled with gold leaf.

Where Books Turned to Ash

Pause a moment on Bebelplatz to admire the State Opera and other architectural gems, but also to reflect on the dangers of censorship. On 10 May 1933, this was the site of Nazi Germany's first full-blown book burning. In the square's centre, Micha Ullmann's minimalist subterranean memorial, **Empty Library**, commemorates this chilling event.

01 Book ahead for the lift ride to the glass dome of the 1894 **Reichstag**, home to the Bundestag (German parliament) and the historic anchor of the post-reunification federal government district.

04 Check out the exhibits, some free, at the **Humboldt Forum**, a cultural complex inside a newly built replica of the Prussian city palace, especially *Berlin Global* and the ethnological collections.

02 Follow in the footsteps of kings, Napoleon and Hitler while strutting through the **Brandenburg Gate**, Berlin's only remaining 18th-century city gate and now a cheery symbol of German reunification.

03 Detour to **Gendarmenmarkt**, Berlin's grandest square, bookended by two domed churches and anchored by a columned concert hall. Climb the tower of the Französischer Dom for stunning bird's-eye views.

05 Get whisked up the space-agey **Fernsehturm** (TV Tower), Germany's tallest structure, for unparalleled views from its rotating observation deck, and a restaurant-bar led by star chef Tim Raue. Buy tickets online to save money.

FROM LEFT: MO PHOTOGRAPHY BERLIN/SHUTTERSTOCK, THOMAS KURMEIER/GETTY IMAGES

01 There's no better place to come to grips with the Berlin Wall's complexity than the **Gedenkstätte Berliner Mauer**, a 1.4km open-air exhibit with preserved Wall remnants and powerful personal stories.

02 Once part of the Wall's death strip, **Mauerpark** now hums with Berlin's free-spirited energy, especially on Sundays when a flea market and outdoor karaoke draw huge crowds of locals and tourists.

03 Drop by the **Tränenpalast**, an original border pavilion, where East Berliners once said tearful goodbyes to visitors from the West, to grasp the emotional toll of the city's division.

04 Get a Cold War crash course at the free outdoor exhibit at **Checkpoint Charlie**, the main Allied border crossing between East and West Berlin. The nearby Mauermuseum details remarkable escape tales.

05 Admire colourful murals while strolling along the **East Side Gallery**, the longest surviving stretch of the Wall (1.3km). Each artwork has a QR code with background info.

FROM LEFT: MISTERVLAD/SHUTTERSTOCK, BLAKE HORN FOR LONELY PLANET.

BERLIN WALL
Demystified

HISTORY | LANDMARKS | MEMORIALS

It sliced through streets, separated families and turned Berlin into the Cold War's most visible fault line. For 28 years, the Berlin Wall was both a physical barrier and a symbol of oppression. Today, a few relics bear witness to this bizarre era.

Trip Notes

Getting around Many hotels and hostels offer free or low-cost bikes for guests. Otherwise, use Uber or the local Jelbi app to locate the nearest bike or e-bike from current bike-sharing services.

When to go Anytime works, just maybe not in a downpour.

Memorial tip Among memorials to those who died trying to escape over the Wall, *The Parliament of Trees* by Ben Wagin packs the most visceral punch.

Why Did the Wall Go Up?

In the 1950s, the growing economic gap between capitalist West Germany and communist East Germany sent a wave of mostly young, educated East Germans westward in search of better opportunities. To halt this exodus of talent and labour, the East German government came up with a drastic solution: build a wall.

The Green City

FROM CITY NOISE TO NATURE'S CHORUS

Berlin treats nature like a daily habit, not a weekend luxury. Forests sit beside U-Bahn stations, lakes double as swimming pools and picnic spots, and parks stitch whole districts together. It's a city where 'heading outdoors' usually means staying in town.

Green, Everywhere You Look

The numbers back up the vibe. Berlin has more than 2500 public green and recreation spaces. Forest covers almost 20% of the city, while surface water spans about 5967 hectares. Taken together, forests and waterways account for roughly a quarter of Berlin's footprint, before you even count parks, allotments and green courtyards. That kind of green-blue baseline shapes how people move, meet and unwind.

Big Backyards Right in Town

One signature park in particular shows how outsized urban nature feels in Berlin. **Tempelhofer Feld**, the former airfield turned adventure playground, offers more than 300 hectares of open runway for kites, skating, gardening and sunset loops on a bike. A 2014 referendum protected it from development (for now), keeping the field as Berlin's shared backyard.

Each of the city's parks has its own flavour. **Tiergarten**, the 210-hectare 'green lung' between Brandenburg Gate and the Zoo Berlin, has a stately character, with memorials, boating ponds and long tree-lined paths. **Volkspark Friedrichshain** is full of local community flair, with barbecue areas atop its hills built from wartime rubble, an open-air summertime cinema and picnicking by the fairy-tale fountain. Even **Mauerpark**, wrested from a section of the Berlin Wall 'death strip', is now a green oasis and public playground, especially during the Sunday flea market and karaoke.

Forests & Lakes

On the city's western edge, **Grunewald** sprawls across roughly 3000 hectares of pines and sandy trails, with the sparkling Havel River peeping through clearings. All over

Left Volkspark Friedrichshain
Centre Krumme Lanke
Right Berlin Wall Trail

town, locals cool off at dozens of lakes, from woodland-ringed **Krumme Lanke** and **Schlachtensee** to vast **Müggelsee**, Berlin's largest lake, in the historic southwestern suburb of Köpenick. **Strandbad Wannsee**, the oldest of the city's lakeside lidos, comes with a 1km-long sandy beach, water sports and a nudist section. Each summer the health authority monitors the water quality of dozens of official bathing sites.

Green Routes

If you like to wander, Berlin literally maps green into daily life. Twenty *Grüne Hauptwege* (Green Main Paths) – a network of green, mostly traffic-free routes totalling roughly 550km – link parks, waterways and neighbourhoods, including the 160km **Berlin Wall Trail** that loops along the former border. Sadly, Berlin is lagging behind other capitals when it comes to bicycle superhighways. Even the modest plan to build about 100km of commuter corridors by 2030 has been shelved due to budget constraints and shifting political priorities under a new conservative city government.

> Taken together, forests and waterways account for roughly a quarter of Berlin's footprint.

Everyday Rituals

Berlin's love of nature isn't just about leisure. Allotment gardens, rooftop beehives, urban farms and composting projects are part of everyday life. Street trees (more than 430,000 at last count) shade beer gardens and streetside cafes, and community gardeners tend raised beds on Tempelhof's tarmac. In Berlin, nature isn't an escape: it's part of daily life.

Green Oddities

Like the city itself, Berlin's green side also has its quirks. In Charlottenburg, the tiny **Ziegenhof goat farm** hides between apartment blocks, with friendly goats munching hay and kids feeding them carrots. Out on **Tempelhofer Feld**, resident sheep step into action as natural lawnmowers in spring, while across town **Domäne Dahlem** is a working eco-farm on the grounds of a medieval estate. Throughout Berlin, some 880 allotment garden colonies form leafy, pint-sized worlds of vegetable plots, garden gnomes and weekend huts – small, neighbourly escapes that feel miles from the urban rush.

BERLIN
Icons

01 Cloud Piercer
Space needle meets disco ball with a rotating restaurant-bar on top – the TV Tower, Germany's tallest structure, clocks in at 368m.

02 Unity Arch
A prime go-to for golden-hour selfies, the Brandenburg Gate frames Berlin's past and present in one elegant triumphal arch.

03 Techno Cathedral
Hyped but still happening, Berghain is the mother ship of techno beats. Survive the door and earn bragging rights for life.

04 Cult Snack
Street-food royalty since 1949, *Currywurst* is a snappy sausage drenched in curry-dusted spiced tomato sauce, best gobbled with fries.

05 Power Perch
A glass crown for democracy, the Reichstag dome literally lets you look out over Berlin and down on the politicians below.

06 Egyptian Supermodel
With high cheekbones and flawless eyeliner since 1345 BCE, Nefertiti still makes audiences swoon from her perch at the Neues Museum.

07 Wrap Star

Messy and gloriously lowbrow, the Berlin-style doner kebab is an anytime hunger fix, especially after a questionable 5am dance floor exit.

08 Border Canvas

The Berlin Wall remnant turned East Side Gallery is perfect for selfies, pondering Cold War history and tracking down that famous 'kiss mural'.

09 Local Lifeline

Berlin's spin on late-night convenience stores, Spätis dole out beer, snacks and gossip, and often double as impromptu bars and therapy rooms.

10 Crosswalk King

East Berlin's beloved Ampelmann traffic-light figure still struts his stuff in a jaunty hat thanks to a grassroots campaign.

01 MEUNIERD/SHUTTERSTOCK, MADDYZ/SHUTTERSTOCK. **02** SERGII FIGURNYI/SHUTTERSTOCK, JOINTSTAR/SHUTTERSTOCK. **03** SL_PIXELFACTORY/SHUTTERSTOCK. **04** ROBERT NEUMANN/SHUTTERSTOCK. **05** NIKADA/SHUTTERSTOCK. **06** BPK/AGYPTISCHES MUSEUM UND PAPYRUSSAMMLUNG, SMB/MARGARETE BÜSING. **07** ALIZADA STUDIOS/SHUTTERSTOCK. **08** MADDYZ/SHUTTERSTOCK, CHRISTO GEORGIEV/SHUTTERSTOCK. **09** BLAKE HORN FOR LONELY PLANET. **10** MEUNIERD/SHUTTERSTOCK

Listings

BEST OF THE REST

 Sublime Plates

Oukan €€€
This dimly lit, Zen-style Japanese fine-dining shrine in Mitte serves meticulous plant-based plates inspired by ancient Buddhist temple cuisine and accompanied by a wine or tea pairing.

Luna D'Oro €€
Inside the glamorous, century-old Clärchens ballroom, this restaurant presents nostalgic German fare with a theatrical, modern twist; the Königsberger Klopse (veal dumplings in caper sauce) and the German-style jelly are classics.

Veronika €€€
Enjoy cosmopolitan yet relaxed global fine dining at Fotografiska in the former Tacheles art squat amid velvet seats and sensual lighting. Wrap up with cocktails in the upstairs bars.

Michelberger €€
This anytime spot near the East Side Gallery serves elevated comfort food rooted in regional goodness, often with ingredients from its own farm, amid the charm of a converted factory.

 Bars & Beer Gardens

Prater €
Berlin's oldest beer garden in Prenzlauer Berg has seen beer-soaked days and nights since 1837 and is still a charismatic spot for guzzling beneath the ancient chestnut trees.

Bellboy Bar €€€
Sassy staff, theatrical design and unique drinks combine at this chic Gendarmenmarkt watering hole that oozes all the lascivious seductiveness of a 1920s booze parlour. Don't get lost finding the toilets.

Lerchen&Eulen €
This friendly pub near Markthalle Neun plies an international crowd with cold Augustiner beer, kick-arse cocktails and fair-trade coffee, all at friendly prices and amid vintage furnishings.

 Labels to Larders

Kurfürstendamm
This famous retail strip near Zoo Station is a power-shopper's dream, with plenty of opportunities for coffee or aperitif breaks.

Frau Tonis Parfum
At this 'scent-sational' made-in-Berlin perfume boutique near Checkpoint Charlie, a scent test identifies a matching fragrance and bespoke blends can be created in just one hour.

Markthalle Neun
Find quality produce, fish, meats and all things artisanal at this historic Kreuzberg market hall with its own brewery and lots of kitchens.

 Royal Encounters

Schloss Charlottenburg
Peek at art, treasures and period rooms on a tour of this baroque palace ensemble, and soak up the grandeur of the Prussian royals.

Pfaueninsel
Detour to Lake Wannsee for close-ups of this storybook island with its whimsical snowy-white palace, built by a king for secret rendezvous with his mistress. Very *Bridgerton*.

 Urban Nature Nooks

Schlossgarten Charlottenburg
Lounge like royalty by the carp pond surrounded by fragrant flowers beds and baroque

splendour after a spin around the glitzy royal apartments of Schloss Charlottenburg.

Volkspark Friedrichshain

Watch an outdoor movie, snap pictures with a fairy-tale fountain, or simply get lost in Berlin's oldest public park, with more locals than tourists and two postwar rubble heaps disguised as hills.

Tiergarten

Prussian rulers once hunted boar and pheasants in one of the world's largest urban oases, which is laced with romantic waterways, dotted with memorial statues and anchored by the Siegessäule victory column.

Architectural Icons

Jüdisches Museum

The angular, gleaming Jewish Museum by American-Polish architect Daniel Libeskind stands as a powerful metaphor for the fractured yet enduring journey of Jewish people in Germany over the past 1700 years.

Haus der Kulturen der Welt

Hugh Stubbins' curvaceous building in the Tiergarten, lidded by a seemingly gravity-defying parabolic roof, houses this well-respected cultural centre focused on global ideas, migrant stories and fresh ways of seeing the world.

Down by the Riverside

Holzmarkt

Grab a beer or pizza at this beloved riverside hangout, a deliberately ramshackle wonderland of recycled wood, funky architecture and arty installations north of the East Side Gallery.

Badeschiff

Beat the heat, Berlin-style, at this cargo boat turned pool moored on Kreuzberg's Spree banks, the centrepiece of a beach club with cocktails, bites and sometimes open-air parties.

Lido Berlin

Live-Music Venues

Lido Berlin

This 1950s Kreuzberg cinema has been recast as a rock-indie-electro-pop hub with mosh-pit energy and a crowd that cares about the music.

Uber Arena

This crown jewel of Berlin's large arenas is the place to catch global stars and home games of the city's pro ice hockey and basketball teams.

Berliner Philharmonie

A classical concert at the Kulturforum is ear-candy at its finest. Free chamber-music recitals take place in the foyer at 1pm on Wednesdays between September and June.

Tours

Fork & Walk Tours

Led by in-the-know locals, these flavour-packed tours serve Berlin on a plate, mixing classics and foodie trends with juicy stories of the city's culture, people, street art and current topics.

Alternative Berlin Tours

Not your run-of-the-mill tour company, this excellent outfit's lineup includes a street-art tour, a deep dive into the 'real Berlin' soul and a tour that spotlights its sub- and alternative cultures.

Day Trip to **POTSDAM**

DAY TRIP | ROYALS | LAKES

Potsdam, 25km southwest of central Berlin, is Berlin's top day trip, luring visitors with its splendid gardens and palaces. Headlined by Schloss Sanssouci, Frederick the Great's jewel-box retreat, the ensemble garnered Unesco World Heritage status in 1990.

How to

Getting here Hop on S-Bahn S7 or regional trains for the 25- to 40-minute ride to Potsdam Hauptbahnhof (ABC ticket required). From there, it's a 15-minute ride on bus 695 to Schloss Sanssouci.

When to go Crowds are smaller on weekday mornings. The gardens are especially beautiful from mid-April (cherry blossoms) through early October (autumn leaves).

Bicycle rental Explore more of beautiful Potsdam by bicycle, available from **Pedales** at Potsdam Hauptbahnhof.

Carefree Retreat

The biggest stunner, and what everyone comes to see, is **Schloss Sanssouci**. Designed in 1747 by Frederick's friend Georg Wenzeslaus von Knobelsdorff, this rococo palace was where the king came to be *sans souci* (without cares). It sits daintily above vine-draped terraces with the Frederick's grave nearby and gives way to an enormous park, dotted with numerous other palaces and outbuildings.

A standout on the audioguided tour of Sanssouci's dozen rooms is the **Konzertsaal** (Concert Hall), whimsically decorated with vines, grapes and even a cobweb where sculpted spiders frolic. The king himself gave flute recitals here. An intimate highlight is the circular, cedar-clad **Bibliothek** (Library), lidded by a gilded sunburst ceiling. Frederick would seek solace here amid 2000

Coffee with Dragons

A lovely spot to refuel during your Sanssouci exploration is the charmingly old-school cafe-restaurant in the **Drachenhaus**, a miniature palace with dragon-shaped roof ornaments. About 1.3km west of Schloss Sanssouci, it serves coffee, homemade cakes and seasonal cuisine, outside on the terrace under a leafy canopy in summer.

Above left Schloss Sanssouci
Above right Bibliothek (Library)
Left Konzertsaal (Concert Hall)

leather-bound volumes ranging from Greek poetry to the latest releases by his dear friend Voltaire. Another standout is the **Marmorsaal** (Marble Hall), an elegant white Carrara-marble symphony inspired by the Pantheon in Rome.

Prussian Pagoda Dreams

The 18th-century European fad for the Far East is on full display in the **Chinesisches Haus**. The cloverleaf-shaped pavilion is one of the park's most photographed buildings thanks to its whimsical exterior, featuring gilded 'Chinese' figures sipping tea, dancing and playing musical instruments amid palm-shaped pillars – an ornate fantasy filtered through Western eyes. The collection of fine porcelain inside can be visited from May to October.

Power Palace

Schloss Sanssouci looks almost dainty compared to the **Neues Palais** (New Palace) with its made-to-impress dimensions, soaring dome and frilled exterior. It took just six years

The Scoop on Sanssouci

All palaces are closed Monday, except the Neues Palais, which is closed Tuesday.

The **Sanssouci+ ticket** (spsg.de), a one-day pass to all palaces around Potsdam, is available online, at Park Sanssouci's visitor centres in the Neues Palais and behind the Historische Mühle, and at each palace.

Entry to Schloss Sanssouci is by timed ticket only. To secure your slot in advance, you need to buy the Sanssouci+ ticket online.

Palaces in Park Sanssouci are fairly well spaced – it's almost 2km between Schloss Sanssouci and the Neues Palais.

Picnicking in the park is permitted, but cycling is limited to Ökonomieweg and Maulbeerallee.

Left Chinesisches Haus
Below Holländisches Viertel (Dutch Quarter), Potsdam

to build, a show of Prussian power following its victory over France in the bloody Seven Years' War. Frederick the Great used the palace mostly for official functions and to host visiting family and friends. Only the last German Kaiser, Wilhelm II, made it his family residence, at least until his abdication in 1918. On the guided 'Grand Tour', admire the extraordinary artistry and craftwork typical of the 18th century. The shell-adorned **Grottensaal** (Grotto Hall) and the **Marmorsaal** (Marble Hall), lit by massive chandeliers, are out of this world. Among the residential quarters, the lavish **Unteres Fürstenquartier** (Lower Royal Suite) gives you a sense of the luxury once enjoyed by the Prussian royals, as does the apartment of Prince Heinrich, Frederick's brother, that can be visited on a separate tour from April to October.

Dutch Treat

Away from Sanssouci, a distinctive part of central Potsdam is the **Holländisches Viertel** (Dutch Quarter) – minus the clogs and tulips. This charismatic cluster of 134 gabled red-brick houses was commissioned around 1730 by Friedrich Wilhelm I to accommodate Dutch artisans recruited to support the city's expansion. The area lies just southeast of the Nauener Tor city gate. Stroll down central Mittelstrasse and its cobblestone side streets, popping into galleries, boutiques, restaurants and cafes.

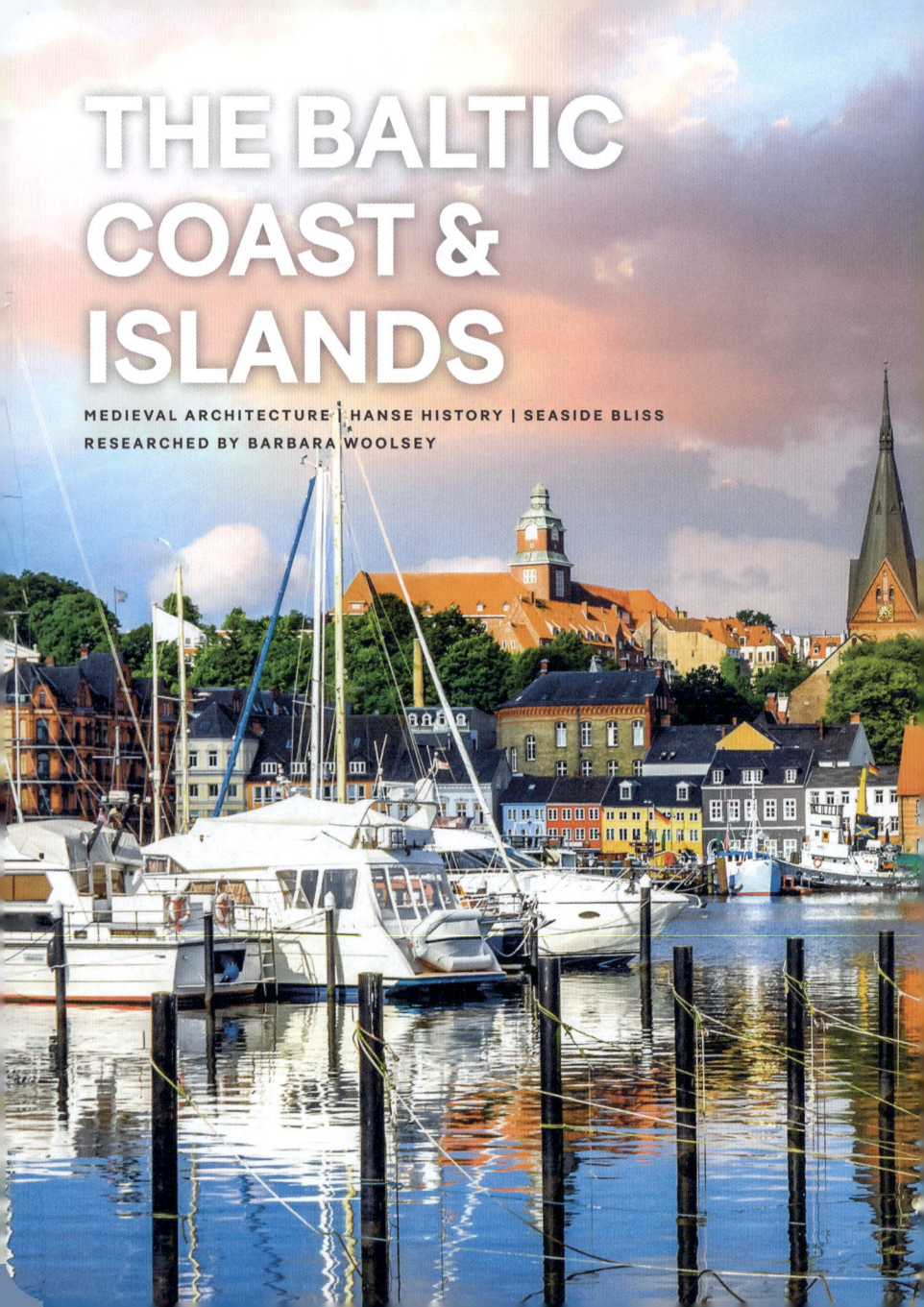

THE BALTIC COAST & ISLANDS

MEDIEVAL ARCHITECTURE | HANSE HISTORY | SEASIDE BLISS
RESEARCHED BY BARBARA WOOLSEY

- **Trip Builder** (p72)
- **Practicalities** (p73)
- **Epically Medieval** (p74)
- **Modern German History** (p78)
- **Great Outdoors** (p80)
- **German Riviera** (p82)
- **Listings** (p84)

THE BALTIC COAST & ISLANDS
Trip Builder

See the chalk cliffs that inspired Friedrich's masterpiece at **Jasmund National Park** (p79).
🚗 1½hr from Stralsund

Cycle around Germany's car-free paradise, **Hiddensee Island** (p81), after taking a horse-drawn carriage ride.
⛴ 2hr from Rügen

Trace medieval sailors' footsteps at the impressive **Europäisches Hansemuseum** (p76).
🚆 2hr from Rostock

Discover the sunny seaside's dark history at Rügen's **Dokumentationszentrum Prora** (p79).
🚗 45min from Stralsund

Discover Germany's sunniest spot, **Usedom Island** (p83), then ferry-hop to Poland.
⛴ 3½hr from Rügen

Coastal Mecklenberg-Western Pomerania, also known as the German Riviera, is a spectacular stretch of the *Ostseeküste* (Baltic Sea Coast) with clean white sands and sparkling seas. Northern Germany's beachcombing season is short but sweet across resort towns on the mainland and islands – all just a couple of hours' from Poland's border.

FROM LEFT: DIEGO GRANDI/SHUTTERSTOCK, RICOK/SHUTTERSTOCK
PREVIOUS PAGE: SINA ETTMER PHOTOGRAPHY/SHUTTERSTOCK

Practicalities

ARRIVING

Rostock Frequent direct trains depart from Berlin and Hamburg (both two hours) and around the region, including hourly connections from Stralsund (one hour).

Adler-Schiffe Regular ferries connect Stralsund, Rügen Island, Hiddensee Island and Świnoujście (Polish/German border).

FIND YOUR WAY

At least every coastal (or island) town has at least one tourist office. It's always worth stopping in.

MONEY

Plan to use cash. Exchange facilities are rare in rural areas and on islands (except for main towns such as Binz).

WHERE TO STAY

Island	Pros/Cons
Rügen	The largest and most developed island. Crowded in peak season.
Hiddensee	Secluded, natural landscapes. Only accessible by ferry.
Usedom	Best weather and close to Poland. Less scenic beauty.

EATING & DRINKING

Seafood restaurants, from fancy to simple, are everywhere. Sea-facing cafes are a coast specialty, and afternoon coffee and cake is a German ritual.

Fischbrötchen (fish sandwiches) are the perfect beach snack from harbourside stalls. Smoked fish (eel, trout, mackerel) from traditional ovens is a speciality in seaside towns; it's enjoyed warm or cold with potato salad and *pils* (beer).

Best Fischbrötchen Fischhalle (p85)

Must-try smoked herring Fischer-Hütte (p85)

GETTING AROUND

Car Most convenient on limited time. Go electric – northern Germany has good charging stations and infrastructure.

Bicycle Excellent routes abound. The well-paved 1000km **Baltic Sea Cycle Route** starts near Denmark and ends near Poland.

Bus Services connect practically all communities (though sometimes sporadically).

JUN–AUG
Crowded resorts, warm(ish) weather. Book accommodation well ahead.

SEP–NOV
Windy and cool and less crowded. Perfect spa time.

DEC–FEB
Off season. Many restaurants and spa-less resorts close.

MAR–MAY
Nature blooms. Bring a jacket for unpredictable weather.

09 Epically MEDIEVAL

VILLAGES | ARCHITECTURE | HISTORY

The Hanseatic League was a powerful confederation of merchant guilds and market towns during the Middle Ages. At its height, it connected more than 200 places across the Baltic and North Seas. Today, Hanse's legacy endures across alluring seaside towns abounding in medieval architecture.

How to

Getting here Regional trains travel regularly from Rostock to Stralsund and Greifswald (€16.20, one hour).

Getting around Most regional train stations are located only 1km or 2km from their town's historic centre. Walk (or rent a bike) for sightseeing.

Regional ticket Go in on an MV-Ticket with up five other passengers (€25) for regional travel. Ask others waiting on the platform – it's a well-known budget hack among holidaying pensioners.

Stralsund

Stralsund was once the Hanseatic League's second most important member, after Lübeck (Hanse's former capital). Its square gables interspersed with turrets, ornate portals and vaulted arches make it one of northern Germany's leading examples of *Backsteingotik* (classic red-brick Gothic gabled architecture). Savour historic attractions along cobblestoned alleys.

The UNESCO World Heritage–listed **Alter Markt** (Stralsund's main square), a 20-minute walk from the train station, is a hub of architectural treasures. The massive 14th-century **Marienkirche** is a superb example of north German red-brick construction. Climb the tower for a sweeping view of the town's red-tiled roofs and nearby Rügen Island.

Nearby **Nikolaikirche**, another masterpiece, dates from 1270. The church's interior is awash

☼ Lübeck

Though not on the Baltic Coast, nearby Lübeck (a three-hour train ride from Stralsund) is a small harbour city – its Trave River flows into the Baltic Sea. This former Hanse capital city is famed for its magnificent **Altstadt**, while lesser-known medieval wonders include the former **Heiligen-Geist-Hospital** that once treated sailors, and hidden Gothic courtyards such as the **Flüchtingshof**.

Above left Stralsund **Above right** Nikolaikirche **Left** Alter Markt

with colour and filled with art treasures. The main altar (1708), designed by baroque master Andreas Schlüter, shows the eye of God flanked by cherubs and is capped by a depiction of the Last Supper. The main portal is reached through an entrance off the Alter Markt.

Greifswald

The old university town of Greifswald, south of Stralsund, was left largely unscathed by WWII thanks to a courageous German colonel who surrendered to Soviet troops.

The former Hanseatic city's skyline – as perfectly captured by German Romantic painter Caspar David Friedrich – is defined by three churches: the **Dom St Nikolai** (nicknamed 'Long Nicholas'), **Marienkirche** ('Fat Mary') and **Kirche St Jacobi** ('Small Jacob').

The richly ornamented buildings ringing the **Markt** hint at Greifswald's stature in the Middle Ages. Several red-brick gabled houses (now cafes and restaurants) are relics of Hanseatic merchants' days, when they were combined living and storage spaces.

Best Feudal Experiences

Visit one of Germany's most high-tech attractions, Lübeck's **Europäisches Hansemuseum**. The state-of-the-art, 'personalised' exhibition unfolds according to your choice of a Hanse city and theme.

Drink rum like a sailor on terraces across **Flensburg**'s cobblestone streets. Near Denmark's border (four hours' drive from Stralsund), the *Rumstadt* (Rum City) was the prosperous centre of the 18th-century Caribbean liquor trade.

Explore **Wieck**, the photogenic centre of Greifswald's fishing village. Beyond the harbour, hike to the ruins of a 12th-century Cistercian monastery and a wonderful hidden beach.

Discover Rostock's **Kulturhistorisches Museum Rostock** (cultural history museum) in a former medieval convent. Historic vaulted interiors and medieval altarpieces showcase sacred sculptures and art.

Left Dom St Nikolai, Greifswald
Below Alter Hafen (Old Harbour), Wismar

Greifswald also has a pretty harbour in the charming district of **Wieck**; the entire area is worth a stroll.

Wismar

One of the prettiest towns along Germany's Baltic Coast, small, photogenic Wismar's gabled facades and cobbled streets make it quintessentially Hanseatic. It joined the League in the 13th century, but it spent most of the 16th and 17th centuries as part of Sweden; reminders of this era are all over town. The entire **Altstadt** was World Heritage–listed in 2002.

Wismar has been long popular with filmmakers, and its picturesque **Alter Hafen** (Old Harbour) starred in the 1922 movie *Nosferatu*. It holds the town's unofficial mascots or, rather, maritime protectors: the '**Swedish Heads**', two baroque wooden busts of Hercules in front of the **Baumhaus** (Tree House).

Old Wismar's centrepiece is the **Markt**. The attractive square is dominated by the 1602 **Wasserkunst** (waterworks), an ornate, 12-sided well that supplied Wismar's drinking water until 1897 and is the town's landmark. Behind it stands the red-brick **Alter Schwede** (Old Swede). Dating from 1380 and featuring a striking step buttress gable facade, the building is a nod to Swedish rule – '*Alte Schwede*' is also a term of endearment in German meaning 'old fellow'. The Old Swede houses a restaurant and guesthouse, as well as a Swedish Head replica.

10 Modern German HISTORY

HISTORIC SPA TOWNS | WWII & GDR RELICS | GERMAN CULTURAL LEGACY

The recent history of this region is defined by changing socio-political tides. In the 19th and early 20th centuries, spa towns were beloved by German and Russian aristocrats. During WWII the coast saw heavy naval activity, then, under East German rule, resorts became state-controlled. Beyond lounging on beautiful beaches, discover hidden histories and a few mysteries along the shore.

How to

Getting here Direct UBB (*ubb-online.com*) trains from Stralsund stop at coastal resorts before terminating in Świnoujście. Regular ferries run to Usedom from Rügen.

Getting around A bicycle is your best friend on the islands. Look for **Usedom Rad** (*usedomrad.de*) rental machines (€12 a day). On Rügen, bikes are available at rental shops around ports/stations.

Electric buses These are increasingly used around the islands. Look for the charging symbol on the side.

Retro resorts The sands of **Travemünde** once drew everyone from Dostoyevsky to Norwegian painter Edvard Munch, the Mann brothers and Europe's elite artists, writers and intellectuals. For a period of the 19th and early 20th centuries, it was Germany's St Tropez. There's an unmistakeable sense of past sophistication and nostalgia, particularly across an excellent range of four- and five-star wellness hotels boasting saunas and steam rooms.

Rügen's largest and most celebrated seaside resort, **Binz** is an alluring confection of ornate, white Victorian-era villas, pale sand and crystal-line water. Its roads are signed in Gothic script and lined with pines and chestnut trees. A highlight is strolling its 4km-long beach promenade, lined with *Bäderarchitektur* ('resort architecture'), an elegant, retro-cool style unique to the Baltic coast.

Exploring Romanticism The German Romanticism period, drawing heavily on dreamy idealism and gut-wrenching emotion, dominated the late 19th century. Romantic intellectuals adored the Baltic Sea coast, including Germany's best-known landscape painter, Caspar David Friedrich. Visit **Jasmund National Park** on Rügen to see one of his great muses, the Königsstuhl white cliffs, which he depicted in the iconic painting *Chalk Cliffs on Rügen* (1818).

Dark Baltic history Rügen's WWII history casts some darkness in the sun. Prora, just north of Binz, bears testament to Nazi plans for the world's largest resort: six hideous, gargantuan six-storey buildings by the sea. The **Dokumentationszentrum Prora** here offers the engrossing MACH I Urlaub (Power Vacation) exhibition, taking a deep look into how Rügen holidays played into Nazi, then later East German, propaganda.

Best Historical Experiences

On **Prora**, stay in the Nazi-envisioned 'workers' resort', now Germany's largest DJH youth hostel.

Peenemünde on Usedom is the 'birthplace of space travel'. At the **Historisch-Technisches Museum**, find out how the V2 rocket was developed here.

At the historic **A-ROSA Altes Kurhaus** in Binz, try luxury thalassotherapy: natural Baltic Sea–based treatments. Salty water, algae and mud therapies were adored by holidaying aristocrats.

Gorch Fock 1, a WWII-era training ship, is a three-masted steel barque steeped in history. The Russians took it as war booty and it sailed to Ukraine and the UK before ending up in Stralsund (its original home port).

Above Binz

11 GREAT Outdoors

RUGGED LANDSCAPES | PRISTINE FOREST | AERIAL HEIGHTS

Beyond its cute medieval villages, the Baltic Sea coast offers incredible encounters with untouched nature. Hiking trails abound and are properly signposted and mapped. There are outdoor activities for every desire, from the best of *Waldeinsamkeit* (the ritualistic German tradition of enjoying solitude in nature) to adrenaline-pumping heights. Though lesser known than forests in, say, Scandinavia, those in Germany's northern wilderness make it a true delight.

How to

Getting here Hiddensee ferries leave Rügen up to 12 times daily year-round. Services from Stralsund run up to three times daily (April to October).

Getting around Public transport is infrequent around conservation areas – explore with a vehicle.

Trains and horses Relax in Molli's retro salon car from Bad Doberan to Heiligendamm and take the 'Rushing Roland' train across Rügen. Horse-carriage rides on Hiddensee are €8 an hour in a group with other passengers.

Top left Skywalk, Jasmund National Park Bottom left Hiddensee Island

Reclusive hikes Woodsy trails abound across the Baltic Sea coast – tourist offices in main villages will guide your way. Among the highlights is the **Peenetal Trail** along the Peene valley; its surrounding wetlands are known as the 'Amazon of the North'. The trail runs for 70km, but you can choose a segment to walk (or cycle). It's also a bird-watcher's dream; expect sea eagles, kingfishers and cranes.

Canvas-worthy cliffs On Rügen Island's northeast, the rugged natural beauty of **Jasmund National Park** has inspired some of Germany's most revered 19th-century Romantic paintings. Jasmund's *Stubbenkammer* (Parlour Room) inspired Friedrich's famous *Chalk Cliffs on Rügen*. Also check out the *Königsstuhl* (King's Chair); at 117m, it's Rügen's highest point. The 'skywalk', a steel-suspension viewing platform that extends over the cliffs, makes nature viewing accessible (though at times crowded). According to folklore, Swedish king Charles XII, exhausted from battling Denmark, used the King's Chair as his La-Z-Boy – hence the nickname. Others say the moniker derives from an ancient ritual of elected kings climbing these cliffs from the sea to represent thronal ascension.

Engine-free living Explore **Hiddensee Island**, *'Dat söte Länneken'* (the sweet little land), 45 minutes by ferry from Rügen and much mythologised in Germany's cultural imagination. This tiny, car-free wonder measures 18km in length and 1.8km in width, but its hiking trails are an epic pop-up book of fairy-tale landscapes. Windswept trees, mauve heathlands (blooming from late summer to early autumn) and shapeshifting dunes abound.

Best Open-Air Experiences

Visit the **Darss-Zingst Peninsula** during spring or autumn to catch some 60,000 cranes during migration. The picturesque area is home to the Neues Kunsthaus Ahrenshoop artist colony on a windswept beach.

In primeval Rügen forest, an extraordinary spiralling treetop walk leads to the 30m-high **Aussichtsturm Adlerhorst** observation deck. The vertigo-inducing ramp goes for 600m – it's not acrophobia-friendly, but it is wheelchair- and stroller-accessible.

Scenic flights in a light plane are a wonderful way to see the spectacular Baltic coastline in all its glory.

Germany's oldest seaside resort, **Heiligendamm**, was called the 'White Town by the Sea'. Try a seawater spa treatment.

German RIVIERA

SEASIDE RESORTS | ECO-TRAVEL | SEAFOOD GALORE

Welcome to Germany's coastal paradise, where East German heritage defines the ports and resorts of a unique Baltic seafaring region. Holiday cottages, slow life on bikes and dazzling, clean white coasts attract holidaying Germans, Nordics and Poles, but word's slowly getting out. Take this itinerary and go island hopping.

Trip Notes

Getting around Although you'll appreciate having a car, regular rail services do connect the region with Hamburg, Berlin and other northern cities (Rostock and Stralsund most frequently).

When to go The beach season goes from mid-June to early September.

Ferries These connect all three islands with punctual, daily services. International ferries to Trelleborg (Sweden) and Rønne (Denmark) sail from Rügen. You can also sail from Usedom to the Polish border.

⚓ Neuendorf

Neuendorf, in southern Hiddensee, is one of the island's smallest villages and a place I recommend. In this old fishing village, there are not even streets, only a few houses and a port with a few boats. Come here by bike or ferry and visit the shop of Gesine, a fisherman's wife who prepares excellent smoked fish and other fish dishes. Nothing fancy, but she knows her business.

Cathrin Brandes *is a cookbook author and chef. (@cathrinbrandes; @stranddistel_hiddensee).*

02 Warnemünde is about promenading, eating fish, sipping cocktails and lazing in a *Strandkorb* (sheltered straw 'beach basket' seat) on its long, wide and startlingly white beach with a Hugo cocktail (prosecco, mint and elderflower syrup) in hand.

03 On car-free **Hiddensee**, a tiny island off Rügen's west coast, go hiking and cycling across remote, woodland landscapes; taking a horse-drawn carriage is a fun, novel delight.

01 See where iconic German writer Thomas Mann spent his happiest days in **Travemünde**, with its 4.5km of beach. Germany's St Tropez is a 1½-hour train ride from Hamburg and three hours from Rostock.

04 Nicknamed *Badewanne Berlins* (Berlin's Bathtub) in the prewar period, **Usedom** is a holiday spot revered for its 42km-long beach. Discover bathing culture among grand villas and historic promenades once favoured by German emperors.

05 Cross into Poland, visiting **Świnoujście** on the island Usedom, which was split by a new international border after WWII. Polish heritage includes heaped *pierogi* platters, artisanal amber jewellery and folk performances during summer.

FROM LEFT: JUERGEN WACKENHUT/SHUTTERSTOCK, ARTONO/SHUTTERSTOCK, ANDREAS WOLOCHOW/SHUTTERSTOCK

Listings

BEST OF THE REST

Castles

Putbusser Schlosspark
This 75-hectare English-style park on Rügen is filled with exotic botanical species. With unexpected bucolic countryside vibes, its towering castle casts cool shade over leafy surrounds – the perfect beach break.

Jagdschloss Granitz
This grandiose, 1723 hunting palace in Binz was once an alfresco playground for German nobility pursuing deer, foxes and hare. Built atop a 107m-high hill, it gets snickers for its phallic shape.

Museums

Ozeaneum
A state-of-the-art museum with an underwater world of Baltic, North Sea, Atlantic and even polar creatures. Peek into a tank keeping thousands of herring destined to drop down northern gullets. Humboldt penguins are a highlight.

Pommersches Landesmuseum
An outstanding Greifswald museum with a glassed-in hal that links three Franciscan monastery buildings. There's a major gallery of paintings, including half a dozen by Caspar David Friedrich, plus history and natural-history exhibits.

Passat
Travemünde takes great pride in its historic four-masted sailing-ship-turned-museum, which used to voyage around South America's Cape Horn in the early to mid-20th century. A regular passenger ferry crosses the river to the ship.

Schleswig-Holsteinisches Freilichtmuseum
Not directly on the Baltic coast, but close enough (a two-hour drive from Rostock). At this busy ethnographic attraction, beekeepers, bakers, potters and other artisans showcase regional traditions in 70 reassembled historic houses.

Rügen Delicacies

Fischräucherei Kuse €
A fish-smoking joint, directly on Binz' beach promenade, serving the island's tastiest, cheapest grilled specialities. The fifth-generation family business fishes its own crustaceans and doles them out daily.

Rügener Insel-Brauerei
The beer garden at the award-winning brewery offers refreshing escape from the coastal sun. The craft brewery specialises in a wide range of deliciously thirst-quenching beers made with Baltic ingredients.

Freustil €€€
One of the region's top restaurants has value to match its relaxed vibe. Exquisitely prepared

Passat

seasonal dishes are sourced locally and prepared with creativity. Request an outdoor table – enchanting during long summer nights.

Hiddensee Restaurants

Fischimbiss 'Zum Süder' €

At this no-frills fish snack bar in a southern Hiddensee country house, fresh, local catches are made into *fischbrötchen* (fish sandwiches) and grilled platters. Outdoor, sea-facing tables are a favourite stop for cyclists and hikers.

Sommerpalast und Eis Manufaktur €

Cycle up and order from the whitewashed villa window of this charming ice-cream cafe – in English, the 'Summer Palace'. Serves small-batch, artisanal flavours from regional ingredients: sea buckthorn, elderflower or berry sorbet, perhaps.

Stranddistel €€

Stranddistel, or 'Sea Holly' in English, is a boho-chic restaurant focused on regional sourcing with creative twists. Find pizza made with Baltic ingredients (smoked herring, salami from local sheep) and an expansive, laid-back terrace.

Stralsund Restaurants

Fischhalle €

Of the plentiful harbour stands hawking smoked fish in Stralsund, Fischhalle is the pick. Choose your pleasure (smoked fish for a picnic, perhaps) from the glass-fronted counters and sip a beer while waiting for your order.

Schipperhus €€

Just back from the main waterfront, and a little quieter as a result, Schipperhus does the usual fish and schnitzel fare better than most; the canalside terrace is lovely on a sunny day.

Speicher 8 €€

Simply roasted fish is one of the stars of this excellent casual restaurant in an old turreted

Jagdschloss Granitz

waterfront building. There are great tables out the front; order a beautifully presented fish platter for two.

Other Mainland Restaurants

Fischer-Hütte €

In Greifswald's charming harbour village of Wieck, excellent smoked-fish stands abound – the 'Fisher's House' specialises in smoked herring. Start with Wieck-style fish soup and move onto the house speciality.

Medinis €€€

Haute food is still catching on in Rostock, but this contemporary Italian fine-dining restaurant in Heiligendamm delivers refined dishes with Baltic twists and an excellent wine list. It's near the beach promenade to boot.

Brasserie €€€

These terrace views in Warnemünde are worth it alone, but the food is also excellent. Seasonal produce goes into menus that feature locally caught seafood. Enjoy a long lunch with wine overlooking the yacht harbour.

Café Glücklich €

Amid a few galleries, this artful cafe serves Wismar's finest coffee. Traditional German breakfasts are as beautiful as they are delicious. Cakes and crumbles demand room for dessert.

HAMBURG

MARITIME HERITAGE | AWESOME ARCHITECTURE | WILD NIGHTLIFE
RESEARCHED BY BARBARA WOOLSEY

- **Trip Builder** (p88)
- **Practicalities** (p89)
- **Hidden Gems** (p90)
- **Ride the Night** (p94)
- **Audiovisual & Arty** (p96)
- **Speicherstadt & HafenCity** (p98)
- **Listings** (p100)

Climb the 'mountain path' at the **Hamburg Bunker** (p93) and relax in the rooftop garden.
🚆 20min from Central Station

Go clubbing (p95) or cafe-lounging (p101) in **St Georg**, Hamburg's LGBTIQ+ district.
🚆 10min from Central Station

Go inside the **Dockland** (p92) building and seek out its panoramic harbour terrace.
🚆 30min from Central Station

Visit the palatial hidden courtyard of Hamburg's **Rathaus** (p92).
🚶 15min from Central Station

HAMBURG
Trip Builder

Visit the **Auswanderermuseum BallinStadt** (p97) and trace the steps of German migrants to the Americas.
🚆 15min from Central Station

Germany's largest port boasts historical cosmopolitanism and affluence. This is a city with a story to tell as a destination primely anchoring European maritime heritage, past and future. Hamburg's 'gateway to the world' has bait for every interest.

FROM LEFT: SON-MEDIA/SHUTTERSTOCK, JJFARQ/SHUTTERSTOCK
PREVIOUS PAGE: X TORBEN KNAUER/SHUTTERSTOCK

0 — 1 km
0 — 0.5 miles

Practicalities

ARRIVING

Hamburg Airport Fly in from most European cities. Other direct international flights include Dubai, Doha and Istanbul, though none from North America.
Hamburg Central Station Reached from Berlin and Frankfurt by direct train (approximately three hours).

FIND YOUR WAY

Hamburg Central Station has free wi-fi and lots to kill time in the direct vicinity, including waterfront walking paths and St Georg.

MONEY

Dive pubs aside, cards are accepted almost everywhere (MasterCard and Visa; American Express less so). Carry a little cash.

WHERE TO STAY

Place	Pros/Cons
Altstadt	Excellent transport. Walking distance to most attractions. Feels touristy.
Speicherstadt & HafenCity	Close to museums. Lacks locals/neighbourhood personality.
St Pauli & Reeperbahn	Vibrant neighbourhood vibes. Noisy on weekends.
Altona & Elbmeile	Residential feel and quality dining. A train ride from inner city.

EATING & DRINKING

Visiting without trying a *Fischbrötchen* (fish sandwich) is sacrilege. Seafood is an obvious favourite, but don't miss traditional northern specialities.

If there's a quintessential Hamburg dish, it's *Labskaus*, a sailors' stew of potato, cured beef, herring and beetroot. Hamburg is also famous for its *Franzbrötchen* (essentially, a cinnamon-filled croissant), allegedly originating in local bakeries during Napoleon's occupation.

Best Labskaus Das Dorf (p101)
Must-try Fischbrötchen Fischmarkt (p91)

GETTING AROUND

Walking and cycling The city centre is easily walkable; renting a bike expedites sightseeing.

Public transport Trains, buses and trams go everywhere; bikes board free on weekends and in August.

Taxi and Uber Taxis are expensive but necessary outside the city centre. Ubers are cheaper, but due to local regulations are scarcely available.

JUN–AUG
The busiest time. Book ahead for most things.

SEP–NOV
Can be lovely, but is cold. Nightlife still rocks; less-crowded museums.

DEC–FEB
Quietest time to visit. Christmas markets brighten things.

MAR–MAY
Similar to autumn: chilly but sometimes delightful.

Hidden GEMS

HISTORY | FREE SITES | MUSEUMS

Trust Hamburg – a city hellbent on keeping its individuality and counterculture – to keep some of its best experiences away from prying eyes. Behind unmarked doors, and with little pomp and circumstance, you'll find the port's rebellious, adventure-loving soul.

How to

Getting around
Sightsee on foot where possible and you'll be rewarded with a deeper understanding of each neighbourhood's personality.

When to go Consider visiting outside of busy summer season, but bring layers, including a waterproof coat and sturdy shoes for all-weather sightseeing.

Guided tours
Hamburg's stockpile of scenes can require navigational help. Consider interest-specific tours of St Pauli counterculture, craft beer, the Beatles in Hamburg etc.

'After Hours' Harbour Tradition

Hamburg's legendary **Fischmarkt** is the perfect excuse to stay up all Saturday night. Every Sunday in the wee hours (5am to 9.30am during summer), some 70,000 locals and visitors descend upon the harbour's crowded, fast-paced scene. Hilariously, many visitors are not your average early birds but partygoers fending off hangovers with fish sandwiches. Running since 1703, the market has, in recent years, become Hamburg's de facto 'after hours' Sunday party. Survive loud and boisterous *Marktschreier* (market criers), strong fishy grilling and live German-pop bands in the **Fischauktionshalle** (Fish Auction Hall) – while nursing a throbbing headache – and you might feel invincible.

Weird Science

Hamburg's long history of engineering and trade-driven innovation has fostered

Hamburg Fight Club

The entrance to **Zur Ritze**, an iconic Reeperbahn dive, is marked with painted legs spread wide. Punks and, sometimes, local celebs get tipsy inside. Its basement is an active **boxing gym**. Established in 1974 by an East German middleweight, the 'boxing cellar' has trained St Pauli street fighters and bouncers, as well as Mike Tyson, Muhammad Ali and both Klitschkos.

Above left Fischauktionshalle (Fish Auction Hall) **Above right** Boxing gym, Zur Ritze **Left** Fischmarkt

a fleet of science museums with oddball, anti-textbook flair. The supermarket-themed **Deutsches Zusatzstoffmuseum** (German Food Additives Museum) sheds light on the unhealthy artificial additives hidden in our meals. Meanwhile, the **Medizinhistorisches Museum** (Medical History Museum), at the Hamburg University Teaching Hospital, is a treasure trove of bizarre exhibits – eerie wax figurines and strange instruments tracing medical history from the 19th century.

Stately Secrets

Hamburg's 1897-inaugurated **Rathaus** (City Hall) is a 647-room beehive of secret chambers. Parade through its maze on a guided tour (though only certain rooms are visited as the building still functions as the seat of the Hamburg Senate and Parliament).

Better yet, march straight through the Grand Entrance Hall to take in its **'hidden' courtyard**. The alfresco area is wondrous, and one of Hamburg's most relaxing, free-to-enjoy spots.

Expect the Unexpected

Discover Hamburg's busy, experimental craft-brewing scene: Germany's first organic brewery **Wildwuchs Brauwerk** and beer-sommelier-owned **Kehrwieder Kreativbrauerei** stand out.

The futurist-looking **Dockland** office building has a free public-access terrace offering incredible harbour perspectives.

Skip a touristy harbour cruise to board one of the (much cheaper) **HADAG commuter ferries**.

Score some of Hamburg's best river views from the **Altonaer Balkon** (Altona Balcony). The hilltop park is elevated 27m above the Elbe.

Catch a St Pauli FC soccer match at **Millerntor-Stadion** where punk locals reject traditional hooligan culture, waving rainbow, LGBTIQ+ flags bearing the club's skull-and-crossbones logo.

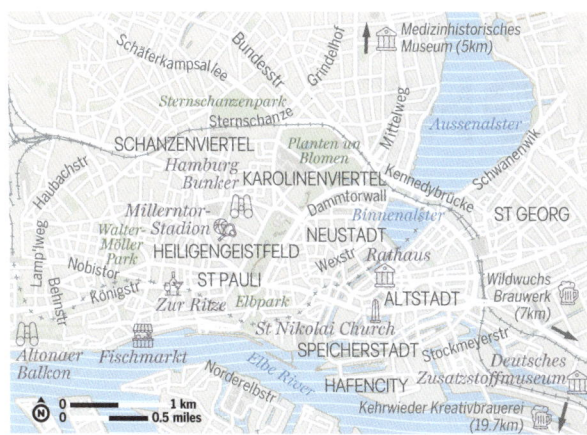

Left Altonaer Balkon (Altona Balcony)
Below St Nikolai Church

Comfy chairs and tables overlook the eternally gorgeous **Hygieia Fountain**, featuring a bronze of the Greek goddess of health in remembrance of Germany's 1892 cholera epidemic. More than 17,000 people fell ill through drinking water; over 8605 people (many working class) lost their lives.

WWII Relics

As a crucial strategic defence position during WWII, Hamburg is loaded with wartime reminders.

St Nikolai Church was the world's tallest building from 1874 to 1876, and it remains Hamburg's second-tallest structure. Today, its bombed-out remains encompass a war memorial and crypt history museum. Take the lift up St Nikolai's 76.3m-high **observation tower** inside the surviving spire for awesome views. Down below, walk among the church's naval ruinous remnants in an **open-air courtyard**. It's free to enter and often holds pop-up exhibitions.

The brooding **Hamburg Bunker**, a former air-raid shelter, is a WWII relic full of surprises and historical footnotes. Climb the 300-plus steps of the concrete 'mountain path' to a **rooftop urban garden** offering unparalleled 360-degree city views. Along the way, there's a cafe with excellent views, historical displays and a bird's-eye peek at the Millnertor-Stadion soccer stadium and Hamburg's tallest building (though publicly closed), the TV Tower.

14 Ride the NIGHT

DIVE BARS | LIVE MUSIC | UNDERGROUND CLUBS

Nightlife in Hamburg, with its cool cocktail bars and amazing live-music venues, goes far beyond the Reeperbahn. That said, a bad-decisions bar romp around the red-light district (Titty Twister Bar, anyone?) is, for many, a partygoer's rite of passage. Despite this, Hamburg's egalitarian spirit is well represented by nightlife, offering something for every mood and sailor's wage.

How to

Getting here Bar-hopping in St Pauli is effortless, with pubs on almost every corner. Clubs are in outer, industrial areas, requiring taxi service on speed dial.

When to go Hamburg's nightlife is a 24/7, year-round affair. Weekends are busiest, of course, but finding action on weekdays isn't hard.

Hidden charges Beware of boisterous Reeperbahn doorstaff offering 'free entry'. These clubs are often pretty lame and have a mandatory drink minimum.

Dive-bar wonderland In St Pauli, *Kneipe* bars (dive pubs) are a utopia for cheap, stiff drinks and gruff, quirky locals. Originating from working-class, maritime culture, today they are an (anti-)establishment of local punk culture. What makes a *Kneipe*? Rustic interiors, low lights, trashy toilets and maybe a jukebox or billiards. Smoking indoors is often accepted – card payments aren't. After everywhere else is shut, trust your local St Pauli *Kneipe* such as **St Pauli Eck** and **Golden Pudel Club** to serve till sunrise.

Beatlemania Long before forging rock 'n' roll history, the Beatles paid their dues performing on the famous Grosse Freiheit party mile. On the corner of the Reeperbahn and Grosse Freiheit, stand atop the vinyl-record-shaped **Beatles-Platz**, next to abstract steel sculptures of the band (including a hybrid of Ringo Starr and the band's

original drummer, Pete Best). The band's name is commemorated outside the **Kaiserkeller** and the **Indra** – both have full concert lineups today. The dive pub **Gretel & Alfons** was the Fab Four's favourite haunt – legend has it Paul McCartney ran up (and forgot) a considerable tab here. He eventually paid decades later.

Unlikely beach bars

Undeterred by the active harbour or *Schmuddelwetter* (drizzly weather), Hamburg's city beach is a paradise of sand-covered bars along the banks of the Elbe. Enjoy a beer on a lounger at **Strandpauli** – maybe even a dance party – no matter the weather.

Best After Dark

Start evenings at **Frau Hedi's Tanzkaffee** (Dance Cafe), a docked party boat.

Stashed in Hamburg Bunker, the **Uebel & Gefaehrlich** (Evil and Dangerous) nightclub is a 1000-person-capacity, delirium-inducing spin into Hamburg's electronic-music rave scene.

Catch alt-music concerts, often with art installations, on the **MS Stubnitz**, a docked East German fishing vessel turned event space.

Sprawling warehouse **Südpol** is Hamburg's underground clubbing institution. Find it hidden between off-downtown office complexes.

In **St Georg**, LGBTIQ+ nightlife reigns supreme. Strict door policies protect safe spaces; there's zero tolerance for unruly behaviour.

The Reeperbahn's classiest address, the elegant **Tanzende Tuerme** (Dancing Towers) building, houses jazz lair Mojo Club, Clouds steakhouse and cocktail-heaven Clouds Bar.

Above Strandpauli

15 Audiovisual & ARTY

CONTEMPORARY ART GALLERIES | SENSORY MUSEUMS | MODERN ART

Hamburg's arts and culture scene is here to make you feel things. Emotionally, the city can seem restrained, shaped by northern German stoicism. However, this conceals a deep intensity and a high social conscience fuelling thriving activist and counterculture scenes. A long history of immigration and port life fosters creativity, fringe cultures, and collective cultural expressions speaking louder than personal overtures.

Getting around Get the Hamburg Card to visit museums, with public transport included (from €11.90 a day).

When to go Visit during spring (April to June) and early autumn (September to October) for less-busy viewings.

Art Mile Hamburg's five-pack of renowned art institutions, the *Kunstmeile* (Art Mile), is a contemporary art lover's must-do. With a three-day Art Mile Pass (€35), feast your eyes on them all.

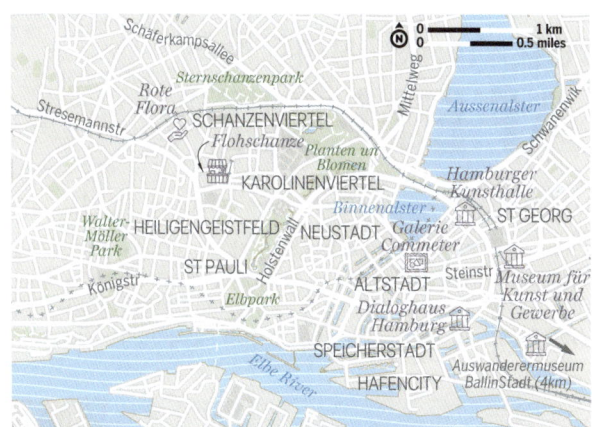

Top left The Rote Flora
Bottom left Hamburger Kunsthalle

The Rote Flora Once a dapper 19th-century theatre but today a rather decrepit building, **The Rote Flora** is Hamburg's most important anti-establishment landmark. Graffiti covered and unkept, the building was occupied by activists in 1989 amid commercial development plans. In 2014 the Hamburg government granted Rote Flora legal protection. Check out a lively programme of activist-led cultural events and performances here.

Arts treasure trove Germany's wealthiest urban economy premises Hamburg's dynamic arts scene. From Renaissance works to medieval art and contemporary works, the world-class **Hamburger Kunsthalle** has a bit of everything, including a memorable 19th-century German Romanticism room filled with Caspar David Friedrich works. The stark white modern cube addition, **Galerie der Gegenwart**, showcases contemporary German artists, while the **Museum für Kunst und Gewerbe** (Museum for Art and Industry) is an artisan-everything paradise. Find handcrafted wares from across different cultures and generations – furniture, fashion, jewellery, posters, porcelain and musical instruments.

'Outsider' perspectives Hamburg's lesser-known perspectives are emphasised on the culture circuit. A bookend for New York's Ellis Island, the **Auswanderermuseum BallinStadt** (Emigration Museum) looks at the exodus of five million Germans to the USA and South America from 1850 to the 1930s. Multilingual displays highlight their voyages and New World arrivals. **Dialoghaus Hamburg** offers a powerful experience by simulating the daily life of visually impaired individuals. Visitors walk through completely dark rooms guided by vision-impaired people.

Best Around the Underground

Schanzenviertel and **Karolinenviertel** are vibrant places to hang out and explore local creativity in independent boutiques, vintage shops and small, independent galleries.

Flohschanze, hosted in a former slaughterhouse, is Hamburg's best Saturday flea market. It's a nirvana for thrifty trinket hunters and vintage junkies, with hundreds of vendors selling their own art or secondhand bric-a-brac.

At **Hijack**'s modern-art gallery, catch exhibitions combined with a nightlife party atmosphere: live singers, salsa dancing and DJs.

The privately run **Galerie Commeter** is Hamburg's oldest gallery. Contemporary arts galore and, unlike most Hamburg galleries, it's free to visit.

16 Speicherstadt & HAFENCITY

FUTURISTIC BUILDINGS | HARBOUR LIFE | OFFBEAT MARITIME HISTORY

Welcome to the waterfront. The seven-storey red-brick warehouses lining the Speicherstadt archipelago are a famous Hamburg symbol. Around the Elbphilharmonie, find Hamburg's crowning architecturally dynamic corner. It's located in the developing HafenCity, an area innovatively and sustainably shaping the city's future.

Trip Notes

Getting around The underground U4 line links HafenCity (Überseequartier station) citywide. Otherwise, it's a 10-minute walk from the city centre.

When to go Avoid tour groups visiting in the morning. The Elbphilharmonie observation deck stays open until 11.30pm daily.

What to bring You'll be mostly outdoors with little shade around; bring sunscreen and a water bottle. If you need a toilet or resting spot, visit the **HafenCity Info Center**.

Golden Hour

However many times you visit the Elbphilharmonie, devote at least one late afternoon to taking a **boat cruise** along the Elbe west of the building (from Landungsbrücken) – the sunset on the glass panels as the city lights begin to wink is pure magic.

Listings

BEST OF THE REST

 Gawk-worthy Architecture

Chilehaus
One of Hamburg's most beautiful buildings is this brick-and-copper beauty. Gaze at its ocean-liner-esque shape, remarkable curved walls like a ship's bow and staggered balconies like ship decks.

St Michaelis Kirche
Der Michel (The Michael) is one of Hamburg's most recognisable landmarks and northern Germany's largest Protestant baroque church. Ascend the tower (by steps or lift) for great citywide vistas.

Alsterarkaden
Stroll this elegant, Venetian-inspired shopping arcade along the waterfront. Renaissance-style columns flank upmarket shops and cafes against the Alsterfleet canal.

Deichstrasse
Get a feel for the old canal and merchants' quarter along this street in the Altstadt (Old City). Restored 18th-century homes now mostly house restaurants.

 Live-Music Venues

Molotow
A hot 'n' heavy indie rock club right on the Reeperbahn. One of the red-light district's better venues, its stage has hosted bands from the White Stripes to the Hives.

Hafenklang
A collective of Hamburg industry insiders presents established and emerging DJs and bands, clubbing events and parties. Look for the spray-painted name on the graffiti-covered, dark-brick harbour shop above a blank metal door.

Docks Prinzenbar
This elegant, baroque club – think cheeky cherubs, stucco flourishes and sparkling chandeliers – with an intimate atmosphere was once a cinema. Electro bashes, concerts and queer parties, just off the Reeperbahn.

Fabrik
A former factory in Altona firmly associated with beautiful sounds. The live music ranges from classical to DJ sets; also hosts theatre and film (with excellent acoustics, of course).

Cascadas
One of the better live-music venues outside of St Pauli, The nightly programme ranges across soul, jazz, Latin, funk, Caribbean and blues.

 Underground Clubs

NCTS
A pop-up industrial warehouse for high-BPM underground beats. The best spot for a bass-heavy night with Hamburg's most discerning and experienced ravers. Difficult door.

Hafenklang

Golden Cut

One of Hamburg's top clubs, with pretty strict door policy and long queues. Local and touring DJs play house, R&B and hip-hop parties; it also hosts big-show after-soirées.

 ## Cocktail Bars

Kyti Voo

A mixed St Georg crowd shaken with a rewarding menu of craft beer and cocktails until very late. At sunnier (or less dark) times, grab a table on the outdoor terrace.

Clockers

Forest-inspired Altona cocktail den winning many mixology awards. Serious concoctions are served between mossy walls, branches and fairy lights.

Le Lion

Easily the classiest, most exclusive bar (by virtue of size) you'll find in Altstadt – no, Hamburg. If there's space and you're nicely dressed, slip into this cocktail lair and order the signature gin basil smash.

 ## Cafes in St Georg

Café Gnosa €

With abstract art and an in-house bakery, Café Gnosa draws an affable crowd. A gay meeting point since the 1950s, it's a popular spot for breakfast and coffee dates.

Das Dorf €€€

There are lots of reasons to visit this wonderfully traditional cafe-restaurant with its pavement terrace and wood-panelled dining room. We love it especially for its homemade bread and northern German specialities such as *Labskaus* stew.

Fraulein Fritz €

Not on the main Lange Reihe stretch, but well worth a visit, it has a changing lunch menu of

Café Gnosa

two options, as well as homemade lemonade. Fast service, high-quality regional produce and affordable.

 ## Fine Dining

Bullerei €€

One of Hamburg's coolest dining spaces, Bullerei inhabits a converted Altona slaughterhouse with buzzy acoustics – don't come for a quiet romantic dinner. Steak and Italian-inflected dishes are on the menu.

The Table €€€

Lauded young German chef Kevin Fehling serves haute cuisine on a single communal table. A beautiful, modern-build dining room and sustainable, experimental dishes echo the restaurant's location in futuristic HafenCity.

Fischereihafen €€€

Near the Elbmeile waterfront and serving Hamburg's finest fish and regional specialities in a maritime-themed, river-facing dining room. Lobster comes in many forms. The Oyster Bar is a gentrified treat.

Deichgraf €€€

In a prime waterside setting in Altstadt, Deichgraf is an old guard on the port city's fine-dining scene. Excels in Hamburg specialities cooked to a high standard.

CENTRAL GERMANY

HISTORY | ARCHITECTURE | LAND OF FAIRY TALES

RESEARCHED BY ANTHONY HAM

- ▶ **Trip Builder** (p104)
- ▶ **Practicalities** (p106)
- ▶ **Discover Goethe's Weimar** (p108)
- ▶ **Explore a Storied Small Town** (p110)
- ▶ **Explore Erfurt's Historical Legacy** (p112)
- ▶ **The Trail of the Brothers Grimm** (p116)
- ▶ **Follow the Bauhaus Trail** (p118)
- ▶ **Listings** (p120)

CENTRAL GERMANY
Trip Builder

Germany's heartland was once divided in two, but since reunification this has become one of the country's most rewarding corners. Cities steeped in history – Weimar, Erfurt and Dessau-Rosslau – yield to postcard-perfect villages such as Quedlinburg, with the historical significance of its story far outstripping its size.

Discover the world of the Brothers Grimm in **Kassel** (p117)
🚆 *2hr from Frankfurt*

See where the Brothers Grimm grew up in **Steinau an der Strasse** (p117)
🚗 *1½hr from Kassel*

FROM LEFT: CAMILO CONCHA/SHUTTERSTOCK, LEV LEVIN/SHUTTERSTOCK, PLAM PETROV/SHUTTERSTOCK
PREVIOUS PAGE: CAMILO CONCHA/SHUTTERSTOCK

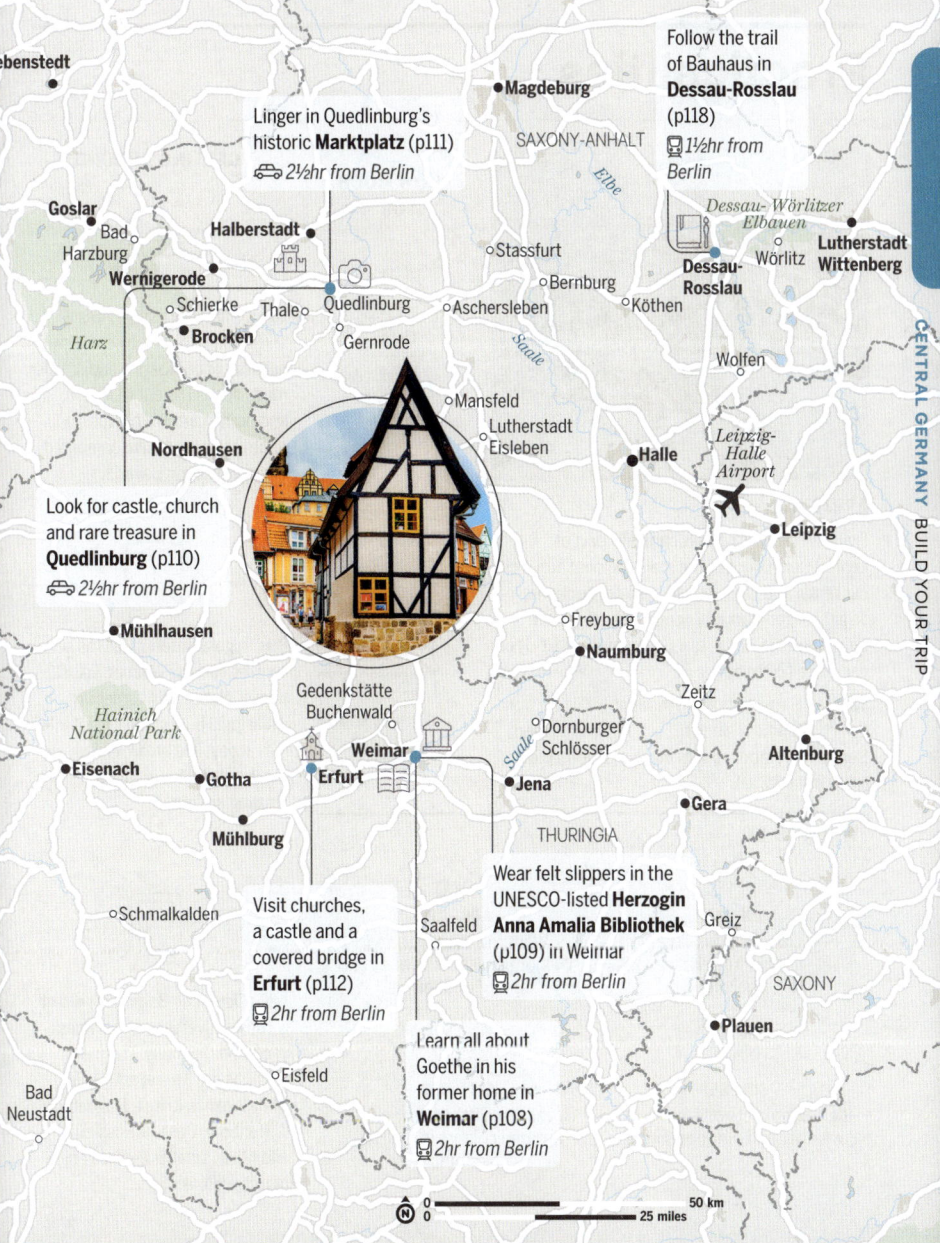

Practicalities

ARRIVING

Frankfurt Airport Not technically part of central Germany, but the main regional hub with car rental and car, bus and train connections. To get to Frankfurt city centre, take the train (20 minutes, €6.60), taxi (20 minutes, €6.60) or car share (20 minutes, €20).

Weimar Hauptbahnhof Frequent trains to/from Erfurt, Frankfurt, Munich, Leipzig, Dresden and Berlin. The station is 1km north of Goetheplatz (walk or taxi €10).

HOW MUCH FOR A

Kiosk beer
€1.50

Toilet at train stations
€1

2nd-class train ticket to Erfurt
€7.80

GETTING AROUND

Car Central Germany is easily and safely explored by car. The network of autobahns and smaller roads spans the entire region, and rental cars are plentiful and relatively inexpensive compared to neighbouring Bavaria.

Bus Regular intercity buses serve centres such as Weimar, Erfurt, Kassel, Halle and Magdeburg, while local buses radiate out into less accessible areas, including the Harz Mountains and Thuringian forest.

Train Deutsche Bahn (DB) directly runs or oversees all services in central Germany. The major rail hubs are Kassel and Halle, while Weimar, Erfurt, Magdeburg, Wittenberg, Dessau-Rosslau and other, smaller centres enjoy regular connections.

WHEN TO GO

JAN–MAR
Few crowds, cross-country skiing and winter heartland cooking.

APR–JUN
Warming temperatures, Walpurgisnacht festivities and spring wildflowers.

JUL–SEP
High-season crowds, but warm weather and outdoor dining.

OCT–DEC
December Christmas markets; autumn colours in the Harz Mountains.

EATING & DRINKING

The Thuringia region, which takes in much of central Germany, has one of Germany's most beloved traditional cuisines. Highlights include Thüringer *Kloss* (a large dumpling made from mashed and grated raw potato and typically served with *Rotkohl*, or red cabbage), *Sauerbraten* (vinegar-marinated pot roast), *Schweinshaxe* (pork knuckle), *Rostbrätel* (pork neck) and dark-beer *Gulasch*. The Thüringer *Rostbratwurst* (a grilled pork and beef sausage usually eaten in a soft white roll with Born Sen, a mustard from Erfurt) has been following the same recipe since 1432.

Best Thüringer Kloss Benediktiner Wirtshaus im joHanns Hof (p120)

Must Try Rostbrätel Brunnenkeller (p121)

CONNECT & FIND YOUR WAY

Wi-fi is widespread and free in hotels, restaurants, shops, cafes and many public areas. Navigation can be complicated in cities with old towns, as some have restricted access as well as one-way streets that are not always clearly marked.

WHERE TO STAY

Accommodation is consistent throughout the region, with everything from modern business hotels to half-timbered guesthouses overlooking cobbled squares.

Town or Village	Pros/Cons
Weimar	Charming old-town. Easy to access by car and get around on foot. Some central hotels can be noisy.
Erfurt	Lots of accommodation choice and compact old town. Access to some hotels by car is complicated.
Kassel	Excellent hotel choices. Driving in the city centre can be difficult.
Quedlinburg	Beautiful old-town setting. Fewer choices than cities.
Göttingen	Fabulous base for the Fairy Tale Road. Better hotels on the city-centre fringe.

DISCOUNT CARDS

Most larger towns have a discount card covering single or multi-day transport and entry to attractions. Check the tourist offices in Kassel, Weimar, Erfurt, Halle and Dessau-Rosslau.

MONEY

ATMs are everywhere, with at least one in most villages. Carry an emergency stash of euros for those out-of-the-way places that don't accept credit cards.

17 Discover Goethe's WEIMAR

HISTORY | CULTURE | ARCHITECTURE

Weimar is a city steeped in history, and Germany's cultural colossus, Johann Wolfgang von Goethe, is at the heart of it. In the 18th and 19th century, he spent much of his life in Weimar: he moved here in 1775, aged 26, and remained until his death on 22 March 1832. He is the lens through which everything else in Weimar makes sense.

How to

Getting here and around Weimar is well connected to other German cities by bus and train. If you do have a car, parking overnight in a city car park costs €15 for 24 hours. Then get out and walk.

When to go Avoid July and August; spring and autumn are ideal.

Discount card The Weimar Card (€32.50) gives 48-hour access to most museums, a free guided walking tour and discounts elsewhere.

Where he lived For 50 years, Goethe lived in the 18th-century **Wohnhaus** (residence) on Frauenplan square, a 'bribe' from Karl August, Grand Duke of Saxe-Weimar-Eisenac, to keep Goethe here, reinforcing the grand duke's dreams of a Weimar-centric cultural revival.

The museum The **Goethe-Nationalmuseum** has the world's largest collection of Goethe manuscripts and artefacts. Plan on a couple of hours here using a free audio-guide. See the study where he wrote *Faust* (1808), the quill and inkstand still on the desk, and the bedroom where he died, still in its original state.

Goethe's first house Goethe lived at the **Goethe Gartenhaus** from his arrival

Top right Herzogin Anna Amalia Bibliothek
Bottom right Wittumspalais

> ## Weimar of the Enlightenment
>
> Goethe was not Weimar's only cultural giant: Schiller, Bach, Liszt, Gropius, Schopenhauer, Kandinsky, Klee and Nietzsche all spent time here, earning the city a reputation as the cradle of Germany's Enlightenment. The **Goethe-Schiller Archive** is the country's oldest literary archive, with over five million artefacts of 18th-, 19th- and 20th-century German literature. Delve deeper into Weimar's rich cultural soil with a visit to the **Schiller Museum**; the **Liszt-Haus**, where composer Franz Liszt lived; and the beautiful **Nietzsche Archiv**, where the philosopher lived out his final years.

in the city until he moved to the Wohnhaus six years later. The spare, cosy cottage is surrounded by the garden that Goethe himself laid out, now part of this 23.5-hectare, UNESCO-listed park.

Palace and library The **Wittumspalais** was the stately home of the Herzogin (Duchess) Anna Amalia. Goethe was a regular in its salons, which still display period furnishings and ceiling frescoes. Don't miss the ravishing, rococo, UNESCO-listed **Herzogin Anna Amalia Bibliothek** (Anna Amalia's Library); only 25 visitors are allowed in at a time, all wearing felt slippers.

18 Explore A Storied SMALL TOWN

ARCHITECTURE | CASTLES & CHURCHES | VILLAGE LIFE

Steeped in history as the 'cradle of the German Reich', Quedlinburg is a beautiful small town just north of the Harz Mountains. Signposts to that history are everywhere, from the imposing castle to churches and half-timbered buildings. Visit its monuments and museums by all means, but don't forget to spend time in Marktplatz, admiring the architecture and watching the world go by.

How to

Getting here and around Easily reached by car, bus or train, but best explored on foot.

When to go Try to come on a weekday in spring (March to May) or autumn (September to November).

Audioguide Quedlinburg has two tourist offices and both offer an audioguide (in English, German or Japanese) covering 20 points of interest across town.

Top left Marktplatz
Bottom left Schloss Quedlinburg

High on castle hill Start atop Quedlinburg's Schlossberg – the sheer, rocky prominence around which the town clusters – at the 10th-century **Stiftskirche St Servatius** (Collegiate Church St Servatii). It's a masterpiece of Romanesque church architecture and features tombs, rare Bibles and a crypt with early religious frescoes. Also here is the **Schloss Quedlinburg**, a Renaissance palace containing the **Schlossmuseum**, which was closed for major renovations when we last visited.

A favourite square As you meander through the quiet streets and canals of central Quedlinburg, little prepares you for **Marktplatz**, the elongated town 'square' that's one of the loveliest in central Germany. Dozens of 16th-century *Fachwerk* (half-timbered) homes and other buildings line the perimeter and, at Marktplatz' northern end, the greenery-cloaked, still-functioning **Rathaus** (1320) is an unusual counterpoint to the half-timbered facades. Immediately behind the Rathaus is the **Marktkirche St Benediktii**, a graceful 12th-century church.

Intimate local corners Nearby, at Breite Strasse 39, is the **Gildehaus zur Rose** (1612). Running off Markt is the tiny **Schuhhof**, a shoemakers' courtyard with shutters and stable-like 'gossip doors'. **Alter Klopstock** (1580), at Stieg 28, has the scrolled beams typical of Quedlinburg.

A fine museum Some of Quedlinburg's 2000 traditional *Fachwerk* houses are more than 600 years old. They're the focus of the **Fachwerkmuseum im Ständerbau**.

The Romanesque Road

The churches of **St Wiperti**, just outside Quedlinburg, and Stiftskirche St Servatius make Quedlinburg a prominent stop on the **Strasse der Romanik** *(The Romanesque Road; strassederromanik.de)*. Divided into northern and southern sections, the driving route connects towns in Saxony-Anhalt that hold significant Romanesque buildings, weaving together 80 sites of historical and architectural interest. Its starting point is Magdeburg, the principal sights of which include the 10th-century **Magdeburger Dom** and the **Monastery of Our Lady**, which now houses an art museum. Other stops include Gernrode, Freyburg, Naumburg and Halle, the foremost Romanesque sight of which is the **Burg Giebichenstein** (Giebichenstein Castle).

EXPLORE
Erfurt's Historical Legacy

OLD TOWN | ARCHITECTURE | FOOD

Erfurt is a gem from the German heartland that sees only a fraction of the visitors it deserves, although word is getting out. Thuringia's capital is a world of churches, and its medieval centre and immense baroque fortress are simply superb.

How to

Getting here and around There are good train and bus connections from major German towns; the compact old city is best explored by walking.

When to go Erfurt's pretty squares are perfect when the sun shines; July and August have the best weather, but May, June and September have fewer visitors.

ErfurtCard Head to the tourist office for a 48-hour ErfurtCard. The standard version (€14.90) provides a free tour (in German) and entry to attractions.

Ancient Churches & Castle

Erfurt's old town is anchored by Cathedral Hill, which is named for **Erfurter Dom**, the 12th-century Romanesque-Gothic Catholic cathedral where Martin Luther was ordained as a priest. The Dom is home to numerous treasures, among them 15th-century Gloriosa, the world's largest free-swinging medieval bell; exquisite stained-glass windows; the 'Wolfram' (an 850-year-old bronze candelabrum in the shape of a man); a Romanesque stucco Madonna; Cranach's *The Mystic Marriage of St Catherine*; and intricately carved choir stalls.

Alongside Erfurter Dom on the hilltop is the late-13th-century **Severikirche** (Church of St Severus), which has its own gems: a stone Madonna (1345), a 15m-high sandstone font (1467) and the sarcophagus of St Severus.

Erfurt Orientation

Build your exploration around Altstadt's squares: **Domplatz**, the largest, sprawling below Cathedral Hill; **Anger**, a transport and shopping hub where old meets new; **Wenigemarkt**, a tiny old market square that's perfect for a casual meal; and **Fischmarkt**, the city's central square with a collection of spectacular historic buildings.

Above left Erfurter Dom
Above right Anger **Left** Severikirche (Church of St Severus)

Beyond Domberg looms the 36-hectare **Zitadelle Petersberg**, one of Europe's most complete and impressive baroque fortresses. Guided tours of its labyrinthine tunnels are organised through the tourist office.

A Medieval Bridge

Spanning the Gera between Wenigemarkt and Benediktsplatz is the photogenic **Krämerbrücke** (Merchants' Bridge), the longest shop-lined medieval bridge in Europe. Built in 1325, the stone bridge is believed to be the only one north of the Alps that's still inhabited. Get a fine view of the bridge by climbing the tower of the **Ägidienkirche** (Church of St Aegidius) at its eastern end.

Jewish Erfurt

Erfurt was once home to a thriving Jewish community, and it was centred on the **Alte Synagoge**, one of the oldest surviving synagogues in Europe. In 1349, a pogrom

Erfurt Festivals

Every year at Easter, the **Thüringer Bachwochen** (*Thuringian Bach Festival; thueringer-bachwochen.de*) brings 17th- and 18th-century music to the city (among other locations significant to Bach's life).

Erfurt's medieval past is revived on the third week of June during the **Krämerbrückenfest**.

At the height of summer, for three weeks in July and August, the **Domstufen Festspiele** (*Cathedral Steps Theatre Festival; domstufen-festspiele.de*) sees operas, children's musicals and other performances take over the steps beneath Erfurter Dom.

Lesser-known music gets a run in September and October during **Güldener Herbst** (*gueldener-herbst.de*), showcasing forgotten operas, cantatas and other compositions across different Erfurt venues.

Left Krämerbrücke (Merchants' Bridge) **Below** Alte Synagoge

prompted the Jewish community to disguise the synagogue as an inn and storage area. The practice continued into the 20th century, ultimately saving the synagogue from destruction during the Nazi era.

Apart from its history, the synagogue's greatest asset is the golden hoard known as the 'Erfurt Treasure'. Unearthed during excavations nearby, the haul included jewellery, cutlery and, most famously, a very rare golden Jewish marriage ring from the early 14th century.

Martin Luther's Erfurt

On the other side of the bridge from the Alte Synagoge is the **Augustinerkloster**, the Augustinian monastery where Luther lived from 1505 to 1511, where he was ordained as a monk and where he read his first Mass and preached his first sermon. You can visit the grounds and church (with its haunting Gothic stained-glass windows) for free, while guided tours take you through the cloister and Luther's cell. There's also a small exhibition on Luther's time in Erfurt.

If you want to spend some time in contemplation on Luther's old patch, you can stay overnight.

20 THE TRAIL OF
the Brothers Grimm

LEGENDS | SCENIC DRIVE | CULTURE

The Märchenstrasse, or Fairy Tale Road, follows the Brothers Grimm and their stories on a magical journey across the central German landscape. The towns you'll explore either capture part of the brothers' lives or draw near to one of their stories.

Trip Notes

Getting here and around You could follow the route by bus, but having your own wheels allows you to travel at your own pace, with greater flexibility.

When to go Best seen in fine weather, the Märchenstrasse is ideal from late spring to mid-autumn.

Information The full Fairy Tale Road runs 600km from Hanau to Bremen, with 50-odd fairy-tale-associated stops. Visit *deutsche-maerchenstrasse.com* for maps and a full list of attractions.

Made for Disney

The remarkable output of Jacob and Wilhelm Grimm arose from ancient German or Hessian storytelling traditions. Their most famous stories included 'Hansel and Gretel', 'Little Red Riding Hood', 'Cinderella', 'Sleeping Beauty', 'Rapunzel', 'Snow White and the Seven Dwarves' and 'Puss in Boots' (among many others).

21 FOLLOW
the Bauhaus Trail

ARCHITECTURE | HISTORY | DESIGN

Part architectural style, part philosophy of life, Bauhaus (literally, 'building house') is one of the most enduring cultural legacies to emerge from central Germany in the 20th century. The Bauhaus approach to design has been hugely influential in modern life, and you'll get to enjoy its earliest (and some of its most memorable) manifestations in Weimar and Dessau-Rosslau.

How to

Getting here and around Direct regional services connect Dessau-Rosslau to Berlin (1½ hours) and other cities. Some Bauhaus sights are distant from the centre, so make use of the city's excellent network of trams.

When to go Avoid July, August and most weekends, though Dessau-Rosslau doesn't see the crowds of other central German cities.

Discount card The Welterbe (World Heritage) Card is available from tourist offices. For €24.90/44.90 you get 24/72 hours of free transport, tours, bike hire and access to all sights.

Top left Bauhaus-Dessau Museum
Bottom left Haus Muche/Schlemmer

Bauhaus Museum Bauhaus reached its creative peak in Dessau. Pick up the Bauhaus beat at the purpose-built **Bauhaus-Dessau Museum**, which opened in 2019 and houses exhibitions curated from a collection of more than 49,000 pieces – the second largest in the world after the Bauhaus-Berlin.

'Bauhaus Building' The next obligatory stop on your exploration of all things Bauhaus is the **Bauhausgebäude** itself. This iconic modernist building, designed by Gropius, was completed in 1926 as the School of Art, Design and Architecture. Grab an audioguide to explore the building and in-house exhibition.

Meisterhäuser Nearby are the **Masters' Houses** – the Gropiushaus, Haus Feininger, Haus Muche/Schlemmer and Haus Kandinsky/Klee – on leafy Ebertallee.

Haus Muche/Schlemmer Of them all, **Haus Muche/Schlemmer** is perhaps the most intriguing, offering as it does a window on some of the early experimental adaptations of the Bauhaus philosophy. While some of its design experiments, such as low balcony rails or room proportions, don't really cut it in the modern world, other features are startlingly innovative. The partially black bedroom here is intriguing – Marcel Breuer apparently burst in to paint it while reluctant owner Georg Muche was away on business.

Bauhaus Living To round out your Bauhaus experience, schedule a visit to the **Siedlung Törten** (Törten Estate), a complete, Bauhaus-designed 314-residence estate for working people that's still lived in (and much visited) today.

The Birth of Bauhaus

Bauhaus was founded in Weimar in 1925 and its defining principle is that 'form follows function'. It was based on practical, anti-elitist principles and the enunciation of a unifying artistic vision that aimed to make functional, accessible, yet human-focused everyday objects and spaces. The Bauhaus school united architecture, painting, furniture design and sculpture into a single discipline. By pioneering mass-production techniques and the integration of art, design and architecture as part of a commitment to improve human life, it's arguably responsible for much of the furniture we buy and the houses we build to this day. For more information, visit *bauhaus-dessau.de*.

Listings

BEST OF THE REST

 Castles & Palaces

Wartburg
This World Heritage–listed castle in Eisenach represents over 1000 years of German history. Goethe stayed at the immense, multi-layered fortress, and Martin Luther translated the New Testament into German here.

Schloss Friedenstein
In Gotha, 26km west of Erfurt, this creaky-floored horseshoe palace – Germany's largest early baroque palace – has 38 glorious and wonderfully preserved baroque, rococo and neoclassical apartments dating from the late 17th century.

Landgrafenschloss
Above Marburg's old town, this 13th-century castle is one of the best places in central Germany for seeing a castle as it was in its heyday. It offers fabulous views.

Schloss Wernigerode
Wernigerode's most impressive sight looks down from a high, wooded peak east of town. Built in the 12th century, it has superb apartments, a banquet hall and a church.

Kaiserpfalz Goslar
Goslar's preeminent symbol in a town that enjoys UNESCO World Heritage status, this palace-castle has an extravagant hall, a sarcophagus containing the heart of Holy Roman Emperor Henry III (!) and evocative church remains.

Burg Giebichenstein
Nearly 3km north of Halle's old-town centre, this castle is considered a Romanesque masterpiece. It was built in the 9th century.

Grüne Zitadelle
The Green Citadel, the last building created by Friedensreich Hundertwasser, is a whimsical fantasy with organically flowing walls set with friezes, 'dancing' windows, golden onion domes and a rooftop garden.

 Musical Masters

Bachhaus
One of Eisenach's principal attractions is the birthplace of Johann Sebastian Bach. Comprising two 15th-century houses knocked together, it houses the world's largest collection of Bach artefacts.

Händel-Haus
Halle's favourite son, Georg Friedrich Handel (1685–1759) is lavishly celebrated in the town of his birth. In the house of his birth, exhibits take you through his life, work and wider significance.

 Nazi Past

Gedenkstätte Buchenwald
Beyond Weimar's cultural and historic treasures lies a staggering testament to the darkest chapter in the city's past: the remains of Buchenwald Concentration Camp. The camp has been preserved almost untouched.

 Traditional Foods

Benediktiner Wirtshaus im joHanns Hof
This cosy courtyard pub is the place in Weimar for Thüringer *Klösse* with *Schweinebacke* (Thuringian pig cheek) and Saale-Unstrut wines.

Zum Weissen Schwan
Goethe himself used to recommend the traditional food at the 16th-century White Swan. Who are we to argue?

Brunnenkeller
Regional classics such as Thüringer *Rostbrätel* (pork neck) served beneath an ancient brick-vaulted ceiling or out on the square in Eisenach.

Alt Naumburg
The in-house restaurant of this superior pension slings Thuringian specialities such as *Rostbrätel* and *Fleischkäse* (meatloaf).

Regionalladen Harz
A few steps off Quedlinburg's Marktplatz, this fine little grocery store sells local delicacies, especially mustards and honeys.

 Local Wines

Rotkäppchen Sektkellerei
Founded in 1856, this local winemaker produces Sekt, the dry, sparkling wine for which Saale-Unstrut is renowned. Take a guided tour.

Weinatelier Rue
Wines from the nearby Saale-Unstrut region are among the 50-odd drops sold by the glass at this atmospheric bar in Erfurt.

 Churches

Naumburger Dom
Naumburg, at the confluence of the Saale and Unstrut, has a striking Renaissance Rathaus and an impressive medieval cathedral that blends Romanesque and early Gothic elements.

Magdeburger Dom
Founded as a monastery in 937 by the Holy Roman Emperor Otto I and later rebuilt as Germany's first Gothic cathedral (and rebuilt again after WWII), the sculptures and crypt here are magnificent.

 Martin Luther's Legacy

Luther's Geburtshaus & Sterbehaus
Re-creating the buildings where Luther was born and died in Eisleben, exhibits include

Hainich National Park

a precious Bible from 1541, the last Luther worked on in his life.

Schlosskirche
This church in Wittenburg is where Luther is said to have ignited the Protestant Reformation when he nailed his Ninety-five Theses to the door.

Stadtkirche Wittenberg
This is where Luther conducted the world's first Protestant worship services in 1521. Other nearby sites of interest include the Lutherhaus (the Luther family home) and the Luthereiche where, in 1521, he burnt his papal bull of excommunication.

 Old Stories

Landesmuseum für Vorgeschichte
Widely considered one of the most significant museums of prehistory in Europe. Highlights include the famous bronze Nebra sky disc and the oldest-known recorded human fingerprint.

 Out in Nature

Hainich National Park
Nature has been left to grow without interference into Germany's largest coherent deciduous forest. It's UNESCO World Heritage–listed and filled with wildlife.

SAXONY

BAROQUE | MUSIC | MOUNTAINS
RESEARCHED BY LEONID RAGOZIN

- ▶ **Trip Builder** (p124)
- ▶ **Practicalities** (p125)
- ▶ **A Gulp of Baroque in Dresden** (p126)
- ▶ **Riparian Bliss** (p130)
- ▶ **Paint Your Hike** (p132)
- ▶ **Sounds Like Leipzig** (p134)
- ▶ **Mountains of Abundance** (p136)
- ▶ **Venture into the German Far East** (p139)
- ▶ **Listings** (p140)

FROM LEFT: ARTONO/SHUTTERSTOCK,
NATALIYA SCHMIDT/SHUTTERSTOCK,
KAY WIEGAND/SHUTTERSTOCK
PREVIOUS PAGE: LEONID ANDRONOV/SHUTTERSTOCK

Enjoy Bach's choir for breakfast and Wagner's orchestra for dinner in **Leipzig** (p134)
🚆 *1hr from Berlin*

Marvel at **Dresden's** baroque cityscape and Saxon treasures (p126)
🚆 *2hr from Berlin*

Ride a steamship along the **Elbe** past vineyards and castles (p130)
⛴ *board in Dresden*

Treat yourself to some extra baroque and stroll into Poland in **Görlitz** (p138)
🚆 *1½hr from Dresden*

Hike through the whimsical rocky terrain of **Saxon Switzerland** (p132)
🚆 *1hr from Dresden*

Explore the castle and hit a hiking trail in **Schwarzenberg** (p136) in the Ore Mountains
🚆 *50min from Zwickau*

SAXONY
Trip Builder

Saxony is about living in style: catching a vintage steamship on the way to a castle, marvelling at Sixtine Madonna, savouring classical music at pedigreed venues, or following the steps of Caspar David Friedrich through the rugged landscapes he glorified.

Practicalities

ARRIVING

Most people arrive in Dresden and Leipzig by train or bus from Berlin. Prague and Karlovy Vary in Czechia are within easy reach of Dresden and the Ore Mountains. Trains running from Dresden to Görlitz continue to Zgorzelec in Poland, where you can change for Wrocław.

FIND YOUR WAY

Hotels and some restaurants provide wi-fi passwords to guests and customers. The Deutsche Bahn app is very useful for planning.

MONEY

Saxony tends to be more expensive than eastern lands on average. Around €5 for a pint of beer is a norm.

WHERE TO STAY

Town	Pros/Cons
Dresden	The Neustadt is cheaper and livelier than the Altstadt, but close to it.
Bad Schandau	Hiking trails, many restaurants and a large spa complex.
Leipzig	Altstadt stay on a reasonable budget. Can be a little noisy.
Schwarzenberg	Fairytale castle town near hiking trails.
Augustusburg	A youth hostel in a royal castle.
Görlitz	Peaceful and affordable, but a bit desolate.

EATING & DRINKING

The culinary landscape blends into Slavic. Brace for *Knödel* (dumplings) and *Sauerbraten* (pot roast).

A nonstandard fermented beer, *Gose,* is making a comeback in Leipzig after decades of obscurity. Main commercial beer brands include Radeberger and Freiberger. Leipzig is also famous for trademark desserts such as *Eierschecke* and *Leipziger Allerlei*.

Best place to try Saxon wine Schloss Wackerbarth (p131)

Must-try Gose beer Gosenschenke Ohne Bedenken (p141)

GETTING AROUND

Train The main railway axis runs from Plauen to Görlitz via Chemnitz and Dresden. All main sights along the Elbe valley are connected by Dresden's S-bahn.

Bus Intercity buses make the trip from Leipzig to Dresden much cheaper and not much longer.

Bicycle The 1300km Elberadweg route cuts through Saxony from Torgau in the northwest to the Czech border.

JAN–MAR
Skiing galore in the Ore Mountains.

APR–JUN
Rapeseed fields and orchards in bloom. Festival season in large cities.

JUL–SEP
Escape summer heat on a steamship journey or a mountain hike.

OCT–DEC
Beautiful autumn in Saxon Switzerland, and miners' parades in the mountains.

22 A Gulp of Baroque
IN DRESDEN

ARCHITECTURE | ART | OPERA

Black against the emerald green of the Elbe valley, the majestic silhouette of Dresden's Altstadt has risen from the ashes of WWII in almost full old-time glory. The baroque old town is brimming with architectural treasures and art collections.

How to

Getting here and around Dresden is roughly halfway between Berlin and Prague. Tram is the main mode of getting around, complemented by S-bahn for longer trips in and out of town.

When to go The best time to go is May and early June when everything blooms and the best city festivals take place.

Budget Dresden City Card is a way to save on transport and museums.

Brühl's Terrace & Residenzshloss

Take a walk on **Brühl's terrace**, a magnificent baroque promenade perched high above the Elbe and dubbed the 'balcony of Europe'. Then descend towards the sombre spire of **Katholische Hofkirche** (Dresden Cathedral), which served as the burial ground for Saxon kings. Those kings appear in their full splendour on the magnificent mural known as the *Procession of Princes* that adorns the outer wall of **Residenzschloss**, the royal castle. Guarded by its massive walls are lavish royal treasuries. The **Historisches Grünes Gewölbe** (Historical Green Vault) is a magnificent collection of art objects that poured into Dresden at the height of its power under Augustus II the Strong. These include crown jewels of Saxon and Polish kings, large diamonds and sapphires, and hundreds of exquisite items made of ivory, silver,

Phoenix City

Once known as Florence on the Elbe, Dresden was flattened by Allied bombing that generated blazes so powerful that the tin roof of Residenzschloss melted away. The painstaking restoration lasted throughout the DDR decades and was renewed with fresh energy after reunification. What you see today has literally risen from ashes.

Above left Brühl's terrace **Above right** Historisches Grünes Gewölbe (Historical Green Vault) **Left** Residenzschloss

amber and more. One floor above it, the **Neues Grünes Gewölbe** (New Green Vault) displays, among other treasures, a cherry stone with 185 faces carved on it and an intricate ivory frigate supported by Neptune's figure.

Zwinger

The sculpture-filled **Zwinger** palace, the Saxon answer to Versailles, is home to the **Gemäldegalerie Alte Meister**, a priceless art collection featuring Rafael's *Madonna* and a lot of Tintoretto's depictions of Italy and Saxony. You'll also find a vast collection of Chinese and European porcelain, as well as the Royal Cabinet of Mathematical and Physical Instruments, containing beautifully designed, sophisticated 18th-century science tools.

Frauenkirche & Albertinum

It's hard to believe, but the enormous baroque **Frauenkirche** just wasn't there in Altstadt's main square, Neumarkt, for six decades. The

What to See in Residenzschloss

You need a separate ticket – for a specific time slot – to visit the **Historisches Grünes Gewölbe**; best secured online at *shop.skd.museum*. Other Residenzshcloss museums are visited on a combined ticket that most prominently includes the New Green Vault, but so much more too. The **Armoury** features extensive displays of firearms and knight armour as well as the Turkish Chamber, the largest collection of Ottoman items outside Turkey. There's also the **State Apartments of August the Strong**, a numismatic collection at **Coin Cabinet** and the **Museum of Prints, Drawings and Photographs**.

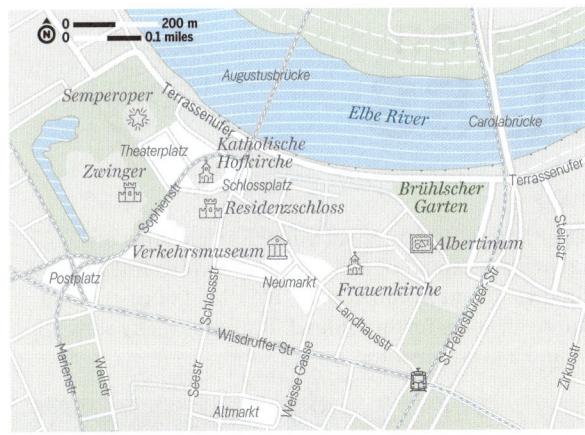

Left Armoury, Residenzschloss
Below Semperoper

18th-century masterpiece was a pile of rubble between its destruction from Allied bombings in 1945 and its magical resurrection in 2004. Behind it, the large art space known as **Albertinum** contains three galleries, including **Galerie Neue Meister**, a collection of German and other Western European paintings from 19th-century Romanticism till the present. Come to see Caspar David Friedrich, Edvard Munch and Claude Monet, as well as AR Penck and Neo Rausch.

In the square by Frauenkirche, the old royal stables house the wonderful **Verkehrsmuseum** (Transport Museum), which covers seemingly every mode of transport, from horse-driven carriages to train, boats and planes.

Semperoper

Polish your evening with a night at the **Semperoper**. Built in 1841 and rebuilt twice over, the magnificent opera house complements the opulence of the nearby Zwinger. Adorned with stone figures of Goethe, Shakespeare, Sophocles and Molière, the neo-Rennaissance building by the Elbe is itself a treat – it's worth visiting on an organised tour during the day even if you have tickets for the evening show. Having hosted premieres by the likes of Richard Strauss, it keeps churning out new and elaborate performances every season.

23 Riparian BLISS

STEAMSHIPS | CASTLES | WINES

Few wheels bring better karma than those of vintage steamships plying the Elbe from the German porcelain capital of Meissen to the whimsical rocks of Saxon Switzerland. Up and downstream from Dresden, it's a land of castles and vineyards: some right by the river, some further inland. Brace for really slow travel, with on-board lunch and a glass of wine.

How to

Getting here and around Board your steamship in Dresden. Buy tickets in advance at saechsische-dampfschifffahrt.de. You can take S-Bahn or bus on the way back, depending on where you go.

When to go Steamships run from April to September.

Duration The trips are long, so plan carefully. Travelling downstream from Dresden, it takes 5½ hours to the final destination – Bad Schandau. Upstream, it's 2¼ hours to Meissen.

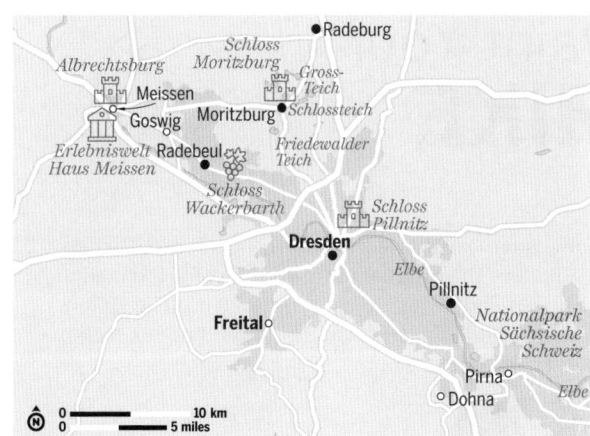

Top left Albrechtsburg castle, Meissen
Bottom left Schloss Pillnitz

Fleet The vintage fleet of Dresden-based Sächsische Dampfschifffahrt (known as White Fleet) is an essential element of the Elbe panorama as seen from Bruhl's terrace at sunset. However, during the day these chain-smoking grand dames from a bygone epoch carry passengers to the castles, vineyards and mountain-hiking spots along the Elbe. They move with utmost grace, which also means unhurriedly. The pace allows you to treat yourself to a filling lunch on the deck and a few glasses of Saxon wine, even on a shorter trip.

Pillnitz One of the least time-consuming jaunts on offer is to **Schloss Pillnitz**, an Orient-themed palace with formal gardens that houses Dresden's Kunstgewerbemuseum, dedicated to the history of design. On the way, you'll pass the Blue Wonder (Lochwitz Bridge), an elegant cantilever truss bridge in Dresden's southwestern suburbs.

Meissen Just as popular is a trip to Germany's porcelain capital, graced by the picture-perfect **Albrechtsburg** castle. Meissen's famed porcelain factory, **Erlebniswelt Haus Meissen**, features a wonderful museum and live porcelain-making displays. This journey goes along vineyard-covered hills rising above Radebeul, where you can stop for a degustation session at **Schloss Wackerbarth**.

Retro transfer In Radebeul, you can also swap your steamship for a steam train running along the narrow-gauge Lössnitzgrundbahn to a station next to **Schloss Moritzburg**, another opulent home of Saxon royals.

Saxon Navy

Launched in 1836, Saxony's White Fleet, comprising nine steamers, two salon and two motor ships, is approaching its 200-year anniversary. Its oldest vessel, *Stadt Wehlen*, turned 150 in 2017. This 'monument in motion', as it is dubbed, appears in full splendour during the **Dresden Steamship** parade and provides moving venues to **Dresden Dixieland Festival**, both held in May.

Catastrophic floods followed by low water periods make navigation on the Elbe unpredictable. Check saechsische-dampfschifffahrt.de for the status quo. When long trips to Saxon Switzerland are cancelled, shorter ones might be still running.

24 Paint Your HIKE

MOUNTAINS | WALKS | ART

Follow in the steps of Caspar David Friedrich and other German artists whose dramatic paintings served as the original tourist adverts for the land of sombre crags and outlandishly eroded forms – Saxon Switzerland. The 116km Malerweg (Painters' Trail) makes a full circle around this mountainous section of the Elbe valley on the border with Czechia.

How to

Getting here and around You can get to Saxon Switzerland by train from Dresden or Prague, but arriving by steamship is way classier.

When to go Late spring and summer are great for hiking, but it's autumn that ushers in proper Romanticist melancholy.

Losing weight You can get your baggage transported from A to B while you're hiking on Malerweg through malerweg-gepaeck transport.de.

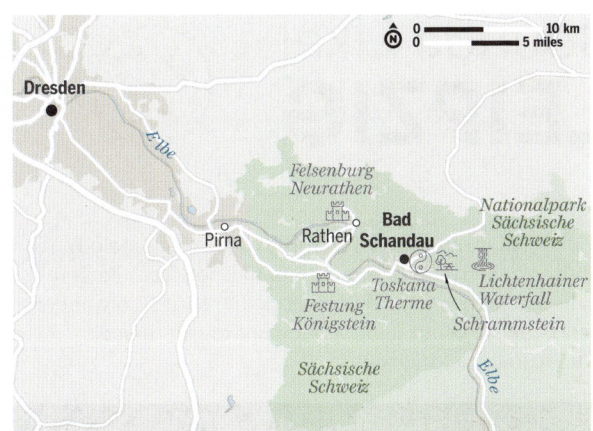

Top left Felsenburg Neurathen
Bottom left Lichtenhainer Waterfall

Practicalities Malerweg is divided into eight sections, with accommodation available in villages along the route. Check saechsische-schweiz.de for details, including which paintings correspond to which section.

Highlights The main highlights fall on stages two and four on the Elbe's eastern bank. The 10.9km stage two passes Bastei, the most striking panorama of erosion forms in the area (also accessible from Kurort Rathen down by the river). A sandstone bridge built in 1851 leads through the rocks to the remnants of the partly reconstructed **Felsenburg Neurathen** medieval castle. The 18.3km stage four runs above Bad Schandau and past **Schrammstein**, another area of whimsical rocks formed by erosion, to **Lichtenhainer Waterfall**, which comes with a small *Biergarten*. This is also the terminal point for **Kirnitzstahlbahn**, a vintage tram route running up into the mountains from Bad Schandau. **Toskana Therme**, a large spa complex on the banks of the Elbe in Bad Schandau, is a perfect place to stretch your tired muscles after the hike.

Königstein Fortress On the western side of the river, **Festung Königstein** is a magnificent eagle-nest castle on a high rock overlooking the vast green expanses below. Its history as a prison since the 16th century is much darker. It sits in the middle of Malerweg's 16.6km stage seven.

⚠ Switzerland Lost & Found

Nostalgic Swiss-born painters invited to teach at the Dresden Academy of Arts after its creation in the 18th century were reputedly responsible for lending their homeland's name to the Elbe valley mountains. But it was the winds of Romanticism that brought some of the grandest 19th-century figures, such Friedrich, Richard Wagner and Hans Christian Andersen, to the area. Tourists of the Romantic age trod the mountains' original trails. The advent of railways left this network unkempt and forlorn, while the Nazis even tried to ban the name Saxon Switzerland. The 21st century saw a revival of hiking in the area.

25 Sounds Like LEIPZIG

MUSIC | MUSEUMS | WALKS

Dance into Leipzig, a city that hums an irresistibly captivating melody as it goes about its daily chores. A plethora of famous composers, from Bach to Mendelssohn-Bartholdy, called Leipzig home. With that pedigree, it's no wonder the city boasts two world-class music venues and a bunch of music-themed museums connected by a dedicated walking route.

How to

Getting here and around Leipzig is one hour by ICE, or two hours by bus, from Berlin.

When to go Everything blooms in May and June, which are also dense with music festivals.

Getting tickets Start your planning by checking out the websites of Gewandhaus and Leipzig Opera, as tickets for the best events sell quickly. Note that cheaper seats intended for youngsters might be too cramped for adults.

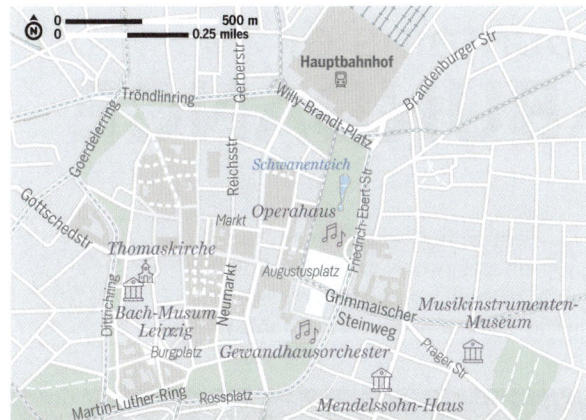

Top left Gewandhaus
Bottom left Thomaskirche

Sunday sessions Try scheduling your Leipzig visit for a Sunday, starting your morning with Mass at **Thomaskirche**, Johan Sebastian Bach's base for 27 years. If they're not away on tour, you'll get to see Thomanerchor, the boys' choir that he conducted during this period.

Notenspur Having done that, hit the Notenspur, starting with **Bach-Museum Leipzig**, an interactive museum across the square where you can listen to much of the great composer's monumental musical heritage. Follow the route to **Mendelssohn-Haus**, where you can try your hand at conducting a virtual orchestra in a state-of-the-art interactive exhibition. Other museums on the route include buildings once occupied by Richard Wagner, Robert Schumann and Edvard Grieg.

Music museum The highlight of Leipzig University's collections at Museen im Grassi is the fabulous **Musikinstrumenten-Museum**, which traces the history of music from medieval times to modernity. Apart from seeing musical instruments from many eras, you can also listen to masterpieces in which they feature.

Orchestral evenings Plan your musical evening in Leipzig well in advance. The city's two main venues face each other in the enormous Augustusplatz. With striking murals inside a glassy, modernist DDR-era building, the **Gewandhaus** is home to its namesake orchestra, which was once led by Mendesohn Bartholdi. The orchestra divides time between its own venue and the **Oper Leipzig**, one of Germany's finest and best known opera stages, across the square.

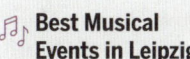 Best Musical Events in Leipzig

Bachfest (May–June) Bach's music in all shapes and forms, from Thomanenchor to jazz interpretations. Also, Bach-pong: a form of beer pong.

Wave-Gotik-Treffen (May–June) A massive Gothic music fest, but it's the audience that rocks most – people dressed in mind-boggling costumes form the weirdest of crowds.

Klassik Airleben (June) Gewandhaus Orchestra picnic performances at the end of the season draw enormous crowds.

A Capella (May–June) Annual vocal competition held in all kinds of venues, from churches to libraries.

Leipziger Markt Music (August) Ten eclectic nights with classical orchestras and indie bands in the city's main square.

 Recommended by Leipzig-based journalist **Anna Toropova**.

26 Mountains of ABUNDANCE

MUSEUMS | MINES | CASTLES

The Ore Mountains (Erzgebirge in German) are not particularly dramatic in appearance, but they are full of wonders. Miners' towns in the highlands, as well as industrial cities in the plains below, feature fascinating museums, castles, visitable mines, spas and many hiking trails.

Trip Notes

Getting here and around A short distance apart by train, Chemnitz and Zwickau are well connected to Dresden. A railway line originating in Chemnitz climbs the Ore Mountains towards Annaberg-Buchholz, where you can catch the frequent bus 415 to Schwarzenberg. The latter has train services to Zwickau.

When to go Late spring is the best time to go.

On foot The Ore Mountains are crisscrossed with well-maintained hiking trails.

Mines of Abundance

The silver mine under the local museum in Annaberg-Buchholz had been forgotten for 500 years before it was rediscovered in 1990. A tour of the zinc mine in Pöhla near Schwarzenberg involves train and boat rides as well as a laser show.

01 Find yourself in an exemplary DDR-era socialist city in **Chemnitz**, complete with a gigantic head of Karl Marx in the centre. Check out SMAC, a huge and fascinating archaeology museum.

02 A shiny castle on a hill, **Augustusburg**, the former hunting lodge of Elector Augustus, is a constellation of seemingly incompatible elements: a Lucas Cranach altar, a motorcycle museum and a wonderful youth hostel.

05 The ornate 12th century Marienkirche graces the well-preserved old town in industrial **Zwickau**. Its other claim to fame is a giant Audi museum.

04 The most enchanting town in the Ore Mountains, **Schwarzenberg** boasts a fairy-tale castle on a rock, the wonderful Perla Castrum museum and the visitable Pöhla zink mine nearby.

03 **Annaberg-Buchholz** is an old mining town high in the mountains with several visitable mines, including one right under the town's museum. A few spa complexes, such as Therme Miriquidi, are in close proximity.

FROM TOP: JANTRAUTSCHOLDPHOTOGRAPHY/SHUTTERSTOCK, AQUATARKUS/SHUTTERSTOCK, AQUATARKUS/SHUTTERSTOCK

VENTURE INTO
the German Far East

BAROQUE | SLAVIC CULTURE | STEAMERS

Take a melancholic trip through the eastern corner of Saxony, Upper Lusatia (Oberlausitz), where Germany blends into a Slavic neighbourhood and baroque towns retain their pre-WWII splendour. Each town here tells a different story, from ethnic heritage to round-the-world travel.

Trip Notes

Getting here & around There are frequent trains from Dresden to Bautzen, continuing on to Görlitz, which has regular train services to Zittau. Bus 10 runs frequently from Zittau to Herrnhut, continuing to Löbau on the Bautzen–Görlitz railway line.

Cycling Also a good idea on this route.

When to go On Easter Sunday, Sorbian men dress themselves and their horses in their vintage best and parade around villages near Bautzen.

Light up Your Christmas

As well as presiding over a global church, Herrnhut also happens to be the birthplace of paper Christmas stars that adorn every German home in December. You can chose yours – they come in all colours and sizes – as well as watch the stars being handmade at Hernhutter Sterne Manufaktur.

Listings

BEST OF THE REST

 Must-Visit Museums

Museum der Bildenden Künste
A cube-shaped modern block inside Leipzig's Altstadt contains a wonderful collection of German art as it evolved from Romanticism to the tortured expressionism and totalitarian art of the 20th century.

Museum für Völkerkunde
The enormous ethnographic collection at Leipzig University's Museen im Grassi is a treat for anthropologists. Items collected by generations of German scholars around the world are on display.

Militärhistorisches Museum Dresden
In a striking old building reshaped by Daniel Liebiskind, Germany's main military museum tells the story of armed conflict dispassionately, showcasing war artefacts from different ages.

SMAC
Occupying a converted department store, this museum literally digs deep into Germany's prehistory, displaying precious finds from excavations from the Stone Age to medieval times.

Industriemuseum Chemnitz
This huge and modern museum inside a vintage industrial space features the history of machinery, from the roots of the Industrial Revolution to modernity.

 Small Cities & Towns Worth Visiting

Plauen
Once the lace capital of Germany, hilly Plauen has a few wonderful museums. The old spa towns of Bad Elster and Bad Brambach in the nearby mountains are also worth a visit.

Freiberg
Home to the ancient Freiberg Mining Academy, this lovely university town has a beautifully decorated cathedral, a fascinating collection of minerals, a visitable mine and its own beer.

Grimma
Sitting by the dreamy Mulde River, picture-perfect Grimma means a lot in Germany's literary and Lutheran history, but it's also just a great place for long walks and bike rides.

Colditz
Schloss Colditz, presiding over this small town reachable from Leipzig, served as a camp for WWII prisoners who made numerous ingenious escape attempts, even building a glider from available materials.

Torgau
Home to an imposing castle of Saxon royals, Torgau features prominently in the story of Martin Luther. It's also the place where Soviet and American troops met at the end of WWII.

 Quirky Museums off the Beaten Track

Terra Mineralia
Nature trumps human-made art in this mind-boggling collection of shiny minerals from around the world. The museum is inside a castle in the quaint university town of Freiberg.

Karl May Museum
In Radebeul, the vintage Wild West is packed into the former house of a German adventure novelist who inspired generations of compatriots with stories of cowboys and Indians.

Deutsche Raumfahrtausstelung
Far, far away in the Ore Mountains, Morgenröthe-Rautenkranz is the home village

of the first German in space, Zigmund Jähn. Now it's the location of a touching exhibition on the German space programme.

Fabrik den Fäden

In Saxony's far western corner, the old industrial city of Plauen celebrates its one-time fame as the lace capital of Germany with this wonderful exhibition inside a former lace factory.

Scenic Beer Gardens

Katy's Garage

With Katy, the red Mini Cooper, overlooking the *Biergarten* from the kitchen roof, this is the mellowest and most-happening place in Dresden Neustadt's nightlife area.

Gaststätte Brauhaus Zwickau

Sitting in the shade of the ornate Dom St Marien in Zwickau's main square, this quaint establishment allows you to combine visual and gustatory delights.

Goldener Anker

This is a very laid-back and somewhat makeshift place on the idyllic bank of the Elbe in the finely revitalised old village of Altkötzschenbroda, inside Radebeul. *Flammkuchens* and Saxon wine are on offer.

Gosenschenke Ohne Bedenken

Head to this out-of-the-centre establishment to try one of Leipzig's beer specialities that almost went extinct. *Gose* is warm fermented beer with nonstandard adds, such as cinnamon.

KultUhr

This laid-back terrace is by a lighthouse-like building above the flower clock, one of Zittau's attractions. Beer, wine and quality food.

The Great Saxon Outdoors

Leipzig waterways

Like the human body, Leipzig largely consists of water. Its lakes and canals comprise an

Muskau Park

intricate network of waterways that allow exploration of cities by paddling or stand-up paddleboarding.

Vogtland Panoramaweg

This 230km circular hiking route connects charming little towns in the rolling hills of Vogtland, a historic region in Saxony's west, as well as the Ore Mountains.

Skiing in the Ore Mountains

They're not the Alps, but the Ore Mountains have a few low-key skiing resorts, such as Oberwiesenthal and Elbenstock. There's also an extensive network of cross-country skiing tracks.

Flora & Fauna

Muskau Park

An eccentric aristocrat is responsible for this extensive English-styled gardens at Bad Muskau in Saxony's northeast. Now spanning the German–Polish border, it's a great place for a long walk and meditation.

Zoo Leipzig

One of Europe's best zoos features an artificial rainforest under a huge cupola that visitors explore by boat. The primate section is equally fascinating.

MUNICH

BEER | ART | HISTORY
RESEARCHED BY MARC DI DUCA

- ▶ **Trip Builder** (p144)
- ▶ **Practicalities** (p145)
- ▶ **Beer in Munich** (p146)
- ▶ **Munich's Oktoberfest** (p148)
- ▶ **The Wittelsbachs' Royal Palaces** (p150)
- ▶ **The Art Scene** (p152)
- ▶ **The 1972 Olympiapark** (p156)
- ▶ **Listings** (p158)

MUNICH
Trip Builder

Wander Munich's former and future Olympic venue, **Olympiapark** (p156), where there's heaps to see and do
🚶 *1min from Pinakotheken tram stop*

Lose yourself in an ocean of art in the **Kunstareal** (p153)
🚶 *1min from Pinakotheken tram stop*

Spend an evening with Munich's lager at the **Chinesischer Turm** (p146) beer garden
🚶 *10min from Tivolistrasse tram stop*

Learn about the rise of the Nazis and Hitler's beginnings in Munich at the **NS Dokuzentrum** (p159)
🚶 *1min from Pinakotheken tram stop*

Drop in on the Wittelsbachs, the Bavarian royal family, at their summer and winter **palaces** (p150)
🚶 *3min from Odeonsplatz U-Bahn station*

▬ Germany's most affluent city and its secret capital, Munich is all about its art, its beer, its glorious (and often inglorious) past and the super-modern blended with the old in a way only Bavarians can do, all experienced with an almost-Mediterranean vibe.

FROM LEFT: YASEMIN OZDEMIR SHUTTERSTOCK, PANI GARMYDER/SHUTTERSTOCK
PREVIOUS PAGE: SINA ETTMER PHOTOGRAPHY/SHUTTERSTOCK, ENGLISH GARDEN SHOWN COURTESY OF THE BAVARIAN PALACE ADMINISTRATION, WWW.SCHLOESSER.BAYERN.DE

Practicalities

ARRIVING

Flughafen München Officially Franz-Josef-Strauss Airport, it's around 30km northeast of the city centre. Hop aboard the S1 or S8 S-Bahn, which take 40 minutes to the Hauptbahnhof.

FIND YOUR WAY

Use the very helpful and easy-to-navigate MVV app to buy tickets and plan journeys through your smartphone.

MONEY

Many of Munich's biggest museums and galleries charge just €1 admission on a Sunday.

WHERE TO STAY

Neighbour-hood	Pros/Cons
Altstadt	Super central. Most expensive part of town.
Westend	Cheapest and biggest choice. Very busy part of the city.
Schwabing	Puts visitors at the heart of the student nightlife action. Not much choice.

EATING & DRINKING

Weisswurst, a grey-white veal and pork-fat sausage, is eaten for breakfast with sweet mustard, a pretzel and a jug of wheat beer.

The big six breweries produce some of the world's best beer by the gigalitre.

Beer gardens are a must-do experience when in the Bavarian capital.

Best pub with history Hofbräuhaus (p147)

Must-try coffee and cake Kuchentratsch (p158)

GETTING AROUND

S-Bahn Light rail system linking rural Bavaria with the suburbs and city centre almost round the clock.

U-Bahn The underground railway serves the centre and inner suburbs.

Tram and bus Trams link the centre with the suburbs. Buses take over from the end of the S-Bahn and U-Bahn lines.

JAN–MAR
Bitterly cold, a chance of snow; bright, crisp days

APR–JUN
Spring arrives with flowers and *Spargelzeit* (asparagus time)

JUL–SEP
Hot, sticky and humid, but September can be pleasant

OCT–DEC
Nights draw in, beer gardens close, and Advent markets spring up

28 Beer in MUNICH

BEER | TRADITION | NIGHTLIFE

Forget the fruity concoctions of Brussels and the Czechs' flavoursome fizz – when it comes to beer, Bavaria has the world's best, and at the centre of the region's proud traditions are the six Munich breweries that are in permanent competition for the title of top tipple. A tankard of creamy lager in a traditional beer hall or garden is the quintessential Munich experience.

How to

When to go Beer gardens across Munich are open from around Easter to early October.

Picnicking Most beer gardens are fine about drinkers bringing their own food, as long as they order a beer. For this, choose tables without tablecloths and cutlery.

Stammtisch This is a table in a beer hall reserved for local drinkers. If you sit in a spot marked as such, you'll soon be asked to move.

Top left Hirschgarten
Bottom left Hofbräuhaus

The big six When locals talk about the 'big six', they mean the breweries allowed to supply beer to Oktoberfest: Augustiner, Hacker-Pschorr, Hofbräu, Löwenbräu, Paulaner and Spaten.

Beer halls The mother of all beer halls, the Altstadt's **Hofbräuhaus** is an unmissable spectacle, even if you don't like beer. Within its traditionally decorated interior, you'll discover a range of spaces in which to do your *Mass* (1L tankard) lifting, including a horse chestnut–shaded garden. An oompah band keeps things swinging in the evenings. This is arguably the world's top beer hall and the biggest in Munich, but others such as the **Augustiner Bräustuben**, near the main train station, or the **Paulaner am Nockherberg**, south of the city centre, offer a less touristed experience.

Beer gardens In the warmer months, lager imbibing largely heads outdoors into Munich's beer gardens. Shaded by horse chestnut trees and fairy-lit after dark, these are idyllic spots for nights out on the suds in the muggy southern-German air. One of the best is the **Chinesischer Turm** in the English Garden, with tables gathered around the Chinese Tower folly. Others worth seeking out include the central **Viktualienmarkt** and the **Biergarten am Muffatwerk** with its healthier food options. If you're looking for beer superlatives, the **Hirschgarten** near Schloss Nymphenburg is the world's biggest beer garden, capable of seating up to 8700 drinkers!

Other Munich Lagers

The big six may dominate the beer mats of the Bavarian capital, but there are countless others out there. **Tegernseer** is one of the most popular bottled beers in Munich, though for the pulled version you should head to the **Tegernseer Tal** tavern. Dark and syrupy **Klosterbrauerei Andechs**, from the Andechs Monastery, is a real treat, and still brewed by monks. The **Erdinger Brewery** produces some of Bavaria's best beer, especially *Weissbier*, available in a few select pubs in Munich. The **Weisses Brauhaus**, just off the Marienplatz, sets the standard for wheat beer across the land with its **Schneider Weissbier**.

Munich's Oktoberfest

THE WORLD'S MOST FAMOUS BEER FESTIVAL

Planet Earth's largest mass celebration of beer, and the traditional highlight of Bavaria's cultural calendar, Oktoberfest is one of the best-known annual events in Europe. No other party manages to mix such a level of crimson-faced humour, drunken debauchery and excessive consumption of lager with so much tradition, history… and oompah music.

Left Tapping the first keg
Centre The Festzug (brewer's parade)
Right Ferris wheel at the funfair

A Bit of History

Believe it or not, the world's biggest beer festival started as a simple horse race. In 1810, Bavarian crown prince Ludwig (later King Ludwig I) married Princess Therese of Saxe-Hildburghausen and, following the wedding, a horse race was held at the city gates. The six-day celebration was such a galloping success that it became an annual event, was extended and was moved forward to start in September so that visitors could enjoy warmer weather and lighter nights. The horse race, which quickly became a sideshow to the suds, ended in 1960, but an agricultural show is still part of Oktoberfest.

Ozapft ist's!

As early as mid-July the brewery crews start erecting the tents that almost fill the Theresienwiese, a gravelly open space west of Munich city centre known locally as the Wiesn.

Starting at 10.45am on the first day, the brewer's parade (the Festzug) travels through the city centre from the River Isar to the fairgrounds. This involves many old, brightly decorated horse-drawn carriages once used to transport kegs from brewery to pub and countless felt-hatted tagalongs. When the procession reaches the Wiesn, focus switches to the Schottenhamel beer tent and the mayor of Munich who, on the stroke of noon, takes a mallet and knocks the tap into the first keg. As the beer flows forth and the thirsty crowds cheer, the mayor exclaims: *'Ozapft ist's!'* (literally 'It's tapped' in Bavarian dialect).

The Beer

All the lager pulled at Oktoberfest must have been brewed within Munich's city limits, which restricts the number

of breweries permitted to wet your whistle to six: Hofbräu-München (of Hofbräuhaus fame), Paulaner, Löwenbräu, Augustiner and the lesser-known Hacker-Pschorr and Spaten.

> As the beer flows forth and the thirsty crowds cheer, the mayor exclaims: 'Ozapft ist's!' (literally 'It's tapped' in Bavarian dialect).

The famous 1L *Mass* brought to your table by a Dirndl-trussed waitress contains pretty strong stuff, as the breweries cook up special concoctions for the occasion. The percentage of alcohol starts at around 5.8%, which makes a single *Mass* the equivalent of almost 3.5 pints of most regular beers in Britain, Australia and the USA. Traditionally the most potent brews are piped to the Wiesn by Hofbräu, and the weakest by Hacker-Pschorr.

Not Just Beer

Oktoberfest is not called the world's biggest fair for nothing, and while most visitors' focus is on the *Bier,* there's a lot going on away from the tents. The funfair, with its big wheel, ye-olde test-your-strength booths and scarier 21st-century rides, is an obvious attraction, but magic performances, an agricultural show (more interesting than it sounds) and stalls selling everything from Oktoberfest souvenirs to waffles constitute other minor diversions. The first Sunday sees an impressive costumed procession wind its way through Munich's city centre, a tradition going back to 1835, and the customary religious Oktoberfest Mass is held in the Hippodrom beer tent on the first Thursday. A brass-band concert huffs and puffs beneath the Bavaria statue on the morning of the second Sunday, near the spot from where the gun salute is fired on the last Sunday.

Oktoberfest: Vital Stats

Where At the Theresienwiese to the west of the city centre. Poccistrasse and Theresienwiese are the nearest U-Bahn stations.

When For 16 days up to the first (occasionally second) Sunday in October: 19 September to 4 October, 2026; 18 September to 3 October, 2027; 16 September to 3 October, 2028.

Opening Hours Beer is served from 10am to 10.30pm Monday to Friday, and 9am to 10.30pm Saturday and Sunday. Other attractions and facilities open for longer.

Admission free

Price of a 1L Mass of beer €14.50–16

Attendance Around six million visitors

Amount of beer consumed Between six and seven million litres

Beer tents 35

29 The Wittelsbachs' Royal PALACES

GRANDEUR | ARCHITECTURE | HISTORY

The House of Wittelsbach was the family that ruled over the Kingdom of Bavaria for more than eight centuries until 1918. As Bavarian royals, their home was the Bavarian capital, Munich, where they created two residences: a city-centre winter residence called the, er, Residenz and a lavish summerhouse at Schloss Nymphenburg. The two complexes are now unmissable visitor attractions.

How to

Getting here The Residenz is a short walk from Odeonsplatz U-Bahn station. Tram 17 links Nymphenburg with Karlsplatz, a short walk from the Residenz.

Information Check ticket prices and opening times for Nymphenburg at *schloss-nymphenburg.de,* and for the Residenz at *residenz-muenchen.de*.

Theatre opening times Most of the year, the Cuvilliés Theatre at the Residenz is only open in the afternoons.

Winter palace Munich's top visitor attraction is the **Residenz**, the Wittelsbachs' city-centre mothership and one of Europe's largest palace complexes. Over the centuries, Bavarian dukes and kings turned their noses up at their predecessors' digs and added their own quarters to the palace. The result is a huge warren of wings, halls, churches and chapels that takes a good two hours to see at a canter. The sad side of the story is that much of what you see is actually a post-WWII rebuild as the complex was damaged during air raids in 1945. Standout interiors include the **Antiquarium**, the largest Renaissance hall north of the Alps, Ludwig I's no-holds-barred, neoclassical **Royal Palace** and the baroque **Cuvilliés Theatre**.

Summer palace After that royal bling overload, it's usually a good idea to leave the Wittelsbachs' summer

pad for another day. **Schloss Nymphenburg**, a 20-minute ride west on tram 17, is a baroque masterpiece set in extensive parkland. Highlights of the self-guided tour include the famous **Schönheitengalerie** (Gallery of the Beauties), containing 38 portraits of females chosen by an 'admiring' King Ludwig I, the highly decorative, rococo **Festsaal** (Grosser or Steinerner Saal), which dominates the central section of the building, and the **Chinese Lacquer Room**. After the tour you can wander the folly-dotted grounds, the high point being the **Amalienburg**, a small, wonderfully decorative hunting lodge. It's the work of the Wittelsbachs' favourite architect, Cuvilliés.

François de Cuvilliés

Belgium-born François de Cuvilliés (1695–1768) is the rococo architect who had the greatest influence on the appearance of the Wittelsbachs' Munich residences. He was appointed court architect in 1724 by Maximilian II, but worked under Charles VII and Maximilian III, for whom he created the baroque theatre that now bears his name. He was also responsible for designing the rococo Reiche Zimmer At Nymphenburg, another of his masterpieces is the Amalienburg, but he also created the dreamy Chinese Lacquer Room in the faux Oriental style fashionable at the time.

Above Residenz

30 The Art SCENE

GALLERIES | HISTORY | ARCHITECTURE

They don't call Munich the 'City of Art and Beer' for nothing, and when you're done with the brews, its time for the hues. You'll find every shade under the sun in Munich's celebrated Kunstareal, an entire neighbourhood given over to world-class galleries.

How to

Getting here Bus 100 passes through the Kunstareal on its way between the Ostbahnhof and the Hauptbahnhof. Königsplatz is the nearest U-Bahn station. Trams run along Barer Strasse.

Information The Kunstareal website *(kunstareal.de)* is essential viewing before heading into the neighbourhood.

Tickets As yet, there isn't a single ticket valid for the entire Kunstareal. Each institution has its own pricing and opening hours.

Athens on the Isar

The **Kunstareal** is divided into two areas, the original 'art zone' being the Königsplatz, which was the showcase for royal Wittelsbach art established by Ludwig I in the early 19th century as part of his 'Athens on the Isar' vision. The Doric-columned **Propyläen** is the gateway to the square, which boasts two grand old museum institutions that face off over the lawns, both designed by Leo von Klenze: the oh-so-neoclassical **Glyptothek** is Munich's oldest museum, housing a feast of art and sculpture from ancient Greece and Rome amassed by King Ludwig I, while the **Antikensammlungen** showcases Greek, Roman and Etruscan antiquities. Both are visited on a single ticket.

 The Show Goes On...

Here we have listed the biggest attractions in the Kunstareal, but there are 26 other galleries, museums and venerable institutions. If you visited one a day, you'd need more than a month to see everything. For the full list, see the Kunstareal website.

Above left Kunstareal
Above right Glyptothek **Left** Propyläen

Old Masters

With its vast collection of art from the 14th to 18th centuries, the **Alte Pinakothek** is one of the world's top art museums, and if you're going to choose just one gallery to visit, many would say this should be it. This neoclassical temple to Old European Masters was designed by Leo von Klenze as a purpose-built gallery for the Wittelsbachs' collections. The whole thing got a major revamp a decade or so ago, but instead of a sterile 21st-century makeover, the building's austerity and simplicity were preserved, making it an archetypal European museum experience.

Da Vinci, Cranach the Elder, Dürer, Bruegel the Elder, Rubens, Botticelli, Rafael, Titian, Velázquez, Raphael...the list of big-name artists goes on room after room, every work a priceless masterpiece. There are too many highlights to list, though Dürer's bearded self-portrait, Rubens' monster *Great Last Judgement* and Rembrandt's *Passion Cycle* stick in the memory.

Closing of the Neue Pinakothek

One of Munich's highlights has long been the Neue Pinakothek. Housing the city's collection of van Goghs, Turners and Monets, it took its turn to close for renovation in 2019 (after the long closure of the Alte Pinakothek) and had been scheduled to reopen in 2025 at the latest. However, in 2022 the authorities dropped a bombshell when they put that date back a full four years to 2029. This means that by the time it reopens, the museum will have been closed for a decade. Many claim this is an unacceptable length of time for such a major visitor attraction to be shut.

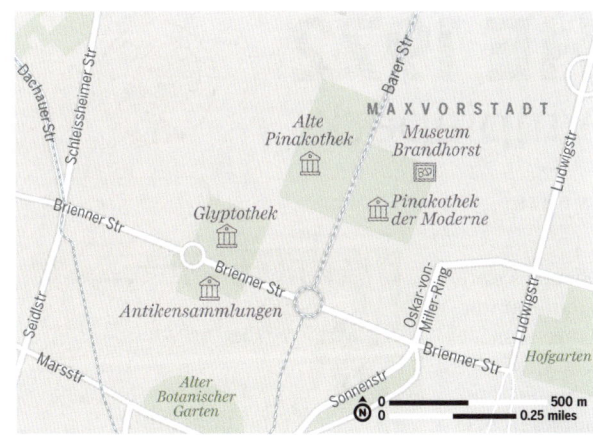

Left Alte Pinakothek
Below Pinakothek der Moderne

Brazen Brandhorst

A bold and aptly abstract building, clad entirely in 36,000 multihued ceramic tubes, the **Museum Brandhorst** jostled its way into the Kunstareal in a punkish blaze of colour in 2009. Its walls, floor and occasionally its ceiling provide space for some of the world's most challenging art. Temporary shows are complemented by changing displays from the Brandhorst's own collections, which feature 1200 pieces from the 1960s to the present day, including many a Warhol, Hirst, Twombly and Katz. There's a cool cafe in the foyer and Munich's best art book shop to peruse.

Four for the Price of One

Germany's largest modern-art museum, the cavernous **Pinakothek der Moderne,** brings together four museums under one roof and is therefore an engaging, all-pleasing mixed bag. The exhibitions would fit into a building 10 times smaller, and it's one of Munich's more exhausting museum experiences, but shows are well curated and thought-provoking.

The **State Gallery of Modern Art** is the high point for most, with works by Picasso, Klee, Dalí, Kandinsky, Warhol, Twombly and Flavin. The **New Collection** is a fascinating parade of applied design, with everything from VW Beetles and Eames chairs to early Apple Macs and Czech Tatra cars.

31 THE 1972 Olympiapark

HISTORY | SPORT | ENTERTAINMENT

The 1972 Summer Olympics were held in Munich, and were significant in that they gave the city a chance to make a historic break with the past. It was the first time Germany had hosted the games since the Berlin Olympics in 1936 with Hitler looking on. Under the motto of the 'Happy Games', the Olympiapark was begun in the late 1960s.

How to

Getting here U-Bahn is the quickest way to reach the Olympiapark. The most convenient stop is Olympiazentrum. Trams 20 and 21 stop at Olympiapark West.

Weather The Olympiapark is largely an outdoor attraction – check the weather forecast before you set off.

Eating Take a picnic. Surprisingly there aren't too many places to eat at the Olympiapark, but there are lawns aplenty for alfresco dining.

The stadium There's a lot to see in and around the **Olympiapark**, but you can visit everything on a whistlestop tour. The centrepiece for the 1972 Games was the **Olympiastadion**, an instantly recognisable structure, especially for football fans with its contorted steel and Plexiglass tent roof. West Germany famously won the 1974 FIFA World Cup here.

Olympic Tower The top attraction here is the 290m-tall **Olympiaturm**. There's a high-speed lift to the three-level viewing platform, 190m above ground, that provides the best views of Munich, bar none.

Olympic Mountain A short walk south of the tower, on the other side of the Olympiasee lake, the **Olympiaberg** (Olympic Mountain) rises

Top right Olympiaturm
Bottom right Olympiapark

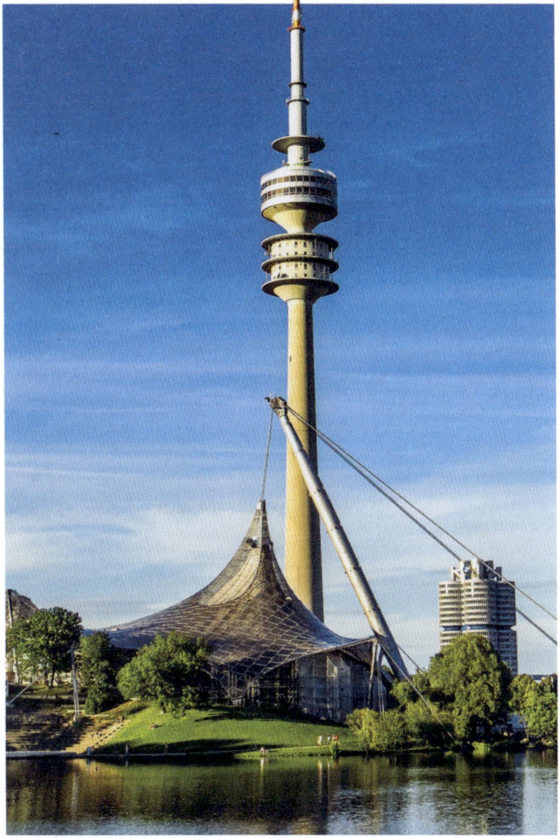

RUDIERNST/SHUTTERSTOCK

RUI VALE SOUSA/SHUTTERSTOCK

Olympics Recycled?

Bavarians are pretty passionate about recycling, but in 2025 Munich's authorities came up with an idea that perfectly combined this with the locals' passion for sport: Munich plans to bid for the 2036, 2040 or 2044 summer games and recycle the 1972 venue for the event. This would be the first time an Olympic venue gets used a second time, which should give Munich an advantage in the bidding process as it avoids the need to build a new complex.

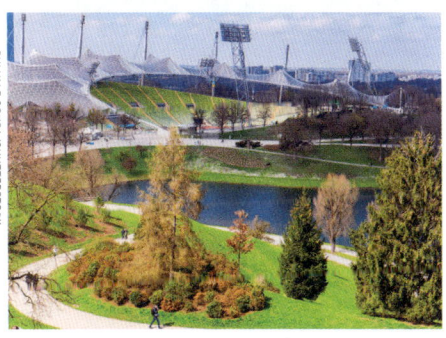

60m into the air and affords views of the park, much of the city and sometimes the Alps in the far distance. Incredibly, the 'mountain' was created in the late 1940s from WWII rubble from the city centre and thus predates even the idea of holding the Olympics here.

Peace Church One of the most intriguing sights at the Olympiapark has nothing to do with the 1972 Games and predates the complex by two decades. Built illegally after WWII by Russian hermit Father Timofey, using debris from what would become the Olympiaberg, the delightfully rural Orthodox **Ost-West Friedenskirche** (East-West Peace Church) burnt down in 2023, but its free museum remains. Efforts are afoot to have the church rebuilt.

Listings

BEST OF THE REST

 Green Spaces

English Garden
The popular, sprawling English Garden is among Europe's biggest city parks – it rivals Hyde Park and Central Park in size.

Theresienwiese
The venue for the world-famous Oktoberfest. At other times, this vast expanse buzzes with concerts, festivals and fairs.

Hofgarten
The most central patch of greenery formerly belonged to the royal Residenz next door. It's the best place in the Altstadt for a park-bench picnic or just a feet-up break between attractions.

 Steeple Views

Frauenkirche
The view from the south tower is the best in the city centre, where nothing taller than its 99m can be built, meaning uncluttered panoramas.

St Peterskirche
Some 306 steps separate you from wonderful vistas from the 92m-high tower of St Peterskirche, central Munich's oldest church (1150).

 World-Class Museums

Deutsches Museum
This unrivalled science museum examines every aspect of tech, mechanics, space, biology and physics in an engaging and entertaining way. Worthwhile kids section.

BMW Museum
Munich is home to BMW and the company's museum is one of the best, featuring whole walls of motorcycles, cut-away engines and famous models from across the decades.

Lenbachhaus
This glorious gallery is the go-to to admire the vibrant canvases of Wassily Kandinsky, Franz Marc, Paul Klee and other members of modernist group Der Blaue Reiter (The Blue Rider).

Sudetendeutsches Museum
Examining the history, culture and fate of the Sudeten Germans who were expelled from Czechoslovakia in 1945, this is one of the best niche museums in Germany,

 Non-Bavarian Eats

Prinz Myshkin €€
One of the city's longest-established vegetarian restaurants, it serves an imaginative menu of health-conscious dishes in a gleaming space.

Il Mulino €€
This much-loved neighbourhood classic has been feeding Italophiles and immigrants from the beautiful country for almost four decades.

Tantris €€€
This double-Michelin-star, psychedelic 1970s retro-resto is one of Germany's best known. Book weeks ahead.

Alois – Dallmayr Fine Dining €€€
Enjoy the double-Michelin-starred menu by head chef Rosina Ostler at this top-drawer Munich stalwart. Book months ahead.

 Coffee & Kuchen

Kuchentratsch €
At this much-celebrated coffee-and-cake halt on the edge of the Theresienwiese, local pen-

sioners earn some euros by baking cakes. The results put many a fancier cafe to shame.

Marais €
Is it a junk shop, a cafe or a sewing shop? Well, it is in fact all three, and everything you see in the converted haberdashery is for sale.

Götterspeise €
A twee, choco-centric cafe serving myriad teas, coffees and cakes from traditional to novelty.

Café Glockenspiel €
This cafe, just off Marienplatz, is a touristy affair, but has excellent views across Munich's main square and of City Hall.

Schmalznudel €
This incredibly popular institution serves just four traditional pastries, one of which, the *Schmalznudel* (an oily type of doughnut), gives the place its local nickname.

Typisch Bayerisch

Schneider Brauhaus €€
The place to come for the *Weisswurst* breakfast – a pair of white veal sausages served with a pretzel, sweet mustard and a mug of wheat beer. Only served until noon.

Bratwurstherzl €€
Wood panelling and an ancient vaulted brick ceiling set the tone of this old tavern with a Franconian focus. Organic sausages are grilled to perfection on an open beechwood fire.

Wirtshaus in der Au €€
This neighbourhood tavern's simple slogan is 'Beer and dumplings since 1901', and it's this time-honoured staple – dumplings – that is its speciality. Chunky tiled floors, a lofty ceiling and a crackling fireplace in winter.

Hotbraukeller €€
This Munich original beer hall reputedly has the city's first beer garden out the back.

NS Dokuzentrum

 WWII Heritage

NS Dokuzentrum
This excellent exhibition, right at the heart of what was once Nazi central in Munich, educates locals and visitors alike about the Nazi period and Munich's role in it.

DenkStätte Weisse Rose
A room buried deep within the main university building examines the role and fate of the nonviolent resistance movement in Nazi Munich. Free.

Dachau Concentration Camp
An S-Bahn and bus ride out of Munich, this concentration camp was the first established by the Nazis. The exhibition here documents the horrific practices established in the camp.

Pre-Loved Finds

Munich Readery
With Germany's biggest collection of secondhand English-language titles, the Readery is the place to go for holiday reading matter. The shop holds events such as author readings.

Flohmarkt im Olympiapark
This huge flea market is held at the large car park on the northwest side of the Olympiapark most Friday and Saturday mornings.

BAVARIA

STORYBOOK CASTLES | HISTORIC TOWNS | RIVERS & MOUNTAINS
RESEARCHED BY ANTHONY HAM

- ▸ **Trip Builder** (p162)
- ▸ **Practicalities** (p164)
- ▸ **Discover a Beautiful Altstadt** (p166)
- ▸ **Enjoy Magical Bamberg** (p168)
- ▸ **A Riverside City** (p170)
- ▸ **Füssen's World Heritage Sites** (p172)
- ▸ **Mad King Ludwig II** (p176)
- ▸ **Northern Romantic Road** (p178)
- ▸ **Southern Romantic Road** (p181)
- ▸ **Bavarian Icons** (p182)
- ▸ **Listings** (p184)

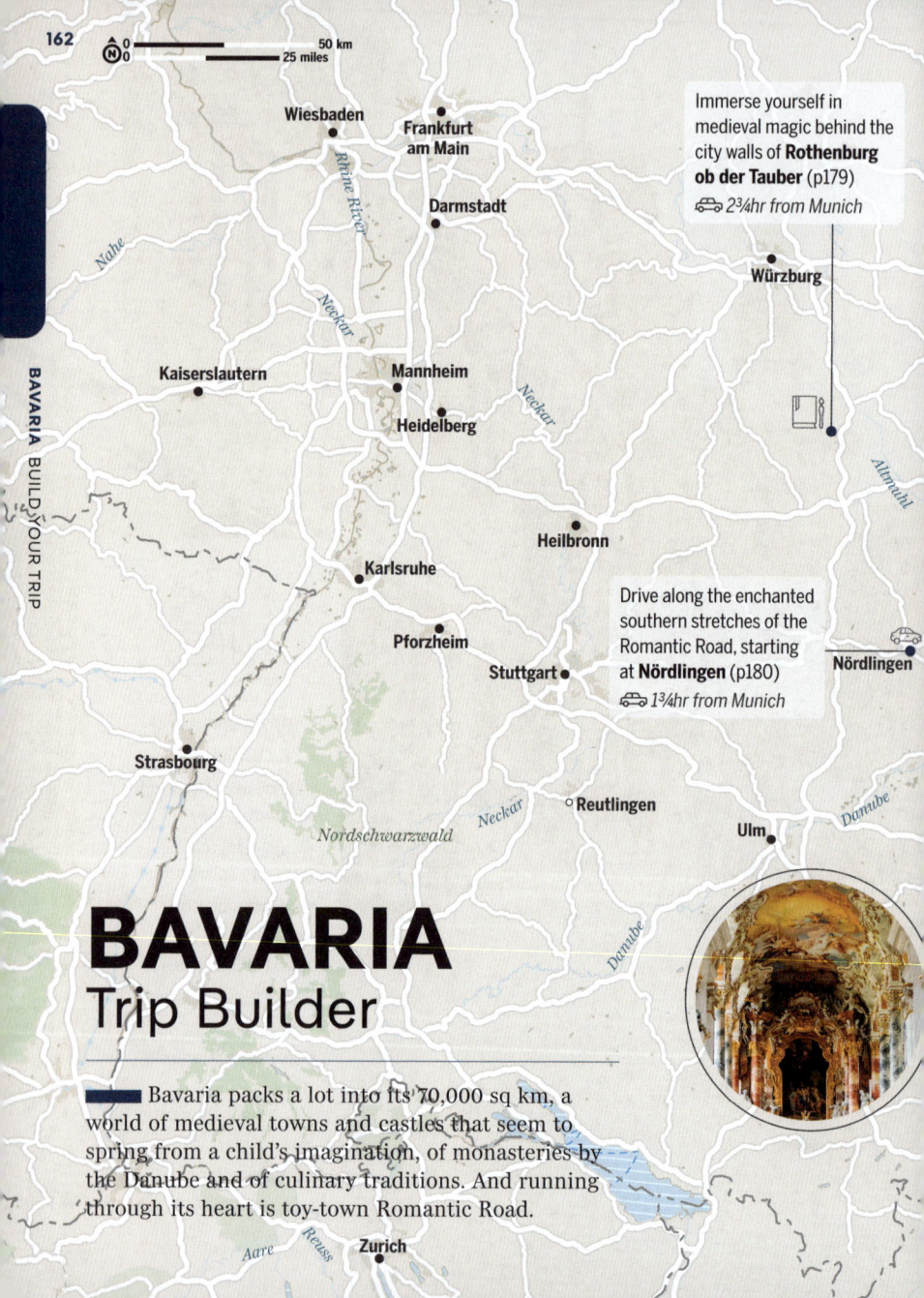

BAVARIA
Trip Builder

Immerse yourself in medieval magic behind the city walls of **Rothenburg ob der Tauber** (p179)
🚗 2¾hr from Munich

Drive along the enchanted southern stretches of the Romantic Road, starting at **Nördlingen** (p180)
🚗 1¾hr from Munich

Bavaria packs a lot into its 70,000 sq km, a world of medieval towns and castles that seem to spring from a child's imagination, of monasteries by the Danube and of culinary traditions. And running through its heart is toy-town Romantic Road.

Explore a medieval town with iconic riverside architecture in **Bamberg** (p168)
🚗 2¾hr from Munich

● Erlangen

● Nuremberg

Visit a castle and track a master painter in **Nuremberg Altstadt** (p166)
🚆 1hr from Munich

Take a boat trip on the Danube to **Walhalla** (p171) and Danube Gorge
🚗 1½hr from Munich

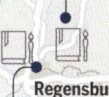
● Regensburg

Spend time exploring the UNESCO World Heritage–listed old town of **Regensburg** (p170)
🚆 1½hr from Munich

● Ingolstadt

● Augsburg

Go on a pilgrimage to the UNESCO-listed **Wieskirche** (p175)
🚗 1½hr from Munich

● Munich

● Salzburg

Enjoy the prototype for Disney's castle at glorious **Schloss Neuschwanstein** (p173)
🚗 2hr from Munich

FROM LEFT: STEVE BARZE/SHUTTERSTOCK, FRANCESCO CARUCCI/SHUTTERSTOCK, BUILDING SHOWN COURTESY OF THE BAVARIAN PALACE ADMINISTRATION, WWW.SCHLOESSER.BAYERN.DE, TRABANTOS/SHUTTERSTOCK, PYMATA/SHUTTERSTOCK
PREVIOUS PAGE: CANADASTOCK/SHUTTERSTOCK

Practicalities

ARRIVING

Flughafen München (Franz-Josef-Strauss Airport), a major international hub. The airport lies around 30km northeast of the centre, accessible via the S1 or S8 S-Bahn. A taxi/rideshare costs €60/45.

Munich Hauptbahnhof This important rail hub in the city centre has services to Berlin (5¼ hours), Cologne (4½ hours), Frankfurt (3¼ hours), Nuremberg (one hour) and more, as well as a handful of international destinations, such as Vienna (four hours).

HOW MUCH FOR A

Beer in a bar
€5

Toilet at train stations
€1

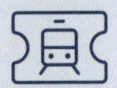

2nd-class train ticket to Nuremberg
€40–70

GETTING AROUND

Train Most medium to large population centres are linked to each other and the remainder of Germany by rail. The Bayern Ticket (aka Bayern Regional Day Pass) gives 24-hour access to all of Bavaria's rail system except high-speed services.

Car With its smooth, fast and laudably toll-free autobahn (highway) system, Bavaria is best explored with a hire car or your own vehicle. In bigger cities, parking can be costly.

Bus You'll only find yourself on a Bavarian bus in the Alps or the Bavarian Forest and possibly if travelling by public transport along the Romantic Road. Larger cities have city-bus systems, but you won't need to negotiate these much.

WHEN TO GO

JAN–MAR
Stunning in the Alps for skiing; Garmisch-Partenkirchen hosts a sledge race (6 January).

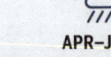

APR–JUN
Temperatures warming, with most hiking trails open by May.

JUL–SEP
Busiest time of year with big crowds but often glorious sunshine.

OCT–DEC
Germany's best Christmas markets, and autumn colours in the Bavarian Forest.

EATING & DRINKING

Bavarian cooking is one of the most distinctive in Germany, and much of it comes from Franconia in the Bavarian heartland. Highlights include Nürnberger *Rostbratwurst*; the *Coburger*, Bavaria's longest sausage; *Klössen* (Franconian dumplings); *Maultaschen* (pork-and-spinach ravioli) and other hearty, more recognisably Bavarian dishes, such as schnitzel, wild boar and snails, best enjoyed in a medieval, wooden-beamed cellar in winter. Given the region's world-class winemaking tradition, dishes are not just paired with fine wines but also cooked with them: bratwurst in wine, for example, or *Mostsuppe* (wine soup).

Best Nürnberger Rostbratwurst Metzgerai Ludwig Walk (p185)
Must-try Mostsuppe Bürgerspital Weinstube (p185)

CONNECT & FIND YOUR WAY

It's easy to get online in Bavaria, with widespread (free) wi-fi in hotels, restaurants, shops, cafes and many public areas. Not all navigation apps pick up the old-town one-way streets, so get out and walk.

WHERE TO STAY

Bavaria has outstanding accommodation. Larger cities obviously have the biggest choice, but there's nothing like sleeping in a 16th-century, half-timbered inn after the day-trippers have left.

Town/Village	Pros/Cons
Nuremberg	Walkable Altstadt (Old Town) and excellent public transport. Busy streets are difficult for those with a car.
Dinkelsbühl	Less busy alternative to Rothenburg; charming places to stay inside the walls. Can also get busy in summer.
Füssen	The essential base for visiting Neuschwanstein and Höhenschwangau. You must book ahead in high season.
Garmisch-Partenkirchen	Beautiful alpine gateway and excellent base for visiting nearby towns and Zugspitze. Accommodation is spread out over a large area.
Bamberg	Stay in the old town centre with plenty of choice. Driving the old centre can be complicated, so park and walk.

DISCOUNT CARD

Many Bavarian tourist towns (including Nuremberg, Bamberg, Garmisch-Partenkirchen, Passau and Füssen) offer a card covering free or discounted entry to attractions and local public transport.

MONEY

Credit cards are accepted in most places, but carry a stash of euros for the occasional place that prefers cash. Even most smaller towns have at least one internationally enabled ATM.

32 Discover a Beautiful ALTSTADT

CULTURE | ARCHITECTURE | CHRISTMAS

Nuremberg's Altstadt (Old Town) is one of Germany's largest and most beautiful. Crowned by a soaring fortress and animated by ghosts of celebrities past, it's a fascinating place to explore and admire the superb architecture at every turn.

How to

Getting here and around Nuremberg has regular trains to/from major German cities. Walk the Altstadt, and take trams to outlying attractions. Many travellers use Nuremberg as a base instead of Munich; direct trains run from Nuremberg to Munich's airport.

When to go December, for the world-famous Christmas Market.

Nürnberg Card Good for two days of public transport and admission to all museums and attractions.

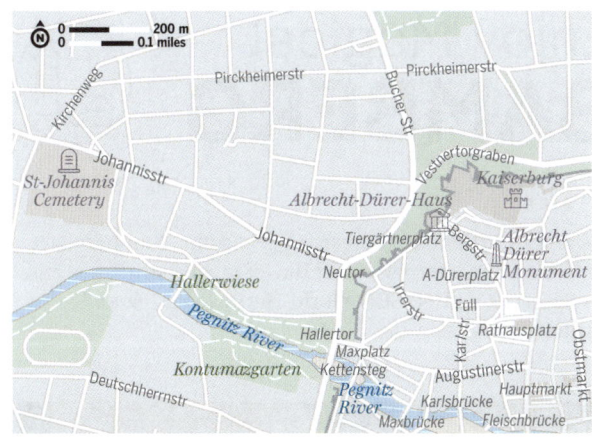

Top left Kaiserburg
Bottom left Albrecht-Dürer-Haus

Walk the old town Straddling the river and covering a larger area than some smaller Bavarian towns, Nuremberg's expansive and remarkably well-preserved old town is simply superb. Begin at the Hauptbahnhof and meander north. Take the little backstreets and stop to admire the half-timbered homes and stone churches.

Castle on a hill The **Kaiserburg** watches over the Altstadt as it has done for centuries – originally built in the 12th century, it was rebuilt after WWII. Begin your visit with the renovated residential wing (Palas) with its lavish Knights' and Imperial Hall, a Romanesque double chapel and the Kaiserburg Museum. Enjoy panoramic views of the Altstadt from the Sinwell Tower, or peer 48m down into the Deep Well.

Albrecht Dürer's Nuremberg Back down in the Altstadt, follow the footsteps of Germany's most revered master artist, who was born in the city in 1471. Set aside at least a couple of hours for **Albrecht-Dürer-Haus**; the hands-on demonstrations in the re-created studio and print shop on the 3rd floor and the attic gallery featuring copies and originals of Dürer's work are highlights.

One of the prettiest squares in Nuremberg's Altstadt, Albrecht-Dürer-Platz has the **Albrecht Dürer Monument**. The great man is buried in crowded, medieval **St-Johannis Cemetery**.

Nuremberg's Christmas Market

Of all Germany's Christmas markets, many agree that **Nuremberg's** is the best. The event takes place on the Hauptmarkt, against the backdrop of the city's medieval splendour. Fairy-lit stalls proffer everything from Yuletide baubles and roast chestnuts to toffee and bottles of mead, as Nuremberg's very own bratwurst and *Glühwein* (mulled wine) scent the chilly air. And, of course, it wouldn't be complete without a nativity scene. The market opens 1 December (or sometimes a couple of days earlier) and runs until Christmas Eve. For more information on the event, visit christkindlesmarkt.de.

33 Enjoy Magical BAMBERG

ARCHITECTURE | CULTURE | BEER

■ The epicentre of Bavaria's north and the heart of Franconia, Bamberg is a disarmingly beautiful architectural masterpiece that the last two centuries seem to have overlooked. It well deserves its UNESCO World Heritage listing and is one of Germany's most attractive towns.

How to

Getting here and around
Bamberg has frequent rail connections to major German cities. Once in town, you can only really explore the Altstadt on foot.

When to go Christmas is a magical time to be in Bamberg. July and August have the best weather, but can be ridiculously crowded.

BAMBERGcard Covers entry to most museums, a two-hour city tour and free local public transport.

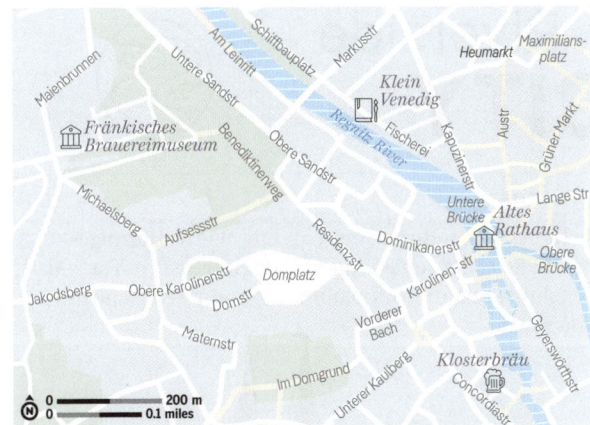

Top left Altes Rathaus
Bottom left Klosterbräu

Altes Rathaus If you've seen any images of Bavaria, the chances are that you've seen Bamberg's **Altes Rathaus**. Built to span an artificial island in the Regnitz River in 1462, it's a classic multistorey half-timbered structure magically overhanging the river. The interior boasts a remarkable collection of porcelain pieces and an opulent rococo hall, but the highlight has always been the view from the pedestrian-only Greyerswörthbrücke. Tip for photographers: zoom in all you like, but a wide-angle lens that takes in both banks of the river is the money shot. The Rathaus is also known for its gloriously frescoed facades – note the cherub's leg cheekily protruding from the east-facing wall. And while tourists are busy snapping away, locals often come to the island to relax and chill with a bottle of wine around sunset.

Bamberg's Little Venice On the east bank of the Regnitz, between Markusbrücke and Untere Brücke, you'll find an enchanted collection of small, half-timbered cottages known as **Klein Venedig** (Little Venice). Once home to a community of fisherfolk, the homes perch atop poles anchored in the river's rushing waters. Some have tiny gardens, and red geraniums cascade from flower boxes during summer months. The best views are from Untere Brücke near the Altes Rathaus, and Am Leinritt on the opposite bank.

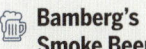

Bamberg's Smoke Beer

Bamberg is one of Germany's most beloved beer towns. Dive deeply into the world of Franconian brewing at the **Fränkisches Brauereimuseum**. Having learned about the history of local beers, it's time to zero in on Bamberg's famous *Rauchbier*, literally 'smoke beer'. The smoky bouquet comes from the malt being smoked over beechwood. **Klosterbräu** is Bamberg's oldest brewery (1533) and is perfect for a tour and sampling. To broaden your beer horizons, the Bamberg tourist office has put together a self-guided BierSchmecker tour, which includes a tankard of the local brew at four of the breweries.

34 A Riverside CITY

ARCHITECTURE | SCENERY | HISTORY

Sitting pretty astride the Danube, Regensburg and its World Heritage–listed tangle of old streets feel like some some kind of hidden treasure. The old bridge across the Danube sets up a magnificent panorama, and a river journey to some incredible sights is a must.

How to

Getting here and around Regensburg is well connected by road and rail to Nuremberg, Passau, Munich and Frankfurt am Main. The town centre is ideal for walking.

When to go Danube tours tend to be crowded in July and August. In May and August/September, Dult is Regensburg's answer to Oktoberfest.

Cycling Regensburg is a cycling city and you can rent two-wheelers at Bikehaus at the train station.

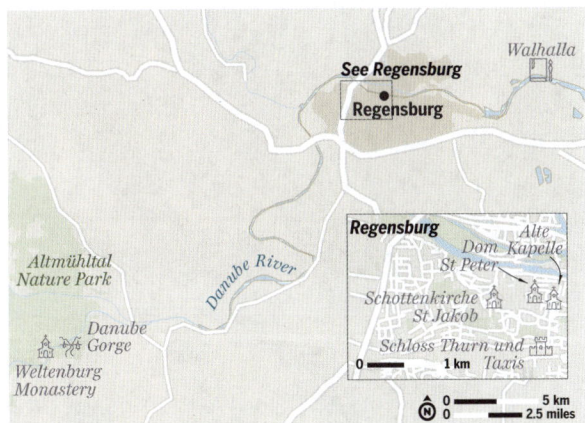

Top left Dom St Peter
Bottom left Alte Kapelle

A beautiful palace In parkland near the train station, the **Schloss Thurn und Taxis** became, in the 19th century, one of the most modern palaces in Europe. Tour the state rooms, treasury and carriage museum and prepare to be dazzled.

Regensburg's churches The austere Catholic **Dom St Peter** dominates the city skyline and is a masterpiece of the Gothic style, with few rivals for grandeur in Bavaria. Nearby, the over-the-top **Alte Kapelle** has vaulted Gothic ceilings. **Schottenkirche St Jakob** is the pinnacle of Romanesque architecture in Germany.

Walhalla Follow the Danube downriver to Walhalla. Modelled on the Parthenon in Athens, Walhalla rises from the riverbank like an apparition from another place and time. It was built by Ludwig I and dedicated to the giants of Germanic culture.

Danube Gorge and monastery Upriver, visit dramatic **Danube Gorge** and **Weltenburg Monastery**. The tour by **Schifffahrt Klinger** runs on Saturdays only from late May until mid-September. Weltenburg Monastery sits on a tight bend in the river and is Bavaria's oldest monastery. Weltenburg is famous for its brewery, and the monks still brew up the Weltenburger Kloster Barock Dunkel, a supreme dark beer said by some to be unsurpassed in Central Europe. Relax in the restaurant and beer hall.

~~~ The Danube

Most rivers in Germany run south to north, but the Danube is an exception, running roughly west to east. It rises in Furtwangen im Schwarzwald, in the Black Forest in Baden-Württemberg, and ultimately passes through 10 countries along its route to the Black Sea. It is Europe's second-longest river, running for 2850km. In Bavaria, the main places to access the Danube are Passau and Regensburg, where the river flows through the heart of town; the superb Danube Gorge at Weltenburg southwest of Regensburg; and Donauwörth (p180), part of which inhabits an island in the Danube.

35 FÜSSEN'S
World Heritage Sites

ARCHITECTURE | HISTORY | CULTURE

▬ Down in Bavaria's far south, the small town of Füssen is the gateway to some major attractions, all of which are inscribed on UNESCO's World Heritage List. Spend a couple of days here and you'll feel like you're living in a fairy tale.

How to

Getting here and around Füssen is the southernmost point on the Romantic Road, with good bus, train and road connections.

When to go There's no quiet period for visiting Neuschwanstein and Hohenschwangau, but summer can be uncomfortably busy and you'll need to reserve tickets ahead.

Early start If you want to visit Neuschwanstein and Hohenschwangau in a single day from Munich, you'll need to start very early. The first train leaves Munich at 4.39am (change in Buchloe), reaching Füssen at 7.21am.

The Classic Photo

As you climb the hill towards Neuschwanstein, resist the urge to go straight for the castle. Instead, follow the signs for **Marienbrücke** (Mary's Bridge), which spans the spectacular Pöllat Gorge over a waterfall just above the castle. Ludwig apparently enjoyed coming up here after dark to watch the candlelight radiating from the Sängersaal. The bridge rises high above the gorge – it's not one for those with a fear of heights, especially when thronging with visitors – but there's no better angle to see the castle in all its glory.

Schloss Neuschwanstein

Ludwig II's fairy-tale **Schloss Neuschwanstein** is Bavaria's most visited attraction, and as it comes into view for the first time it is instantly obvious why. This is

Füssen to the Castles

It's just under 4km from the centre of Füssen to the car parks, bus stop and ticket office for Schloss Neuschwanstein and Schloss Hohenschwangau. You can walk, cycle, drive, take a bus, or take a taxi (€12 to €20 one way). Hourly buses 73 and 78 *(bahn.de)* serve the castles from Fussen Bahnhof.

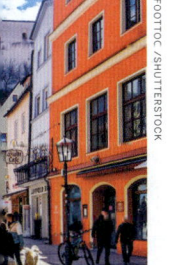

Above left Marienbrücke
Above right Schloss Hohenschwangau (p175) **Left** Füssen old town

the castle of Disney inspiration, and the castle that kids might draw with princesses letting down their hair from a tower, or with a dragon climbing the ramparts. Some have described it as the world's best castle.

The most impressive room is the **Sängersaal** (Minstrels' Hall), the frescoes of which depict scenes from the opera *Tannhäuser*. Don't miss Ludwig's Tristan and Isolde–themed bedroom, dominated by a huge Gothic-style bed crowned with an intricately carved, cathedral-like spire, and the grotto, with more references to *Tannhäuser*. The Byzantine-style **Thronsaal** (Throne Room) boasts an incredible mosaic floor containing more than two million stones. The tour ends with an interesting 20-minute film before you're unleashed into the gift shop.

Schloss Hohenschwangau

You get two castles for your money, and Hohenschwangau's 'other' castle is just

Best View Near Füssen

Some 5km northeast of Füssen, off Route 17 (which connects Füssen with Steingaden), lies the small baroque church of **St Coloman**. The church dates back to the 17th century and has an extravagant baroque interior, though the door is rarely open. But the view from the road between Route 17 and the church has extraordinary views – of the church, the Alps and even a distant Neuschwanstein. If you're lucky enough to be here on a day when the sun is shining and there's sun on the peaks, the results are magnificent.

Left St Coloman **Below** Museum der Bayerischen Könige (Museum of the Bavarian Kings)

as interesting, if not as dreamily storybookish, as Neuschwanstein. King Ludwig II grew up at **Schloss Hohenschwangau** and later enjoyed long summers here until his death in 1886. Some rooms have frescoes from German mythology, including the story of the Swan Knight, Lohengrin.

Not far away, save time for the **Museum der Bayerischen Könige** (Museum of the Bavarian Kings), which takes you through the storied history of Ludwig II and those who sat on his throne before and after his reign.

Join the Pilgrims at Wieskirche

The pilgrimage church **Wieskirche**, around 25km northeast of Füssen, is one of Bavaria's best-known baroque churches. Built around the site where an 18th-century farmer saw his Christ statue shedding tears, it draws more pilgrims than tourists. Inside the almost circular structure, eight snow-white pillars are topped by gold capital stones and swirling decorations. The unsupported dome's surface is adorned with a pastel ceiling fresco that vividly recreates the resurrection of Christ.

Mad King Ludwig II

FEW HISTORICAL CHARACTERS CAST SUCH A LONG SHADOW OVER BAVARIA AS KING LUDWIG II. Almost everywhere you go in Bavaria, there's a story attached to King Ludwig II. Thankfully, for all his fantasies and eccentricities, he left behind a peerless architectural legacy, one where the aesthetics often seem best suited to some kind of magical fairy tale. As you can imagine, his life was itself a fascinating story.

Left Wood engraving of King Ludwig II
Centre Schloss Berg
Right Schloss Linderhof

The Early Years

Where did the grandiose vision that gave birth to Schloss Neuschwanstein and other stunning architectural creations come from? Prinz Otto Ludwig Friedrich Wilhelm was a sensitive soul, fascinated by romantic epics, architecture and music, but his parents, Maximilian II and Marie, took little interest in his musings and he suffered a lonely and joyless childhood. In 1864, at 18 years of age, the prince became king.

At first, Ludwig was an enthusiastic leader. But Bavaria's days as a sovereign state were numbered, and he became a puppet king after the creation of the German Reich in 1871 (which had its advantages, as Bismarck gave Ludwig a hefty allowance). Ludwig withdrew completely to drink, draw up castle plans and view concerts and operas in private. His obsession with French culture and the Sun King, Louis XIV, inspired the fantastical palaces of Neuschwanstein, Linderhof and Herrenchiemsee – lavish projects that left a legacy that rippled down through the years, even as it doomed the monarch during his lifetime.

The Fall of King Ludwig II

Contrary to popular belief, it was only Ludwig's purse – and not the state treasury – that was being bankrupted through all this castle construction. However, by 1886 his ever-growing mountain of debt and unpredictable behaviour put him at odds with his cabinet. The king, it seemed, needed to be 'managed'. In January 1886, several ministers and relatives arranged a hasty psychiatric test

that diagnosed Ludwig as mentally unfit to rule (this was made easier by the fact that his brother had been declared insane years earlier). That June, he was removed to Schloss Berg on Lake Starnberg.

Did he ever get to enjoy the architectural confections that would ultimately lead to his downfall? For all the coffer-depleting sums spent on Schloss Neuschwanstein, the king spent just over 170 days in residence at his beloved castle.

Death

Every year on 13 June, a stirring ceremony takes place on the eastern shore of Lake Starnberg, 100km northeast of Füssen. A small boat glides towards a cross just offshore and a plain wreath is fastened to its front. A single trumpet cuts the silence as the boat returns from this solemn ritual in honour of Ludwig II.

The cross marks the spot where Ludwig died under mysterious circumstances in 1886. No one knows what happened that night, except that Ludwig and his doctor took a Sunday evening lakeside walk and were found several hours later, drowned in just a few feet of water. That summer, the authorities opened Neuschwanstein to the public to help pay off Ludwig's huge debts.

> His obsession with French culture and the Sun King, Louis XIV, inspired the fantastical palaces of Neuschwanstein, Linderhof and Herrenchiemsee – lavish projects that left a legacy.

Schloss Linderhof

South of Oberammergau, in a wide valley hemmed by peaks rising over 1700m in places, World Heritage–listed **Schloss Linderhof** is arguably Ludwig II's most fantastical creation. A compact little jewel-encrusted safe box of weird and wonderful trinkets, it's Ludwig II's smallest palace, and the only one he lived to see fully built. Completed in 1878, it climbs a steep hillside in a fantasy landscape of French gardens, fountains and follies. The vast private bedroom has a 500kg chandelier. Other highlights include the gilded Audience Room, extravagant Hall of Mirrors and the mad king's conch-shaped boat.

36 NORTHERN
Romantic Road

VILLAGES | CULTURE | HISTORY

Welcome to Germany at its most enchanting, with storybook medieval gems cutting a swathe through the heart of Bavaria. This is the Germany many expect to see, with the Romantic Road's perfectly conserved towns delivering on all the clichéd promises seen pretrip on Instagram.

Romantic Road Stats

From the vineyards of Würzburg to the foot of the Alps, the 460km Romantic Road (Romantische Strasse; *romantischestrasse.de*) is by far Germany's most popular tourist route. It passes through 29 cities, towns and villages, as well as 22 castles and palaces and four UNESCO sites in a ribbon of half-timbered quaintness.

Trip Notes

Getting here and around To make all the stops along this northern section of the Romantic Road, you really need your own wheels.

When to go Avoid July and August, if you can, when Rothenburg is simply overwhelmed by visitors. Spring and autumn weekdays are ideal.

Romantic Road Coach This bus service combines with rail to cover most of the route. Some services operate as day trips from Würzburg or Frankfurt.

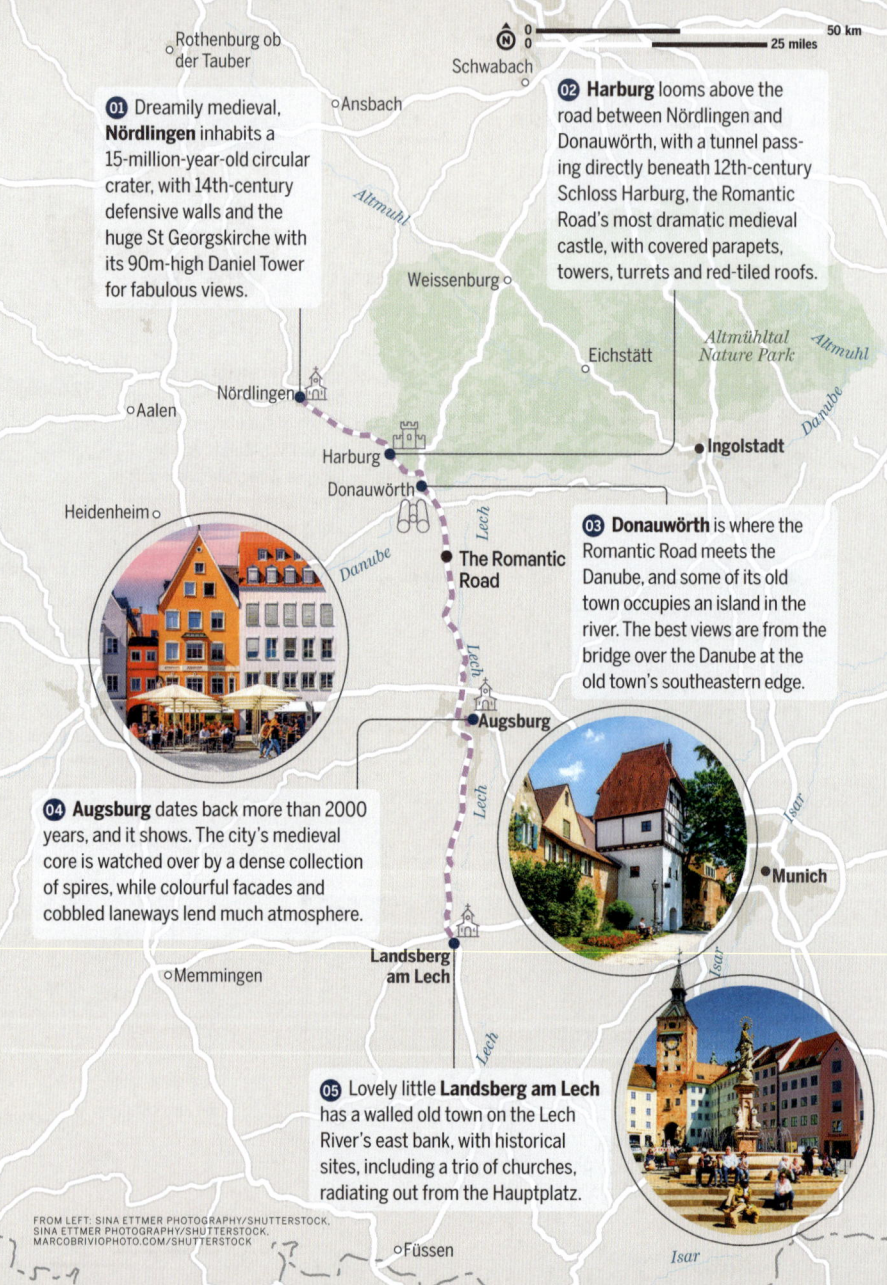

SOUTHERN
Romantic Road

HISTORY | CULTURE | ARCHITECTURE

From the Bavarian heartland, the Romantic Road continues its enchanted path towards the Alps. With the possible exception of Nördlingen and Donauwörth, the towns in this region are less known and receive fewer visitors than those further north, but they're every bit as beautiful.

🏠 Nördlingen from the Air

At the end of the wonderful 1970s film *Willy Wonka & the Chocolate Factory*, Wonka, Charlie and his grandpa smash through the chocolate factory's glass roof in the Wonkavator and the scenes that follow feature an aerial view of Nördlingen (pictured above), with its circular layout and red roofs clearly visible. Munich boy Michael Bollner played Augustus Gloop.

Trip Notes

Getting here and around Having your own vehicle really makes this itinerary work, though you could also base yourself in Augsburg and make day trips by bus or train.

When to go All the towns have excellent Christmas markets in December. July and August can be busy, but months either side should have plenty of sunny days.

Oktoberfest You could combine the Southern Romantic Road with Munich's Oktoberfest. Augsburg has lots of accommodation and is a good alternative base.

BAVARIAN
Icons

01 Schloss Neuschwanstein
In this land of castles, it takes a lot to stand out, but Neuschwanstein is a true Disney fairy tale.

02 Zugspitze
Germany's highest mountain is accessible by cable car, and the views of glaciers and seemingly endless mountain summits is Germany's best.

03 Schnitzel
The humble schnitzel is a miracle of simplicity and a regional obsession; it adorns many a Bavarian menu.

04 Beer tankard
Munich isn't the only town with a beer festival – Straubing (Gäubodenfest) and Regensburg (Dult) have much-loved events; Bamberg is also a beer legend.

05 Bamberg's Altes Rathaus
It's the classic vision of a Bavarian Altstadt: colourful, ancient, half-timbered, frescoed and perched over the Regnitz River.

06 Käthe Wohlfahrt Shop (Rothenburg)
Bavaria's Christmas Markets are among the world's best; this Rothenburg shop (with outposts elsewhere) keeps the magic running all year.

07 Vineyards
Bavaria has exceptional winemakers, but those of Franconia belong in a class of their own; Würzburg and surrounds are the epicentre.

08 Bratwurst
Germany's ultimate street food has much-loved regional variations (especially in Nuremberg and Coburg) and is a traveller's staple.

09 Cable cars
Wherever there's a mountain, the Bavarians seem to have built a cable to ferry skiers and sightseers to the top.

10 Half-timbered houses
Nothing whispers Bavarian quite like a *Fachwerk* (half-timbered) home; the Romantic Road has more than anywhere.

11 Snow sports
The Alps are Germany's winter sports playground; Bavarian children learn to ski soon after walking.

12 Medieval walls
Medieval defensive walls encircle many Bavarian towns, and they're even visible in some cities; Rothenburg, Dinkelsbühl and Nördlingen are standouts.

01 ALEH VARANISHCHA/GETTYIMAGES, 02 PHOTOGRAPHY IS ON/SHUTTERSTOCK, 03 ETORRES/SHUTTERSTOCK, 04 PICTURE ALLIANCE/GETTYIMAGES, 05 FROLOVA, ELENA/SHUTTERSTOCK, 06 SINA ETTMER PHOTOGRAPHY/SHUTTERSTOCK, 07 CANADASTOCK/SHUTTERSTOCK, 08 FOOD IMPRESSIONS/SHUTTERSTOCK, 09 BERNHARD SCHAFFER/SHUTTERSTOCK, 10 ECSTK22/SHUTTERSTOCK, 11 CAVAN IMAGES/ROBERT NIEDRING PHOTOGRAPHER/GETTY IMAGES, 12 BY-STUDIO/SHUTTERSTOCK

Listings

BEST OF THE REST

Museums & Galleries

Deutsche Bahn Museum
At Nuremberg's Hauptbahnhof, this museum is terrific, with plenty of history and two halls of fabulous locos and rolling stock.

Richard Wagner Museum
This musical museum is housed in a Bayreuth mini-mansion the composer built with money given to him by Ludwig II. His unmarked, ivy-covered tomb is out the back.

Audi Factory
If you're a devotee, head for Ingolstadt's Audi Factory. It charts the company's humble beginnings in 1899 to its latest dream machines.

Churches & Monasteries

Eichstätt Dom
Highlights of Eichstätt's richly decorated 11th-century cathedral include a magnificent 16th-century stained-glass window by Hans Holbein the Elder and a carved sandstone altar.

St Martin Church
At the southern end of Landshut's Altstadt, the church's spire, the world's tallest brick structure (130.6m), rises in Gothic splendour.

Dom St Stephan
Dominating Passau's Domplatz, this baroque marvel has an interior filled with a cornucopia of saints and cherubs and a monster organ.

Castles & Palaces

Residenz
Würzburg's vast World Heritage–listed, 18th-century Residenz is one of Germany's most beautiful baroque palaces, with an amazing staircase, the world's largest fresco (by Tiepolo) and lavish halls.

Schloss Herrenchiemsee
Often the last of Ludwig II's mad mansions that tourists see, this opulent palace is the most Versailles-like of all his pads. Incredibly, Ludwig blew more cash on it than on Neuschwanstein.

Cable Cars

Tegelbergbahn
Close to Füssen, this cable car climbs Tegelberg (1881m) to the Tegelberghaus mountain chalet. From the summit, the views extend forever. Hike back down (or to Oberammergau) from the top.

Jennerbahn am Königssee
One of Bavaria's most spectacular rides is a stunning complement to a boat ride on Königssee. For the best views of Königssee, walk 550m (20 minutes) to Königsblick (1874m).

Natural Beauty

Zugspitze
Climb by cable car or cogwheel train (Zahnradbahn) up Germany highest mountain (2962m). The top station has unforgettable views.

Königssee
Take a pleasure boat along the fjord-like Königssee to St Bartholomä church and hamlet to listen to Echo Wall and enjoy a meal and beer.

Jewish Bavaria

Jüdisches Museum Franken
A quick U-Bahn ride from Nuremberg in Fürth, the museum chronicles Jewish life in the region from the Middle Ages to today.

Nazi History

Reichsparteitagsgelände
Much of the footage of Nazi rallies, with marching masses bearing swastika banners, was shot

here in Nuremberg. Visit the excellent Dokumentationszentrum (Documentation Centre).

Dokumentation Obersalzberg & Eagle's Nest
Southeast of Berchtesgaden, visit the superb exhibition then climb to Hitler's mountain hideout at 1834m above sea level.

Opera Houses & Theatres

Festspielhaus
Wagner designed his own festival hall in Bayreuth and it's the main venue for the July–August Wagner Festival. Join a daily tour.

Markgräfliches Opernhaus
Wagner shunned Bayreuth's World Heritage–listed opera house, despite it being one of Europe's most opulent baroque theatres.

Passionstheater
The world's most famous Passion Play takes place every 10 years (next in 2030) at the 4500-seat Passion Play Theatre. In between, there are other performances and a guided tour.

Beer & Wine

Kellerwald
Literally a 'cellar forest', 24 beer cellars create the world's largest beer garden in Forchheim.

Gäubodenfest
Small Straubing hosts Bavaria's second-largest beer festival, a 10-day blow-out in mid-August. Over one million drinkers descend on town.

Landbierparadies
Behind Nuremberg's train station, try more than 50 of Franconia's obscure beers.

Juliusspital
This appealing Würzburg *Weinstube* (traditional wine tavern) has a fabulous list of local Franconian wines paired with excellent local dishes.

Bürgerspital Weinstube
This Würzburg place has one of the most extensive lists of local wines in Bavaria, with Franconian wines (and food).

Festspielhaus

 **Eating**

Metzgerai Ludwig Walk
This Nuremberg purveyor of fine meats has a deli and a street-facing counter where it serves bratwurst, schnitzel and Leberkäse in rolls.

Bratwursthäusle
The bratwurst grilled at this rustic little Nuremberg inn sets the standard for the world.

Goldenes Kreuz
Just off Marktplatz in Coburg, GK serves Franconian food, including bratwurst, as well as *Klössen* (dumplings) served with roast meats.

Backöfele
This Würzburg bastion of regional cooking serves schnitzel, snails, bratwurst in wine and boar.

Bürgerspital Weinstube
Aromatic and unmissable, this medieval Würzburg dining experience offers superb regional dishes, including *Mostsuppe* (wine soup).

Café Central
If you're on a mission to try Bavaria's best apple strudel or Black Forest cake, visit this Dinkelsbühl classic.

Haus Appelberg
This fine Dinkelsbühl traditional choice serves local fish, Franconian sausages and *Maultaschen* (pork-and-spinach ravioli) paired with Franconian wines.

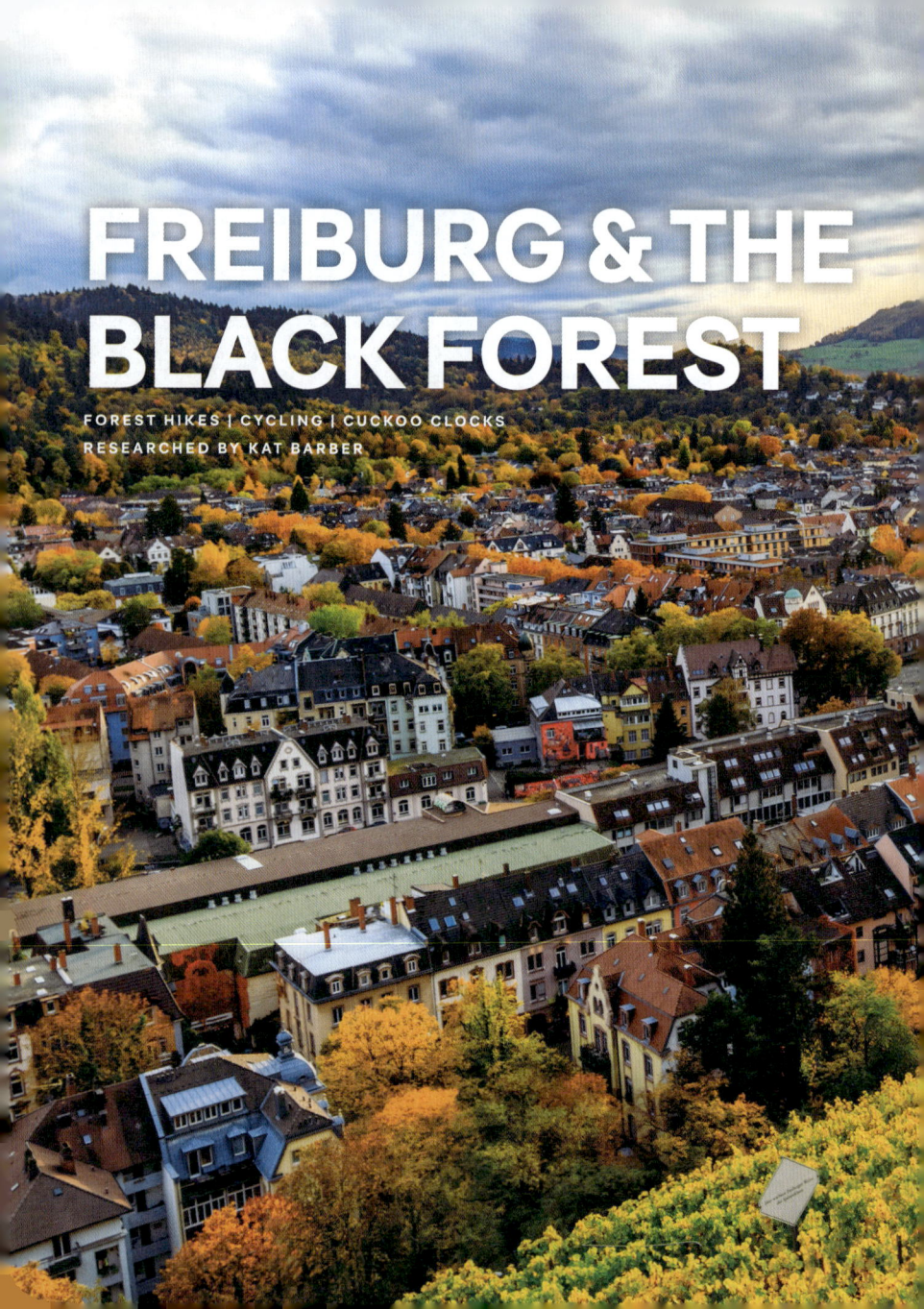

FREIBURG & THE BLACK FOREST

FOREST HIKES | CYCLING | CUCKOO CLOCKS

RESEARCHED BY KAT BARBER

- **Trip Builder** (p188)
- **Practicalities** (p190)
- **Eat at Freiburg's Münster Market** (p192)
- **Snowshoe through the Forest** (p194)
- **Bake Your Own Black Forest Cake** (p196)
- **Race Downhill on a Toboggan** (p198)
- **Gorgeous Gorge Hikes** (p200)
- **Cycle Around Lake Constance** (p204)
- **The History of the Cuckoo Clock** (p206)
- **Listings** (p208)

FREIBURG & THE BLACK FOREST
Trip Builder

Soak up the relaxed vibes in Freiburg, then hike, bike or simply explore the enchanting Black Forest region. From colourful half-timbered-house villages to tranquil turquoise lakes, this region reaches high to snow-covered mountains and down into the depths of ancient gorges.

Eat your way around the **Münster market** (p192) in Freiburg
🚆 2hr from Frankfurt

Try snowshoeing through the snow-covered forest in **Feldberg** (p194)
🚗 50min from Freiburg

Race your mates down Germany's longest **toboggan run** (p198) in Todtnau
🚗 40min from Freiburg

Bake your own Black Forest cake at **Cafe Zimmermann** (p197) in Todtmoos
🚗 1hr from Freiburg

Practicalities

ARRIVING

Freiburg HBF (Breisgau) Train Station Regular high-speed connections to a number of German cities, including Berlin, Cologne and Frankfurt, as well as Basel in Switzerland and Strasbourg in France. From Freiburg, the Höllentalbahn runs a scenic route through the Black Forest, via Titisee to Donaueschingen.

Frankfurt am Main Airport The closest major airport, with international connections all around the world. From the airport, a direct Deutsche Bahn train connects to Freiburg in just over two hours.

HOW MUCH FOR A

Pretzel €1.50

Schnitzel and chips €17

Pint of beer €4.20

GETTING AROUND

Train The best way to get to the Black Forest (in sustainably minded Freiburg, trams and bikes are the main mode of transport). Trains connect to larger towns in the Black Forest such as Baden-Baden, Offenburg, Titisee-Neustadt and Donaueschingen.

Bus There is a very well-connected bus system through the Black Forest, and with the KONUS card you can enjoy unlimited free travel. Plan your route at *bahn.de*.

Car A car will be helpful if you plan on really exploring the region. It will allow you to travel at your leisure, stop in tiny villages and pack more into your day.

WHEN TO GO

JAN–MAR
The winter months are peak snow season across the region.

APR–JUN
Spring has sprung, so have the tulips and the white asparagus *(Spargel)*.

JUL–SEP
Summers are mild, the perfect time to get out hiking, cycling and swimming.

OCT–DEC
Christmas markets bring joy and festive cheer to the long, cold winter nights.

EATING & DRINKING

In this region, you can sample both Badish and Swabian cuisine. Look out for *Spargel* (white asparagus) in spring, plus *Maultäschen* (large meat-filled ravioli in an onion melt), *Knöpfle*, also called *Spätzle* (cheesy egg pasta), and *Flammkuchen* (crispy thin pizza topped with onion and ham). And let's not forget the ultimate on-the-go snack – a pretzel – and, of course, the region's most famous export, the decadent Black Forest cake. Local tipples include the cult beer Rothaus, as well as punchy schnapps made from the numerous fruit orchards.

Best Black Forest cake Cafe Zimmermann (p197)

Must-try beer Rothaus (p208)

WHERE TO STAY

The sheer size of the Black Forest surprises many travellers, so it's best to pick somewhere near the attractions or hikes you'd like to do.

CONNECT & FIND YOUR WAY

Wi-fi Most hotels offer free wi-fi and some towns such as Freiburg have free public wi-fi. Smaller villages and hiking trails may have patchy coverage, so set up roaming data or purchase an eSIM.

Navigation German street addresses always put the street name before the house number, and individual apartments aren't numbered – instead, they use the resident's surname to mark postboxes and doorbells.

Town	Pros/Cons
Freiburg	The largest city in the area with the best transport connections, accommodation options, nightlife and amenities.
Triberg	A kitsch tourist town but the stunning waterfalls, museums, eateries and a supermarket make it a good base.
Baden-Baden	The northernmost Black Forest town, it's a good choice if you like spas, art, culture and great restaurants. Accommodation can be expensive.
Todtnau	A good spot for visiting Feldberg's snowfields, or to ride the toboggan. Quiet in the off-season.
Gegenbach	A picturesque half-timbered town that makes a great jumping-off point. You'll need a car to get around.
Heidelberg	This bustling university town is stunning. Few cheap accommodation options in the centre.

FREE PUBLIC TRANSPORT

All guests staying at hotels throughout the Black Forest will receive a KONUS Card. It gives you free travel in 2nd class on public transport for the duration of your stay.

MONEY

Save money with the Schwarzwald card. It gives you free admission to more than 200 attractions throughout the Black Forest on any three days within a year. Always carry at least a little cash.

38 Eat at Freiburg's Münster MARKET

LONG SAUSAGES | LOCAL PRODUCE | TOWERING CHURCH

Freiburg's **Münster market** is a feast for the senses. Set against the Gothic spires of the Freiburg Münster (cathedral), this local produce market buzzes with locals and visitors sampling regional delicacies from local producers and food trucks. Spend the morning filling your stomach before exploring Freiburg's cute canal-lined alleyways, hilltop lookouts and historical sights. Come hungry and get ready to taste the Black Forest.

How to

Getting here The market is impossible to miss as it takes over the cobbled main square around the church. It's a 15-minute walk from Freiburg HBF or one minute from the Bertoldsbrunnen tram stop.

When to go The market takes place every day except Sundays and public holidays from 7.30am to 1.30pm (till 2pm Saturdays).

Don't forget Not all vendors accept cards, so bring cash and a reusable shopping bag for your purchases. Try to visit early to beat the crowds.

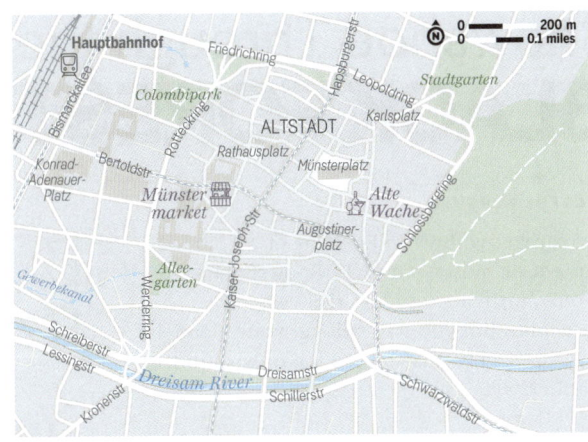

Top and bottom left Stalls at Münster market

To Market

With approximately 130 stalls offering fruit and vegetables, cheeses, flowers, breads, wine and meats from the surrounding area, you won't leave hungry. A market has been held here since the Middle Ages, when carvings at the entrance of the cathedral were used as a rudimentary bread-measuring tool, ensuring customers were getting what they paid for, since many couldn't read.

Five of the Best

Lange Rote Easily the most famous item at the market is the iconic *Lange Rote*, a 35cm-long spiced bratwurst sausage served in a crusty roll and topped with tomato sauce or mustard.

Stefan's Kasekuchen A long line always snakes away from Stefan's bright-yellow cheesecake truck. Join the queue to try the deliciously creamy cheesecake that was founded right here at the market, before it gained a cult following across Germany.

Tofu wurst Vegetarians and vegans can head to Tofu wurst for their meat-free version of the *Lange Rote*.

Baden wine It's never too early for a sip of a crisp white wine. Stop by the wine stands to sample Baden wine or, in autumn, pick up a bottle of *Federweisser* – wine at the beginning of the fermentation process with a light, tingly taste.

Cheese Don't miss stopping by the cheesemongers to sample local varieties such as *Hübschentäler Bergkäse* (Beautiful Valley Mountain Cheese), *Felsbrocken* (an aged hard cheese) and *Ziegenkäse* (goat cheese), made in the nearby alpine regions.

 Local Loves

While the *Lange Rote* is a real classic from the traditional sausage food trucks, I also love the *Merguez*. It's a lamb- and beef-based spicy sausage.

If you time it right, visit the **Freiburger Weinfest**, the city's famous wine festival, held in the same spot at the Münster market. It's held in early July every year and showcases over 400 local wines, live music and performances.

Don't miss **Alte Wache**, a popular wine bar on the Münsterplatz. Try its local invention, the 'Kalte Sophie', an iced slush wine drink, available in summer.

Recommended by **Lena Hug,** *local photographer.* @freiburg.streets

39 Snowshoe Through the BLACK FOREST

SNOW | WINTER HIKE | PEACEFUL PURSUIT

If you're not keen on careening downhill on skis or a snowboard, snowshoeing might be more your style. Snowshoeing along wooded trails is a serene, intimate and less risky way to explore the Black Forest in winter. But you will still get your blood pumping and your senses will be in overdrive, with the only sound being the crunch of snow underfoot.

How to

Getting here
Snowshoeing trails are well marked around the major ski-resort town of Feldberg, which is just under an hour's drive from Freiburg or two hours from Stuttgart.

When to go Consistent snow falls between December and March. Venture out in the mornings for pristine snow and quieter trails.

Where to rent gear
Rental outlets at snow resorts, ski schools and visitor centres (including Haus der Natur in Feldberg) offer snowshoe and pole rental.

What to expect Far from the ski lifts, snowshoeing is a deeply immersive and restorative way to connect with the natural soul of the Black Forest. Despite its odd name, snowshoeing is essentially just winter hiking with large lightweight frames strapped to your boots. There are thousands of kilometres of trails across the Black Forest, and it's recommended to stick to the trails marked with pink signs to ensure you don't disturb hibernating animals.

Gentle jaunt The scenic 3km **Seebuck Route** is a great beginner's trail. The walk takes around 1½ hours and features a manageable 170m ascent. It's a well-signposted circular route and access is easy, starting right behind the Haus der Natur in Feldberg. Start by heading up the Seebuck summit, before turning at the Feldbergturm and descending the southern slope back to the start.

Level up Feeling energetic? Tackle the longer **Feldberg summit tour**, a 9km circular route with 320m in elevation gain. Plan for around 3½ hours' walking time. This trail also kicks off at Haus der Natur, with numerous climbs on the way to the highest of Feldberg's four peaks, the 1493m Wechtenkante. Enjoy the views across the snow-covered Alps on clear days, then refuel with a *Kaffee und Kuchen* (or something stronger) at **St Wilhelmer Hut**. After that, it's all downhill back to the trailhead.

Top left The Black Forest in winter
Bottom left St Wilhelmer Hut
Above Feldberg summit tour

All the Gear No Idea

For snowshoeing, you'll need a pair of sturdy, waterproof boots, strapping to them a pair of snowshoes, which are lightweight frames (around 60cm x 20cm) with a large footprint that allows you to tread on top of the snow rather than sink into it. Add a pair of trekking poles for stability and you're set. You might need to adjust your walk to a little wider than normal, but you'll get the hang of it in no time. One final piece of advice – falling to the ground in snowshoes is easy; getting back on your feet again is a little harder.

40 BAKE A Black Forest Cake

DECADENT DESSERT | BAKING | CULTURAL ICON

The decadent Black Forest cake is far from a touristy treat; it's a cultural treasure you'll find in bakeries throughout the Black Forest. While we recommend sinking your teeth into as many pieces as your appetite allows, attending a baking workshop at Cafe Zimmermann will teach you how to recreate it back home. Roll up your sleeves and discover the secrets of the famous *Schwarzwälder Kirschtorte*.

How to

Getting here Cafe Zimmermann is in Todtmoos in the southern Black Forest region, an hour's drive from Freiburg.

When to go Cake-making classes run Tuesdays at 3pm year-round, but are especially popular in the summer cherry season.

How much The 45-minute workshop costs €17.50 and includes a hot drink, a slice of Black Forest gateau and a recipe. Book online at *cafe-zimmermann-todtmoos.de*.

Top left *Schwarzwälder Kirschtorte* (Black Forest cake) **Bottom left** *Kirschwasser* (cherry brandy) **Above** Cafe Zimmermann

Baking since 1913 Todtmoos is a small village in the depths of the southern Black Forest. Here, at fourth-generation, family-run **Cafe Zimmermann**, they've been kneading and baking since 1913. And their beloved Black Forest cake has history embedded between its layers of sour cherries, whipped cream, rich sponge, cherry brandy and chocolate shavings.

Learn from the masters This goes beyond a simple cooking class; it's a chance to connect with locals, step behind the counter and partake in a rich culinary tradition. This is hands-on, sugar-filled travel at its best. You'll definitely get a newfound appreciation for the work that goes into the cake. Workshops are run by master bakers, who claim it's easier than you think. The workshop dives into the local history of *Schwarzwälder Kirschtorte* and offers a masterclass on how to perfect and decorate the indulgent cake. And of course, you'll get a chance to sample a slice after the theoretical part of the course, as well as a printed recipe to take home. Courses are in German, with English offered on request.

Across the region Other small bakeries and traditional guesthouses host intimate baking classes. Places that'll show you to to whip, fold, and layer like a pro include **Cafe am Eck** in Baiersbronn in the region's north; **Hotel Hirsch** in Enzklösterle and **Erich's Schnapshäusle G'scheiter Beck** in Feldberg.

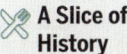

A Slice of History

The Black Forest cake is said to have originated in 1915 when pastry chef Josef Keller created an early version at Café Ahrend in Bad Godesberg. His single-layer cake is seen as the precursor to the multi-tiered classic we enjoy today. The name is said to have come from the black chocolate shavings on top, unmistakably reminiscent of the Black Forest, or perhaps its key ingredient – local *Kirschwasser* (cherry brandy). This *Kirschwasser* can only be labelled as such if it was produced in the Black Forest from fruity black cherries grown in the region.

41 Race Downhill on a TOBOGGAN

THRILLING | SCENIC RIDE | ADVENTURE

Get ready for thrills and laughter as you launch yourself down Germany's longest toboggan run. Whizzing down the steep track amid thick forest, this exhilarating ride in Todtnau is sure to get your heart racing. Whether you're a speed demon or just here for the views, racing down this 3km metal rail track is guaranteed fun.

How to

Getting here Todtnau is a 40-minute drive from Freiburg. With no train station in town, you can catch the train to Freiburg, Kirchzarten, Zell or Titisee, then change to a bus to Todtnau.

When to go The toboggan is open year-round from 9am to 4.30pm, weather permitting. Lines can be long in summer, so arrive early.

How much A single ride is €12.50/14.50 for children/adults, which includes the cable-car ascent.

Top left Hasenhorn Rodelbahn
Bottom left Blackforestline

Thrills and spills For kids and big kids at heart, Todtnau's **Hasenhorn Rodelbahn** is a gravity-fuelled toboggan adventure that blends alpine scenery with pure, childlike joy. While roller-coasters are an exhilarating thrill ride, being the driver of your own toboggan sled puts you in the driver's seat. Want to hit 40km/h and feel the G-force against your face? Go for it! Just try to keep 25m from the toboggan ahead. Prefer to mosey down, taking in the scenery as you go? That's cool, too – just keep hold of that brake.

What to expect Start by hopping on a two-seater chairlift, ascending 1065m to the run's summit, where you'll have a chance to catch your breath and enjoy the Black Forest views, or grab a bite at the kiosk. The Hasenhorn observation tower is also worth a quick visit, with its views stretching across Feldberg all the way to the Vosges. When you're ready, grab your sled (single or double if you've got under-eights in tow), buckle in and get ready to zoom. The steel track dips, curves and accelerates as you race back down the mountain for around 10 minutes. The brake is your best friend when those curves get too sharp. And don't forget to smile for the camera near the bottom.

Make a Day of It

While you're in the area, visit the nearby **Todtnauer Wasserfall** (waterfall), which is especially beautiful when icicles form along the rock face. Grab a combo ticket to visit the falls and the **Blackforestline**, Germany's longest suspension bridge. It offers panoramic views and a dose of adrenaline as you cross its 450m length. For family-friendly fun, head 8km further to **Steinwasen Park**, where roller-coasters, wildlife enclosures and alpine scenery make for a thrilling family day out. This southern corner of the Black Forest is the perfect base if you're looking for an adrenaline rush in nature.

42 **GORGEOUS** Gorge Hikes

SCENERY | WATERFALLS | HIKING

Some of the Black Forest's wildest beauty lies below the treetops, carved into steep rock and echoing with rushing water. Gorge hikes in the Black Forest offer refreshing and soul-stirring walks among dramatic landscapes. Think mossy rock walls, waterfalls, wooden footbridges and narrow ravines.

How to

Getting around You will need a car to access all of the gorge hikes due to their out-of-the-way locations.

When to go Plan to visit between April and October. Due to their slippery terrain, the gorges close over the winter months (November to March) for safety reasons.

What to see Keep an eye out for butterflies, birds, wildflowers, blooming perennials and buzzing insects.

Wutachschlucht (Wutach Gorge)

The 'Grand Canyon' of the Black Forest, the **Wutachschlucht** is the region's most famous and extensive gorge. Over millions of years, the Wutach River has gouged a deep canyon through the rock, up to 170m in places, and nature has filled the space with ferns, waterfalls and overhanging rock walls. Step foot into the gorge and take in the unique botany, dip your toes in the cool water and listen to the calls of kingfishers. The hike can be challenging due to the slippery, uneven surfaces and narrow footbridges.

The whole gorge is 30km in length, and you can hike a number of sections, with buses connecting popular starting points to the main car parks. Park at Schattenmühle, a charming old mill, and catch the bus to Boll. From there, follow the gorge along a 10.8km

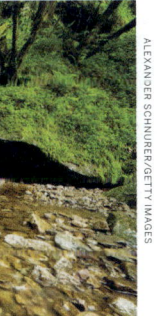

Gear Up

The essential piece of gear for hiking here is sturdy, waterproof hiking boots. Don't forget snacks, water and your hiking poles if you want to look like a local. Start early or visit on a weekday to avoid the crowds. Check conditions at @wutachranger before you start as some trails close after storms or heavy rain.

Top left, top right and bottom
Wutachschlucht

trail back to your car over roughly 3½ hours. If you get lost, just look for the red lozenge symbols on signage.

Ravenna Gorge (Ravennaschlucht)

If Wutachschlucht is wild, **Ravennaschlucht** (Ravenna Gorge) is romantic. Just outside Hinterzarten, not too far from Freiburg, this steep little ravine is known for its ivy-covered rock walls, mini waterfalls and the towering **Ravenna Viaduct** railway bridge at the trailhead. At only 4km in length, it's a great choice for families with adventurous children in tow.

From the car park, the out-and-back trail leads you along a bubbling brook, past mossy boulders and wooden bridges. After ascending steep, narrow stairs, you'll pass remnants of old mills and forges that once powered local industry.

The trail is especially enchanting in winter, when snow blankets everything in a delicate

Wildlife of Wutachschlucht

Wutachschlucht is one of the oldest nature reserves in the state and here you're a silent bystander among nature. The gorge is one of Central Europe's last remaining wild-river landscapes, boasting a fabulous array of flora and fauna. An estimated 10,000 species of arthropods, molluscs and vertebrates live in the region. Experiencing nature also means respecting nature so, when visiting, stay on the paths and keep dogs on the lead to ensure native animals are not disturbed.

Follow the Wutach Ranger @wutachranger on Instagram for the latest updates and tips.

Left Ravenna Viaduct
Below Gauchachschlucht

white dust. Plus, the **Ravenna Gorge Christmas market** that sets up under the viaduct's towering arches on December weekends is one of the most beautiful in the country.

Three Gorges Hike (Drei-Schluchten-Tour)

The Three Gorges Hike takes in the spectacular Wutachschlucht, as well as looping through two of its neighbours: **Gauchachschlucht** and **Engeschlucht**. It's one of the region's most rewarding and stunning day hikes.

Start the circular 9.6km hike by parking at Drei-Schluchten-Halle (Three Gorges Hall) in Bachheim before hiking into Wutachschlucht, passing beneath towering rock galleries and moss-covered boulders. From here, you'll hike upstream along the Gauchach River and enter the hidden and enchanted Gauchachschlucht. It's much narrower than Wutachschlucht and the fallen logs, rustic log bridges and wild flora will make you feel like a character in *The Jungle Book*. You'll soon turn into the third gorge, Engeschlucht, the narrowest of all. Taut steel cables have been installed along much of its slippery, narrow trails, and the quiet, secluded surroundings are the perfect end to the adventure.

43 Cycle Around Lake CONSTANCE

LAKESIDE TRAIL | MULTICOUNTRY | EASY RIDING

The 260km Lake Constance cycle trail is a dream ride for even the most reluctant cyclist. It's flat, scenic and interlaced with cultural gems and – bonus – you can tick off three countries for the price of one, so you likely won't even notice your saddle soreness.

Trip Notes

Getting around You can start from anywhere around the lake, but Konstanz is a popular choice due to its rail links to Freiburg, Stuttgart, Munich, Zurich and Paris.

When to go The weather between May and September offers the best cycling conditions, but it's also when accommodation is priciest and the route is busiest.

Give it a week Allow seven days to complete the loop, building in time for side trips, sightseeing and leisurely lunches.

No Bike? No Problem!

There's no shortage of bike rental and repair shops around the lake. Expect to pay around €15 to €20 per day for a standard bike and €30 to €40 for an e-bike. Helmets, locks, baskets, cargo trailers and child seats are available, too. Ferries across the lake also take bikes, and most hotels have secure bike parking.

The History of the Cuckoo Clock

LOVE IT OR LOATHE IT, THE CUCKOO CLOCK IS A BLACK FOREST ICON.

How did an ornately carved, chirping bird clock from the Black Forest make its way to living rooms around the world? And who first thought it would be a good idea to put a tiny wooden bird in a clock?

The Origin of the Chirping Bird

To understand the origins of the cuckoo clock, start by looking at the environment at the time. In the 18th century, the Black Forest was a poor farming area. During the winter months, when heavy snow blanketed their farms, farmers looked for other ways to earn a living while taking advantage of the local wood supply. Woodcarving and crafting had always been popular, and when travelling clock-peddlers passed through the region, bringing clock technology and trends from other cities across Europe, the Black Forest clockmaking industry was born. The inventor of the cuckoo clock was Franz Anton Ketterer, a clockmaker from the village of Schönwald. His idea was to mimic the call of the cuckoo bird using small bellows and pipes. The design quickly caught on and production took off throughout the area.

German Engineering Meets Art

While the whimsical designs and ornate carvings on the outside are impressive works of art, the clock's inner workings are marvels of early engineering. Weights (often disguised as pine cones) power the mechanism, while wooden gears and a pendulum keep time.

Every hour, a door pops open and a tiny mechanical bird emerges, making its iconic 'cuck-cuck' sound. The call of the cuckoo is still made the same way it was originally, with two bellows sending air through pipes – a similar technology to that found in church organs. The sound is often accompanied by music, dancers or moving figures such as woodchoppers or beer drinkers.

Left and centre The world's largest cuckoo clock, Schonach **Right** U(h)rwaldpfad

The four classic designs include the chalet, modelled on a gabled roof of alpine chalets; carved clocks with ornate birds and leaves; the shield, with a square wooden face and a semi-circle on the top and metal rods as a pendulum; and the modern style, which is more colourful and minimalist.

Cuckoo for Clocks

The cuckoo clock became synonymous with the Black Forest, and travellers in the 19th and 20th centuries took them home as souvenirs, helping their popularity spread globally.

Today, genuine Black Forest cuckoo clocks are still handcrafted in the region, with many workshops remaining small family operations passed down through generations.

Linden is the preferred wood due to its softness, which makes it easiest to carve. The wood is cut and dried for many years before the actual clock is made to ensure it does not crack or splinter. Every cuckoo clock made in the Black Forest must meet high standards of production and mechanical elements to get the seal of approval from the Black Forest Clock Association (VdS), so if you're looking to purchase, always check for the mark of authenticity.

> While the whimsical designs and ornate carvings on the outside are impressive works of art, the clock's inner workings are marvels of early engineering.

Best Places to See Cuckoo Clocks

Take the **U(h)rwaldpfad** in Schonach, an 8.7km hike through the central Black Forest, where locals hang up cuckoo clocks of all shapes and sizes along the route.

Triberg's streets are lined with shops overflowing with clocks in every style

Pay a visit to the **Rombach & Haas** cuckoo-clock workshop in Schonach, pioneers of the modern style.

Step inside the **world's largest cuckoo clock** in Schonach, built by clockmaker Josef Dold and standing 3m tall.

The **Black Forest Museum** in Triberg exhibits four centuries of clocks, alongside historical and cultural items from the region.

Listings

BEST OF THE REST

 ### Beer Gardens

Hausbrauerei Feierling
A local institution straddling Freiburg's canals, this leafy beer garden serves its own unfiltered Inselbier. Lively and central, it's packed on warm evenings with students and families under chestnut trees.

Rothaus
Join a tour of this Black Forest brewery in Grafenhausen, then grab a drink in the shady beer garden and taste what makes its cult beer, the Tannenzäpfle, so special.

Schlossberg
Reach the top of this Freiburg hill after a 30-minute climb (or ascend on the Schlossberg cable car) and be rewarded with stunning views from the hilltop beer garden. Especially popular at sunset.

 ### Swimming Spots

Badeparadies Schwarzwald
This year-round pool complex in Titisee features heated indoor and outdoor pools, a swim-up bar, thunderous jets and an indoor playground with 23 thrilling water slides, a wave pool and loungers.

Titisee
This serene lake offers a swimming beach, pedal boats for hire, lake cruises, restaurants, kiosks and an easy 6km walk around its shores.

Dreisam River
The shallow river running through Freiburg is the perfect place to cool off in summer. You'll find locals reading, skinny dipping and sunbathing on the boulders all along the river's length.

Panorama-Freibad Glottertal
Framed by tall trees, this is one of the Black Forest's most beautiful outdoor swimming pools.

Friedrichsbad
Temple-like Friedrichsbad is a traditional Roman bathing house in Baden-Baden, with a 17-stage bathing regime that includes hot and cold baths, massages and saunas, all done naked.

 ### Unmissable Half-Timbered Towns

Gengenbach
This chocolate-box town is almost too pretty to be real. Pastel half-timbered houses line the main square, and fortified gates and towers stand proudly at the end of cobbled streets.

Schiltach
A fairy-tale village on the Kinzig River, its steep medieval alleys and half-timbered houses make it one of the region's loveliest villages. A preservation order has kept it free from modern renovations.

Tubingen
While not strictly in the Black Forest, Tubingen is one of Germany's most photogenic towns.

Gengenbach

Colourful half-timbered houses line the bustling Marktplatz and overflowing floral baskets brighten the cobbled streets and windowsills.

Eat Like a Local

Gaststätte Griestal-Strausse
Try seasonal ingredients such as the beloved *Spargel* at this homey country tavern in Tuniberg.

Das Blümchen Restaurant
This cosy Freiburg restaurant and beer garden serves up Black Forest cuisine with a twist. With a menu of delicious tapas-style regional dishes, you'll be able to try a bit of everything.

Hofener Hütte
This typical Black Forest mountain hut at 1000m has impressive views over the Dreisamtal. Reach it on two wheels, two feet, or by car from Buchenbach. Try the homemade dumplings or Schwarzwald ham.

Berghütte Lauterbad
This scenic mountain hut just out of Freudenstadt dishes up crispy *Flammkuchen,* coffee, cake and cocktails year-round. Take in impressive views from the sprawling patio.

Eat in Michelin-Star Style

Baiersbronn
Gourmets will be in foodie heaven in tiny Baiersbronn, in the northern Black Forest, with four Michelin-starred restaurants. Pick from Schwarzwaldstube, Restaurant Bareiss, Schlossberg and 1789.

Nigrum
Baden-Baden has a host of gourmet restaurants when you're looking for an unforgettable night out. Nigrum has a moody interior and modern, international set menus.

Hirschen
Set in a 500-year-old house south of Freiburg, Hirschen boasts two Michelin stars for its

Schwarzwälder Freilichtmuseum

five- or seven-course seasonal set menu. The menu is infused with French influences and fresh, regional produce.

Art & History

Schwarzwälder Freilichtmuseum
Fuelled by one man's dedication to preserving Black Forest history, this open-air museum features 26 real homes from the region. Wander through them and witness rural life from the past 600 years.

Museum Frieder Burda
This private collectors' gallery in Baden-Baden features more than 1000 exemplary artworks from the 20th and 21st centuries in an architecturally impressive space.

Black Forest Museum
After visiting Triberg's waterfalls, pay a visit to the Black Forest Museum for a glimpse into the cultural and economic life of the region, including cuckoo clocks, traditional outfits, wood carvings and craft workshops.

Augustinermuseum
Housed in a former monastery in Freiburg, this museum blends Gothic sculpture, religious art and modern exhibitions. Don't miss the striking bird's-eye view of the impressive sculptures from the upper gallery.

Weekend in
HEIDELBERG

HIKING | CASTLE | RIVER PADDLING

Germany's oldest and most famous university town, Heidelberg is beloved for its narrow baroque Altstadt straddling the Neckar River and its dreamy, half-ruined castle watching from above. Channel the spirit of 19th-century romantics who were captivated by its charm as you paddle along the river or hike to the hilltop castle.

How to

Getting here and around Heidelberg is well connected to other German cities by train and is under an hour from Frankfurt international airport. Trams, bikes and e-scooters are your best bets to get around town.

When to go Heidelberg draws millions of tourists every year, so shoulder seasons (April–May and September–October) will be slightly more peaceful.

Say hi The *Brückenaffe* (bridge monkey) statue, the city's good-luck charm, is perched at the entrance to the old bridge.

Hike to Heidelberg's Ruined Castle

Lace up your boots and make your way from Heidelberg's romantic old town up to the summit of the Königstuhl via Heidelberg Castle. While there is a direct funicular, making the 3.8km trek on foot will reward you with views over the castle ruins and the Neckar Valley.

From the Altstadt, ascend the 315-step staircase near the funicular station up towards the castle. The ruined **Schloss Heidelberg** cuts a romantic figure on its hilltop throne. The home of Heidelberg's prince electors since 1225, the castle was destined to become one of the grandest of the Renaissance. It stood proudly for centuries until it was repeatedly attacked and ultimately destroyed by French forces in the 17th century. Inside, you can explore the courtyard, the cellar with the world's

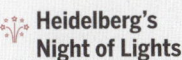

Heidelberg's Night of Lights

Don't miss seeing the castle, the **Alte Brücke** (Old Bridge) and the Altstadt all lit up by fantastic fireworks and illuminations that commemorate the assault on the Schloss in 1693. The event, known as the *Heidelberger Schlossbeleuchtung*, is held twice a year, on the first Saturday in July and the first Saturday in September.

Above left Schloss Heidelberg **Above right** The *Brückenaffe* (bridge monkey) statue on Alte Brücke (Old Bridge) **Left** Alte Brücke

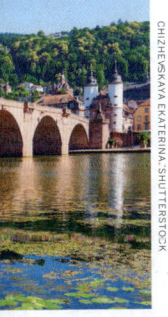

biggest wine barrel (holding 220,000L) and the intriguing **German Pharmacy Museum**. If you want to explore some of the surviving inner rooms, join a guided tour.

From here, continue uphill on the well-marked and shaded 'Königstuhlweg' path up to the **Königstuhl**. This section of the hike is around 3km and can take up to two hours, but is a far less strenuous option than the legendary Himmelsleiter with its 1200 uneven sandstone steps. Rising 567m above the Neckar River, forested Königstuhl offers you sweeping views (especially at sunset), a delicious restaurant and a kiosk.

Captain Your Own Ship

Cruising along the Neckar River is a quintessential Heidelberg experience, providing a unique vantage point on the city's charms. Pay a visit to the 90-year-old **boathouse** (tretbootverleih-hd.de) at the base of the Alte Brücke on the northern bank to don your

≈≈ Unmissable Spots on the River

The Neckarweise is big, free, open grassy area with barbecues, playgrounds and geese, and is a great place for a party or picnic.

The Old Bridge is a must-see, with stunning views, especially at sunset.

Jump in a kayak or hop on a stand-up paddleboard and take in the views of the castle from the water.

Pull in at Neckarorte beach, an artificial beach bar right on the riverbank.

There's a lovely 5km walking trail along the river that loops between two bridges.

Ludger Benighaus from Paddle Tours Heidelberg shares his favourite spots along the Neckar River. @paddle_tours_heidelberg

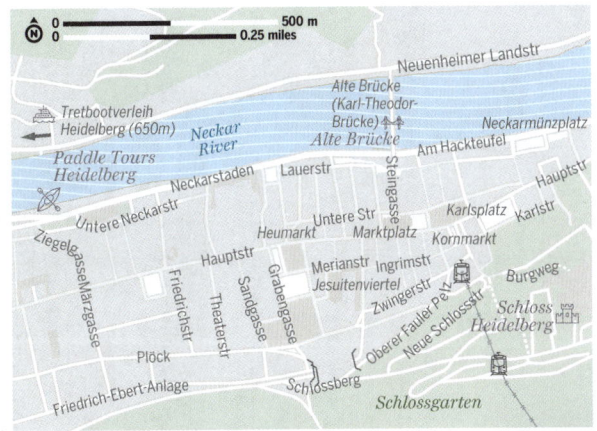

Left Heidelberg at dusk **Below** Motor boats at Tretbootverleih Heidelberg

captain's hat. Fancy a cruise in complete peace and quiet, without the smell of exhaust fumes? Then try a pedal boat and use your leg power to explore the river. Or if you'd like to simply relax and feel the wind in your face, jump in a four-person motor boat and go a little further afield. Motor boats are available for over 18s with a valid driving licence. **Tretbootverleih Heidelberg** opens from 2pm Thursday to Sunday (late April to October) until an hour before sunset.

Paddle the Neckar

The second option on the waters is a kayak, with **Paddle Tours Heidelberg** *(paddle-tours.de; tours €59)* offering tours during the warmer months of April to October. Tours last two hours and no paddling experience is required, with the river's gentle current making it an easy excursion. The views of the Altstadt and Neuenheim, as well as the Alte Brücke and the castle, are fantastic and the friendly guides will teach you about the history of Heidelberg while you paddle. This is Heidelberg at its most tranquil.

COLOGNE & THE RHINELAND

CITY LIFE | INDUSTRIAL HERITAGE | URBANISED NATURE

RESEARCHED BY ANDREA SCHULTE-PEEVERS

- ▶ **Trip Builder** (p216)
- ▶ **Practicalities** (p217)
- ▶ **Cologne Cool** (p218)
- ▶ **Champagne & Altbier** (p222)
- ▶ **Charlemagne's Aachen** (p224)
- ▶ **Cruising into Dragonland** (p226)
- ▶ **Ruhr Reloaded** (p228)
- ▶ **Sibling Rivalry on the Rhine** (p230)
- ▶ **German Beer Primer** (p232)
- ▶ **Listings** (p234)

COLOGNE & THE RHINELAND
Trip Builder

From Roman legions to Ruhr barons, this is a land of cathedral spires, river cruises, beer-fuelled pubs and art-filled industrial halls. Along the Rhine and beyond, Cologne and the Ruhrgebiet serve up history, grit and glamour, plus plenty of surprises.

Explore the world's most beautiful coal mine in **Essen** (p229)
🚆 1½hr from Cologne

Climb a furnace where molten steel once roared at **Landschaftspark Duisburg-Nord** (p229)
🚆 1¼hr from Cologne

Sip, stroll and get merry on an Altbier crawl in Düsseldorf's **Altstadt** (p222)
🚆 30min from Cologne

Feel your spirits soar in the luminous beauty of Cologne's famous **cathedral** (p219)
🚆 4½hr from Berlin

Trace the empire-building steps of Charlemagne in **Aachen** (p224)
🚆 1hr from Cologne

Ride Germany's oldest cogwheel train into **Siebengebirge**'s (p226) dragon country
🚆 40min from Cologne

PREVIOUS PAGE: FRANTIC00/SHUTTERSTOCK
FROM LEFT: ALLAN BAXTER/GETTY, PHOTOGRAPHY IS ON/SHUTTERSTOCK.

Practicalities

ARRIVING

Düsseldorf International Airport and **Köln Bonn Airport** are the main gateways to the region.

Fast ICE and regional RE, RB and S-Bahn trains link all cities and towns in the area and further afield.

FIND YOUR WAY
Major cities like Düsseldorf, Cologne and Essen maintain helpful tourist offices, often at or near the Hauptbahnhof.

MONEY
Even though credit-card use and contactless payment are becoming more common, have some cash in your wallet.

WHERE TO STAY

City	Pros/Cons
Cologne	Major sights, local colour and nightlife. Expensive during trade shows.
Düsseldorf	Sophisticated cosmo vibe; great shopping, culture and pub crawls. Expensive during trade shows.
Essen	Industrial heritage. Offbeat, more low key but less atmospheric and pretty.

EATING & DRINKING

Reibekuchen, also *Rievkooche*, are fried potato pancakes traditionally topped with apple sauce. *Pfefferpotthast* is slow-cooked beef stew spiced with pepper, onions and capers. *Halver Hahn* literally means half a chicken but in reality is a rye roll with cheese, mustard and pickles. And *Himmel un Äd* is mashed potatoes with apple sauce, usually paired with black pudding.

Best craft cocktails Bar Botanik (p234)

Must-try roast pork knuckle Brauerei im Füchschen (p234)

GETTING AROUND

Public transport
All cities and smaller towns are linked through a comprehensive network of buses, trams, U-Bahn (subway) and S-Bahn (suburban) trains.

Tickets
One ticket is valid for travel within an entire network; for example, the VRR network in the Ruhrgebiet/Düsseldorf area, or the VRS network in the Cologne/Bonn region.

JAN–MAR
Short days, long coats. Shorter opening hours at many sights; rural areas hibernate.

APR–JUN
Milder days. Cherry trees pop, beer gardens clink open and moods get a spring upgrade.

JUL–SEP
Sunny, buzzy, outdoor fun and festivals, though thunderstorms can rain on the parade.

OCT–DEC
Autumn colours fade into foggy November, followed by sparkly Christmas season.

45 Cologne **COOL**

CATHEDRAL | ART | KÖLSCH

▬ Founded by the Romans, Cologne (Köln) offers a mother lode of attractions, led by its famous cathedral, with its twin spires dominating the skyline, and an outstanding museum landscape. Cologne's spirited locals are known for their liberal outlook and zest for life.

How to

Getting around Cologne is highly walkable, and places further afield are easily reached by public transport, bike or e-scooter. Radstation behind the Hauptbahnhof rents bikes.

When to go Best from spring to autumn; skip Carnival (before Lent) and December's Christmas market weekends if crowds aren't your thing.

MuseumsCard Good for one-time admission to all municipal museums on two consecutive days, plus free public transport on the first day.

Cathedral Glory

Cologne's geographic and spiritual heart, and its biggest tourist draw, is the magnificent **Kölner Dom** (Cologne Cathedral), a UNESCO World Heritage Site since 1996. Its lacy spires and flying buttresses create a surprising sensation of lightness and fragility, despite their mass and height. That sense of airiness continues inside, where a phalanx of pillars and arches supports the lofty nave. Soft rays filter through stained-glass windows (including a modern one by Gerhard Richter) onto numerous treasures, most famously the **gilded shrine** said to hold the bones of the biblical Three Kings. The **Gero Crucifix**, carved in 970, making it the oldest surviving medieval monumental sculpture, also deserves a close-up. For your fitness fix and sublime views, tackle the thigh-burning 533 steps to the **observation platform** in the Dom's south tower.

Street Art in Ehrenfeld

While Cologne is celebrated for its fine-arts scene, some of its streets are just as expressive. Murals, stencils, stickers and graffiti abound in eclectic-creative Ehrenfeld. A powerful piece is a tribute to local Nazi resistance group Edelweisspiraten beneath Ehrenfeld train station, where the SS hanged 13 of its members.

Above left and left Kölner Dom (Cologne Cathedral) **Above right** The gilded shrine

Kölsch Patrol

Cologne has its own style of beer, Kölsch, which is light, hoppy, slightly sweet and served cool in *Stangen* – skinny, straight glasses holding only 200mL. In traditional Cologne beer halls and pubs, you don't order beer so much as subscribe – the ever-roaming servers, called *Köbes,* will ply you with another round until you signal 'enough' by placing a beermat on top of your glass. Many famous spots cluster in the Altstadt, including top-ranked **Peters Brauhaus** and **Brauerei zur Malzmühle**. If you're pub-hopping, balance your brain with hearty Rhenish dishes such as *Sauerbraten* (vinegar-marinated roast) or *Rievkooche* (potato pancakes).

Shrine to Chocolate

In a sleek riverside temple, the **Schokoladenmuseum** is a sweet celebration of chocolate, the Aztecs' 'elixir of the gods'. Beat the crowds by coming early on a weekday to wander the walk-through chocolate factory,

✧ Odonien: Cologne's Offbeat Fun Zone

In summer, few spots beat **Odonien**'s surreal metal sculpture garden for cocktails, Kölsch or parties. Artist Odo Rumpf turned this former railway lot into an open-air mashup of beer garden, club, concert venue and cultural centre. One day it's a techno rave, the next a robot art show, film screening or flea market. Sip in a bar built into a shipping container and hit the toilets inside a retired circus tiger cage. Hours depend on the weather, so check online or on social media before heading out. If you're into wacky playgrounds, it's definitely worth the trip.

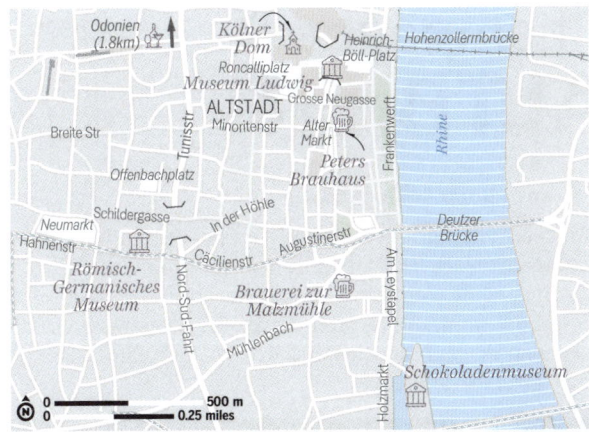

Left Schokoladenmuseum
Below Museum Ludwig

watch truffle-making in action and explore the interactive 'Cocoa's Journey Through Time' exhibition. Cap your tour with a tasting session or strike selfie gold at the 3m-high chocolate fountain.

Hail to the Romans

Under Roman rule, Cologne was a thriving city with temples, paved roads, an aqueduct and stone houses. Finds from that era now fill the **Römisch-Germanisches Museum** (Roman-Germanic Museum), currently exiled to the Belgisches Haus while its 1970s quarters get a facelift. Standouts include a sculpture of Hercules mid-battle with a lion, and a delicate marble torso dubbed the 'Kölsche Venus'. There's also remarkably well-preserved glassware and everyday items such as toys, tweezers and jewellery, the designs of which have barely changed over time.

Modern Masters

Does modern art make your heart skip a beat? Then carve out time for the **Museum Ludwig**, just steps from the Dom. Inside its airy halls, you can binge on Picasso, pop art, Pollock and photography, or linger over German expressionists and the Russian avant-garde. Temporary exhibitions dig into everything from post-colonial critique and identity politics to rising voices in global contemporary art and lesser-known chapters of modernism.

46 Champagne & ALTBIER

ALTBIER BARS | AVANTGARDE ART | BOLD ARCHITECTURE

Düsseldorf may at first seem all buttoned-up business polish, but beneath those Boss suit beats a party-ready heart. The Altstadt's 300-plus bars fuel nights that stretch into morning, while trend-savvy neighbourhoods such as Flingern and Unterbilk, old-school countercultural hubs like Kiefernstrasse and one of Europe's largest Japanese communities inject one of Germany's wealthiest cities with flavour, diversity and edge.

How to

Getting around Rheinbahn operates an extensive network of U-Bahn trains, trams and buses throughout Düsseldorf. Get tickets from bus drivers and station vending machines.

When to go For mild weather, lighter crowds and festivals, aim for spring and early autumn. Business-geared hotels often drop rates in summer.

Boat ride Set sail on the mighty Rhine with Weisse Flotte, which runs boat trips to medieval Kaiserswerth from Burgplatz between Easter and October.

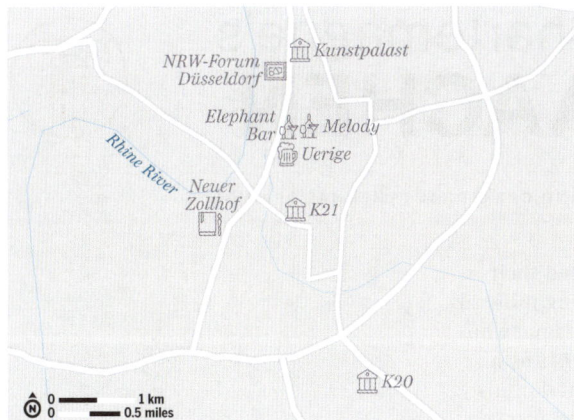

Far left Altstadt nightlife
Left Boat on the Rhine

Altstadt pub crawl Like local rival Cologne's Kölsch, Düsseldorf has its own beer: Altbier, a robust copper-hued ale. A top place for your fix is **Uerige**, a traditional brewpub oozing local colour. Chase your pint with a shot of blood-red Killepitsch liqueur, served opposite – through the window. For cocktails, try tiny, sophisticated **Melody** and/or the more grown-up **Elephant Bar**.

Harbour reimagined Düsseldorf's old Rhine harbour, where dockworkers once hauled cargo, was reborn in the 1990s as **Medienhafen**, a hub for media, design and creative industries. It's an architectural showcase, with Frank Gehry's **Neuer Zollhof** – a trio of warped towers sheathed in stainless steel, red brick and white plaster – drawing the most camera clicks.

Tokyo on the Rhine Immermannstrasse near the main train station is the heart of Little Tokyo. Local faves for slurping ramen include **Takumi** and **Naniwa**, while **Yabase** is tops for sushi and **Sakura Bar** for cocktails.

Art walk Düsseldorf's art scene is a heavyweight, with world-class collections and bold contemporary voices. Kick off at **Kunstpalast**, where centuries of art – including luminous Rubens works – set the tone. Next door, **NRW-Forum Düsseldorf** presents zeitgeist-charged photography, pop culture and digital art. At **K20**, modernist giants mingle with groundbreaking non-Western voices, while sister museum **K21** showcases post-1980s visionaries such as Gursky, Genzken and Paik beneath a soaring glass dome.

 **The Altstadt Beyond Beer**

Beyond the booze and party parlours, the Altstadt tempts with museums, boutiques and historical gems that make a strong case for a daytime wander.

Meander along the **Rheinpromenade** (river walk) from Burgplatz, crowned by the medieval Schlossturm (tower), to the Rheinturm, the TV tower that, at 240.5m, is Düsseldorf's tallest structure.

Pop into the white-stuccoed baroque **St Andreaskirche**, where free Sunday organ concerts fill the nave with rich sound.

Swing by **Markt am Carlsplatz** to stock up on quality produce, wine and artisanal specialities, or to graze on streetfood classics and clever newcomers.

Cool off with a scoop from locally adored **Eiscafe Pia**.

47 Charlemagne's AACHEN

MOMENTOUS HISTORY | GRAND CATHEDRAL | THERMAL SPRINGS

Roman soldiers nursed their battle wounds in its steaming mineral springs, but it was Charlemagne who put Aachen on the map in 794 as his primary residence and capital of his vast Frankish Empire. Today, you can still laze in those same thermal waters and soak up Charlemagne's legacy in the dazzling Dom, around town and in the Centre Charlemagne.

How to

Getting around Aachen's centre is largely pedestrianised and about a 15-minute walk from the Hauptbahnhof, where Radstation rents bicycles.

Fabulous views Head up the Lousberg for panoramic city views (best at sunset), plus peaceful trails and hammocks for maximum chilling.

Museum pass Culture chasers can save a bundle with the 'Six for Six' pass, good for one-time admission to the Rathaus and five museums. Under 21? Yeah – admission is free!

Charlemagne primer

You know the name, but unless you're a history buff, a quick refresher on just why Charlemagne is called the 'father of Europe' probably wouldn't hurt. In comes the **Centre Charlemagne** with interactive exhibits about the man, his legacy and Aachen's own past. The **Route Charlemagne**, a self-guided walk linking key sights, also starts here.

Kings and cathedral

The Route Charlemagne leads past the partly reconstructed **Granusturm** (Granus Tower), the only surviving section of Charlemagne's palace. On the same site looms the grand Gothic **Rathaus** (town hall), topped with statues of kings, many crowned in the **Aachener Dom**. The cathedral is the kind of place where history practically slaps you in the face. Charlemagne was buried here. Thirty kings were crowned here between 936

Beyond Charlemagne

Naturally, Aachen has more to offer than Charlemagne.

Ticket to tranquillity Soak in mineral-rich pools, bake in saunas ranging from toasty to Death Valley hot, and steam away stress at the Carolus-Thermen, Aachen's wellness wonderland for grown-ups.

Printed cookies Don't leave Aachen without trying its beloved Printen – spicy, sweet, gingerbread-like cookies shaped like small loaves and often topped with nuts or chocolate.

Art museums At **Ludwig Forum Aachen**, pop art and other post-'60 styles meet global contemporary voices in a Bauhaus-style former umbrella factory. The **Suermondt Ludwig Museum** showcases medieval sculpture, Old Masters and curiosities in a neo-Renaissance mansion.

and 1531. And for more than 1000 years, pilgrims have flocked to this spot. In 1978, Germany's oldest cathedral became the country's first UNESCO World Heritage Site.

Dom highlights Step through the massive bronze door and into the octagonal **Pfalzkapelle**, Charlemagne's private chapel and the Dom's oldest part. The marble columns are from Ravenna and Rome – a colossal brass chandelier, a gift from Emperor Friedrich Barbarossa, dangles overhead. In the **Gothic choir**, docked to the chapel in 1414, Charlemagne's bones rest in a lavish shrine, accessible only by guided tour, as is his marble throne in the upper gallery.

Above Aachener Dom

48 CRUISING
into Dragonland

BOATING | SCENERY | MYTHOLOGY

Sip a beer while drinking in the Rhine's dramatically shifting scenery on a boat ride south from Cologne or Bonn. Urban edges give way to green slopes framing storybook villages such as Königswinter, the gateway to the Siebengebirge – a myth-laden patchwork of wooded peaks, sculpted valleys and rich wildlife that is one of Germany's oldest nature reserves.

How to

Getting here Scenic floats to Königswinter take about one hour from Bonn and two from Cologne. Return by boat, public transport or Uber.

When to go Köln-Düsseldorfer (KD) runs several trips daily, except Monday, from late April to early October; weekdays are quieter.

Tickets Return fares cost only slightly more, and combo tickets that include the cogwheel train, but not Nibelungenhalle and Schloss Drachenfels entry, are also available.

Siebengebirge Well-marked hiking trails crisscross the Siebengebirge – 40 volcanic hills rising between Königswinter and Bad Honnef in a lush swirl of forest, rocky cliffs and Rhine panoramas. The Grosser Ölberg (461m) may be the highest, but 321m Drachenfels steals the spotlight.

Chug-a-lug Since 1883, the tourist highlight here has been the **Drachenfelsbahn**, Germany's oldest cogwheel train, that chugs from Königswinter to the top of the Drachenfels. About halfway up, it pauses at the gloriously kitschy Nibelungenhalle, complete with dragon murals, Wagner tributes and a pond guarded by a giant stone dragon.

Mock medieval Nearby sits **Schloss Drachenburg**, a

Top right Burg Drachenfels
Bottom right A hiking trail in the Siebengebirge

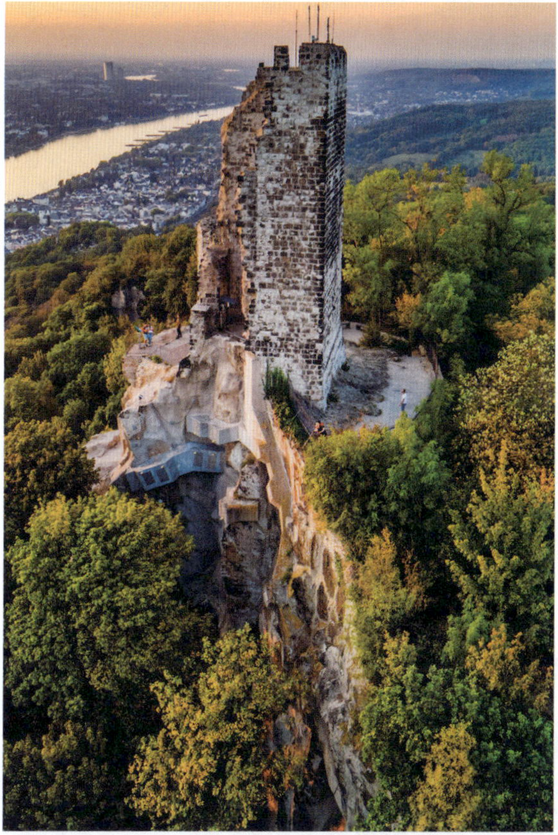

SLAWJANEK_FOTOGRAFIA/SHUTTERSTOCK

MIRA CROZDOWSKI/SHUTTERSTOCK

Siegfried & the Dragon

The Drachenfels looms large in legend as the place where Siegfried, hero of the medieval epic *Nibelungenlied*, slayed a dragon and bathed in its blood to become invincible. Well, almost. A single linden leaf stuck to his back, leaving one small patch untouched. That tiny flaw sealed his fate: later in the story, he's betrayed and stabbed in the back by Hagen, a supposed ally. The tale gripped the German imagination for centuries and inspired Richard Wagner's *Ring Cycle* – imagery later co-opted by Nazi ideology. But at its heart, this is a myth of strength, vulnerability and betrayal that still breathes fire into the Siebengebirge.

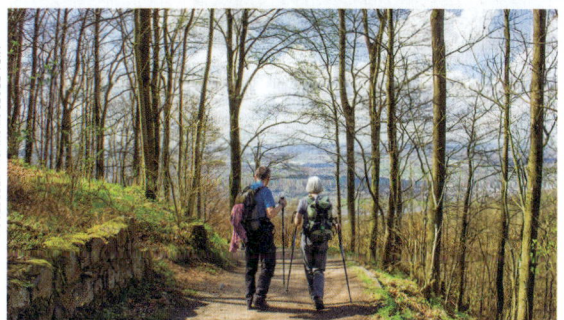

fairy-tale palace masquerading as medieval but actually dreamed up in the 1880s by a local baron and banker with a taste for grandeur. The lovely grounds hold terraces, fountains and a climbable tower.

Real medieval If you think the views from the Schloss are impressive, wait for the knockout panorama along the Rhine from the hilltop ruins of genuinely medieval **Burg Drachenfels**. There's even a restaurant in an incongruously modern glass cube – a welcome sight, especially if you've hiked up instead of hitching a ride on the cogwheel train.

49 RUHR
Reloaded

OFFBEAT | CULTURE | INDUSTRY

Gone are the days when the Ruhrgebiet's blast furnaces, collieries and smelting works powered the German economy. But by fusing its industrial heritage with a progressive mindset, the resilient Ruhr region has been revitalised as an exciting hotbed of art and culture.

🧭 Trip Notes

Getting around Traffic in this densely populated region can be sluggish, so you're usually better off relying on its extensive public transport network.

When to go Spring through autumn is ideal, when you can fold beer garden visits and festivals into your sightseeing adventures.

Football fever Borussia Dortmund tickets are hard to score, but you can still pick up the vibe in countless pubs, or on Alter Markt during special matches.

🏛 Ribbon of Steel & Stories

The **Route of Industrial Heritage** connects hundreds of key sights and attractions across cities such as Dortmund, Essen, Duisburg and Bochum. You can explore by car, bike or public transport. For inspo, go to *route-industriekultur. ruhr*. Most local tourist offices also have plenty of information in English.

03 One of Germany's top art museums, Essen's free **Museum Folkwang** showcases Monet to Richter across 24 themed rooms, with paintings, photos and sculptures arranged to spark dialogue on contemporary issues.

01 If you worship at the ball-shaped altar, visit Dortmund's interactive **German Football Museum**, where the treasure chamber gleams with four World Cup and three European Championship trophies won by Germany's men's team.

04 A 1902 ironworks is now **Landschaftspark Duisburg-Nord**, an adventure playground where you can scale the blast furnace, rappel down a storage bunker or go diving in the old gas tank.

05 Crowning a slagheap, Duisburg's surreal **Tiger & Turtle** sculpture might look like a roller-coaster, but there's no need to buckle up – this track was made for walking.

02 The Ruhrgebiet's sightseeing jewel is Essen's **Zeche Zollverein**, a World Heritage–listed colliery renowned for its Bauhaus-style architecture. Today, it buzzes with museums, art spaces and even a summertime swimming pool.

FROM LEFT: ALFOTOKUNST/SHUTTERSTOCK, SAIKO3P/SHUTTERSTOCK, LFOTOKUNST/SHUTTERSTOCK

Sibling Rivalry on the Rhine

TWO CITIES, ONE RIVER, ENDLESS BANTER.

Cologne and Düsseldorf may only be 40km apart, but they're like two siblings who squabble over everything from beer to Carnival. Ironically (at least for outsiders), they seem to have a lot more in common than they'd ever admit. Both are Rhineland powerhouses: prosperous, cosmopolitan, culturally rich and with egos to match.

Left K21 **Centre** Carnival, Cologne
Right A football match between Fortuna Düsseldorf and the 1. FC Köln

Historic Pedigree

Cologne, the elder sibling, wears its history proudly. Founded by the Romans, it's a city where 2000 years of heritage mixes with a soaring Gothic cathedral, full-throttle Carnival and boisterous beer halls. Düsseldorf is the polished younger sibling, founded 'only' in the Middle Ages and now the state capital of North Rhine–Westphalia, with a sleek business district, fashion flair and a cosmopolitan edge.

Battle of the Brews

Here's where things get seriously serious: Cologne's beloved Kölsch, a pale, crisp ale served in dainty 200mL glasses, is a source of civic pride and EU-protected snobbery. Düsseldorf answers with Altbier, a dark, malty ale that's older in style, bigger in bite and served in squat glasses holding 250mL. Be warned: ordering a Kölsch in Düsseldorf (or an Altbier in Cologne) is definitely a no-no! At best you'll get a withering look from the *Köbes,* as the famously brusque, blue-aproned servers are called in both cities.

Art Attacks

Culture, too, is a point of competitive pride. Düsseldorf hosts Art Düsseldorf, a heavyweight on the international fair circuit, and flaunts top-tier museums such as the Kunstsammlung Nordrhein-Westfalen (K20 and K21) and the NRW-Forum for contemporary edge. Cologne counters with Art Cologne, one of the world's oldest art fairs, plus the Museum Ludwig for modern masters and the Wallraf-Richartz Museum for centuries of European painting. Both cities claim their art scene is better. Both may be right.

For all the ribbing, the truth is that both cities are cut from the same Rhineland cloth: lively, welcoming and confident enough to laugh at themselves.

Carnival Face-Off

Düsseldorf kicks things off with the cheeky awakening of the Hoppeditz, a jester-like figure at 11.11am on 11 November. Its Rose Monday parade is famed for its razor-sharp political floats that gleefully skewer world leaders. Cologne goes full tradition and pageantry with its Dreigestirn (Prince, Farmer, 'Virgin'), showers of Kamelle sweets and its own vast Rose Monday parade. At midnight on Shrove Tuesday, many pubs burn the Nubbel, a dressed straw doll, to symbolically atone for Carnival sins.

Derby Days

Fortuna Düsseldorf and the 1. FC Köln don't clash every season, but when they meet it's with all the passion and theatrical flair you'd expect. Köln clawed its way back into the Bundesliga for the 2025–26 season, while Fortuna currently competes in the 2 Bundesliga, so clashes will only happen via cup draws and relegations. When they do, expect packed terraces, choreo and very selective memories the morning after.

Rhine Cheers

But for all the ribbing, the truth is that both cities are cut from the same Rhineland cloth: lively, welcoming and confident enough to laugh at themselves. The rivalry? Think more good-natured banter than bitter feud. So, whether you're team Kölsch or team Altbier, it's worth raising a glass in both cities.

 Carnival Primer

Known as the 'fifth season', Carnival in the Rhineland is part satirical theatre, part mass street party and all about thumbing your nose at authority before Lent. Festivities ramp up with *Weiberfastnacht* (Women's Carnival) on the Thursday before Ash Wednesday, when neckties are gleefully snipped and beer starts flowing before lunch. Across the region, Rose Monday parades roll out with marching bands, sweets being thrown to the crowds and floats lampooning politics and pop culture. Shrove Tuesday offers one last blowout before Lent begins on Ash Wednesday, when costumes are packed away – at least until 11.11am on 11 November, when the next season is proclaimed.

GERMAN
Beer Primer

01 Pils Power
Crisp, hoppy pale lager traditionally poured into a tall, fluted *Pilstulpe* that keeps the bubbles and shows off clarity.

02 Oktoberfest Classic: Helles
Classic Bavarian lager: smooth and lightly sweet, with strong malt aromas – famously served at Oktoberfest in a hefty 1L *Masskrug* (thick glass or stoneware).

03 Kölsch Character
Cologne's pride: a light, delicate, top-fermented beer that comes in slim, cylindrical *Stangen* (literally 'rods') holding a mere 200mL.

04 Altbier Tradition
Malty, copper-coloured ale from Düsseldorf and surrounds, enjoyed from short, straight-sided beakers holding 200mL or 250mL.

05 Weissbier Whirl
Wheat beer with banana-clove notes – *Hefeweizen* (cloudy, yeastier) or *Kristallweizen* (filtered, fizzier), both served in tall, curvy 500mL glasses with wide tops.

06 Smooth Schwarzbier
The classic vessel for this mellow dark lager with roasty notes is the *Schwarzbierpokal*, a stemmed chalice.

07 Bockbier Strength
Strong, malty lager best enjoyed in a short, wide *Starkbierglas* (goblet or tulip-style) to focus aroma and strength.

08 Berliner Weisse Buzz
Berlin's old-school speciality: a tart, low-alcohol wheat beer, typically mixed with raspberry or woodruff syrup in a wide, goblet-like *Schale*.

09 Smoky Rauchbier
Bamberg smoky speciality, made with beechwood-dried malt, and traditionally served in a half-litre *Seidla*, a sturdy handled mug.

10 Zwickel Freshness
An unfiltered, cellar-fresh lager from Franconia: cloudy, malty, lightly hopped and typically served in rustic half-litre mugs.

01 DMITRY NAUMOV/SHUTTERSTOCK. 02 PANTHER MEDIA GLOBA/ALAMY. 03 FOOD IMPRESSIONS/SHUTTERSTOCK. 04 MANNY GUMINA/SHUTTERSTOCK. 05 MARC VENEMA/ALAMY. 06 ANDREI KUZMIK/SHUTTERSTOCK, MARC VENEMA/SHUTTERSTOCK 07 WIRESTOCK CREATORS/SHUTTERSTOCK. 08 PERFECT-PICTURE-HUNTER/SHUTTERSTOCK. 09 LEEKEOMA/WIKIMEDIA/CC0. 10 DIETMAR RAUSCHER/SHUTTERSTOCK.

Listings

BEST OF THE REST

Classic German Restaurants

Bei Oma Kleinmann €€
This family-owned Cologne restaurant has fed generations schnitzel and other German fare.

Am Knipp €€
Grazers have enjoyed hearty German cuisine at this Aachen inn with beer garden since 1698.

Gasthaus im Stiefel €€
Enjoy regional dishes and house-made schnapps next to Bonn's Beethoven-Haus.

All Night Long

Bootshaus
This high-octane Cologne beat palace is a global heavyweight in the club rankings.

Bumann & Sohn
Köln-Ehrenfeld all-rounder with exposed bricks, beer garden and an eclectic calendar: concerts, parties and DJ nights from hip-hop to house.

AK 47
Like punk rock? Go here. (It's in Düsseldorf.)

Cocktail O'Clock

Bar Botanik €€€
Heavenly hangout in a historical water tower with 360-degree rooftop terrace overlooking Cologne. The cocktail slingers mix like magicians.

Beuys Bar €€€
Chic Düsseldorf lair serves libations such as the popcorn-bourbon-based 'Beuys in the Hood'.

Fcuk Yoga €€
Try the signature gin-based LeGurk at this dimly lit cocktail lair in Essen, complete with speakeasy vibe and crystal chandeliers.

Balke €
Sleek cocktails, bold spirits and handcrafted Balke Gin make this former Dortmund soccer bar beloved for good vibes and top-tier pours.

Rhenish Beer Halls

Peters Brauhaus €€
Behind an ornate facade, this brewpub lures with malty sweet Kölsch and quirky nooks, including a room with a stained-glass ceiling.

Brauerei zur Malzmühle €€
One of Cologne's oldest and best breweries; Bill Clinton grabbed a beer on his 1999 state visit.

Brauerei Im Füchschen €€
Full of local colour, the 'Little Fox' in the Düsseldorf Altstadt is a classic Rhenish beer hall.

Palaces & Castles

Schloss Augustusburg
Fancy yourself on the set of *Bridgerton* at this rococo fantasy in Brühl near Cologne surrounded by manicured gardens.

Schloss Benrath
This *klein aber fein* (small but charming) Düsseldorf park-and-palace combo was once the baroque summer retreat of an art-minded ruler and now hosts summertime garden concerts.

Vogelsang International Place
South of Aachen in Eifel National Park, this hulking modern castle, built as a Nazi party elite training academy, is now an international centre dedicated to tolerance and diversity.

Classical Sound Check

Tonhalle
An expressionist 1920s jewel, Düsseldorf's premier concert hall started out as a planetarium.

Kölner Philharmonie

This subterranean hall's famously sharp acoustics make every concert a proper treat for the ears. On select weekdays, the free Philharmonie Lunch series lets the public sit in on rehearsals.

Offbeat Museums

Archäologischer Park & Römermuseum
Roman-founded Xanten shows off its roots at this re-created settlement where you can wander temples, baths, workshops and an amphitheatre, and the excellent modern museum.

Neanderthal Museum
Learn about our prehistoric cousins at this museum right in the valley near Düsseldorf where the first Neanderthal bones were found in 1856.

Beethoven-Haus
Visit the baroque townhouse in Bonn's Altstadt where the composer of classical music's greatest hits was born in 1770.

Soul of Africa Museum
Spiritual healing, West African vodun, witchcraft and secret societies – this small Essen apartment museum offers a rare glimpse into spiritual traditions and ancestral wisdom.

Festival Fever

Carnival
During the pre-Lent 'fifth season', expect street parades, packed pubs and beer-fuelled chaos, especially in Cologne and Düsseldorf.

Beethovenfest
Bonn celebrates its most famous son with around 60 September concerts in 25 locations.

Cologne Pride
Two weeks of events culminate in the Christopher Street Day parade in early July, which draws around 1.4 million people.

Japan-Tag
Kimonos, karaoke, sushi and samurai – Düsseldorf's one-day May festival is a joyful

Schloss Augustusburg

cultural takeover that's both authentic and wildly fun.

Where it Happened

Historisches Rathaus
The Peace of Westphalia, the treaty ending the Thirty Years' War, was signed here in Münster.

Dokumentationsstätte Regierungsbunker
This atomic shelter is where the Bonn-based West German government would have holed up in the event of nuclear attack.

Friedensmuseum
Exhibition in the surviving tower of the bridge of Remagen documents its pivotal role in WWII.

Quirky Places

Schwebebahn
Hang out in Wuppertal, literally, by riding the retro-futuristic suspended train that's been gliding above the Wupper river since 1901.

Tetraeder
Near Bottrop, a giant steel pyramid graces the top of a slag heap. Climb the slightly swaying skeletal behemoth for panoramic views.

Gasometer
This cylindrical gas storage tank in Oberhausen now hosts immersive exhibitions that blend art, science and environmental themes.

Practicalities

ARRIVING

238

GETTING AROUND

240

SAFE TRAVEL

242

MONEY

243

RESPONSIBLE TRAVEL

244

ACCOMMODATION

246

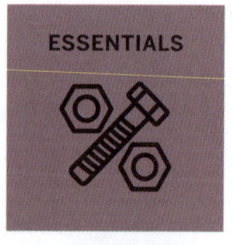

ESSENTIALS

248

LANGUAGE

250

Right Marienplatz, Munich (p142)

EASY STEPS FROM THE AIRPORT TO THE CITY CENTRE

Arriving in Germany by air, you'll likely land at Frankfurt International Airport (pictured below). It's Germany's busiest airport by far (also Europe's sixth-largest). Non-EU passports get stamped at the first entry point in the Schengen area (29 European countries sharing borderless travel). If you're already in Europe, you'll likely come to Germany by plane, or perhaps train, and without crossing customs again.

AT THE AIRPORT

SIM CARDS Mobile providers sell prepaid SIM cards at airport kiosks. Telekom offers the best Germany-wide coverage; Vodafone and O2 are better for travelling around Europe. Ensure your phone is unlocked before travelling.

INTERNATIONAL CURRENCY EXCHANGE (ICE) Outlets are usually found in German airports at arrivals. Traveller-geared **Reisebank** (*reisebank.de*) branches are ubiquitous. Their staffed counters keep longer hours than banks and are usually open weekends.

WI-FI is found at most German airports, train stations and on high-speed trains. Train connectivity can be quite spotty, though.

ATMS in German airports are linked to international networks such as Cirrus, Plus, Star and Maestro. Use your debit (bank) card.

FREE CHARGING STATIONS are widely available at almost every gate in Frankfurt airport. Make sure you bring a universal travel adapter.

CUSTOMS REGULATIONS

Passport checks Once you're in the Schengen area, most travel is borderless. Always keep your passport easily accessible, though, to avoid any issues, especially on trains for spontaneous border controls.

Customs checks Leaving German airports, use the green 'Nothing to declare' or red 'Goods to declare' exits at your discretion – random checks occur at both.

GETTING TO THE CITY CENTRE

Train This is usually the quickest, most convenient and cost-saving option for leaving an airport in Germany. Always check fare zones to purchase the correct ticket and avoid potential fines from train inspectors.

Taxi and Uber The latter is usually cheaper and relatively quick and painless thanks to incoming pick-up areas. During peak times, fares will inflate; this is especially true in Hamburg (regulations have greatly limited Uber's presence).

Carshare apps Self-driving services like Miles and Share Now are increasingly preferred for leaving airports with luggage – they are notably cheaper than ride shares and faster than public transport. Book a vehicle on the spot and pick it up from the airport's designated car park. Sign up at least two weeks before travel for ID verification.

HOW MUCH FOR A...

Train €4.70–14.30

Taxi €35–60

Car share €10–45

Ticket inspections Most German train stations don't use turnstiles, but ticket inspectors will perform random, unannounced checks (and issue fines) during rides.

Frankfurt arrivals Most German airports (including Frankfurt, Berlin, Munich) have train stations providing local, but also long-distance and regional, transport with frequent departures. Depending on your final destination, flying into Germany's largest airport (Frankfurt) and travelling onwards by train can be a climate- and budget-friendly hack.

Plan your journey Download the DB Navigator app for the most up-to-date info on both regional and local public transport (often, Google Maps doesn't even come close).

OTHER POINTS OF ENTRY

Flix SE *(flix.com)* buses and trains enter Germany from various European countries. They are often slower and less comfortable than Deutsche Bahn's high-speed routes, but cheaper (particularly last-minute bookings).

Night trains *(nightjet.com)*, serviced by Austrian rail provider ÖBB via Deutsche Bahn, enter Germany from major European cities such as Basel, Zürich, Vienna, Milan, Venice, Zagreb and Budapest. There are three comfort levels (seat, couchette, sleeper). Common routes include Hamburg to Zürich/Vienna, and Berlin to Paris.

European Sleeper's *(europeansleeper.eu)* 'Good Night Train' is a no-frills (simple couchettes and sleepers) night train, crowdfunded by a Belgian-Dutch collective in 2023. It runs from Amsterdam to Berlin (7½ hours).

Northern Germany's car-ferry ports (such as Kiel, Rostock and Travemünde – Hamburg is not among them) all connect to Scandinavian ports. Some also service Baltic states ports.

Online carpooling providers such as Bla Bla Car *(blablacar.com)* and Mitfahrzentrale *(mifaz.de)* can connect drivers and passengers for long-distance rides across Schengen borders. Most handy for night travel or leaving at specific times; drivers decide the price.

 **TRANSPORT TIPS TO HELP YOU GET AROUND**

Regional transport across Germany is sure to win your appreciation. Flying between German cities isn't always the best option when you consider how much more plentiful and comfortable (and climate-conscious) train and bus services can be. Flying down the autobahn between cities might be dreamy, but parking when you arrive can be an absolute nightmare.

PLANE OR TRAIN?
Planes are often only marginally quicker than trains once security and waits are factored in. Germany's train system is excellent, but can be expensive for last-minute bookings and busy periods (weekends and holidays). Check out the **Eurail Pass** (eurail.com) for unlimited, Europe-wide train travel within a specific timeframe.

DB NAVIGATOR APP
Buy long-distance train tickets through the DB Navigator app. It's an essential tool for reserving seats, checking in, boarding in the right compartment, seeing train delays and filling out compensation forms for disrupted journeys (you might be entitled to a PDF voucher for future travel).

CAR RENTAL PER DAY

from €50

Petrol approx €1.70/litre

EV charging €0.45–0.75/KWh

COACH SEQUENCE Lettered sections (A, B, C etc) are displayed on overhead electronic signs and also via layout (1st/2nd class, bicycle, family/quiet area) on the DB Navigator app. Some trains also split mid-journey and go to different destinations; knowing before boarding is key.

GROUP TICKETS Each German state offers an unlimited regional train ticket for up to five people per day. At provincial stations, passengers often approach each other to 'go in' on a group ticket – it's totally allowed and a good idea. Buy one at the DB Service Centre.

DRIVING ESSENTIALS

 Drive on the right.

 Blood-alcohol limit is 0.05%.

 The speed limit is 50km/h in urban areas and 80km/h on secondary roads.

 On motorways, the recommended speed limit is 130km/h.

 The legal driving age is 18.

Germany's 13,000km cross-country autobahn network is a pride and joy. These public roads are known to be excellent and are always toll-free. Every 40km to 60km, you'll find elaborate service areas with 24-hour petrol stations, toilets and restaurants. Around 70% of the autobahn is without speed limits, though the recommended maximum speed limit overall on motorways is 130km/h. Limit-free routes are indicated with a white circular sign with black lines running diagonally through.

DOWNTOWN PARKING is always limited, especially in a city's Altstadt (historical centre). Parking garages are easiest but expensive; many street meters are now app-based (EasyPark, PayByPhone etc), but require data roaming or wi-fi. On Sundays and holidays, street parking is usually free. EVs often have dedicated (sometimes free) parking spaces. Consider parking in the suburbs and using trains with local commuters.

SPEED CAMERAS are commonplace on motorways and in cities, popping up without warning. While you won't lose points on your home licence, the higher you're driving over the limit, the higher the fine will be.

GERMAN BUSES are cheaper than trains and similarly comfortable (wi-fi, AC etc), but slower (subject to traffic jams). German trains are typically less polluting, running on renewable energy.

KNOW YOUR CARBON FOOTPRINT A domestic flight from Berlin to Munich would emit about 214kg of carbon dioxide per passenger. A bus would emit 33kg per passenger for the same distance. A train would emit about 14kg.

ROAD DISTANCE CHART (KMS) Note: Distances are approximate

	Berlin	Cologne	Dresden	Düsseldorf	Frankfurt am Main	Hamburg	Munich	Nuremberg	Rostock
Cologne	573								
Dresden	191	570							
Düsseldorf	557	40	579						
Frankfurt am Main	546	192	459	247					
Hamburg	290	425	476	409	486				
Munich	585	575	460	608	390	775			
Nuremberg	440	407	315	443	220	590	169		
Rostock	234	600	444	583	661	185	778	634	
Stuttgart	630	370	508	405	205	656	232	212	824

SAFE TRAVEL

Germany is considered a very safe country for living and travelling. Visitors tend to love the ease of all-hours public transport and cities with comfortable walkability. Crime rates are quite low by international standards, but take the usual precautions against petty theft.

RESPECTING RULES Some nightlife establishments are tolerant of public sex and nakedness; therefore, photography is not permitted. If you feel unsafe, look for an 'awareness team' member (sometimes wearing a bright vest) or talk to bar staff. Upon arrival, be prepared for a bouncer to perform bag/body checks.

STAYING SAFE Never leave your drink unattended; GHB drugging has increasingly become a reported problem. Similarly, always keep your belongings with you – a cross-body bag is usually the most convenient. Most nightclubs have a zero-tolerance policy for illegal substance use; if caught, you risk being kicked out.

GETTING THERE Many larger clubs are in less-populated, sometimes-industrial areas. Plan to take an Uber, or know where the nearest public transport stop is. Driving or cycling drunk is punishable (usually by fine). Know your limits as German beer can be a high ABV elixir – drink plenty of water, especially at open-air raves.

Tap Water Though Germans never order it, *Leitungswasser* is clean, drinkable and well-filtered. Carry a bottle and fill it up everywhere; in restaurants, you may pay a small surcharge (€0.50 to €2) for non-bottled water.

Emergency Services Dial 112 for medical emergencies and rescue. For police (reporting a crime), dial 110. For non-life-threatening medical help outside regular clinic hours, call 116 117 for on-call doctors.

BRING YOUR OWN ASPIRIN

German pharmacies don't sell any medications, not even aspirin. Even over-the-counter medications are only available at pharmacies and likely will be in smaller quantities and more expensive than you would pay at home. Pack for aches, pains, allergies and birth control (only available by prescription).

CARRYING MEDICATIONS

Some anxiety and pain medications are considered illegal narcotics in Europe. Possession is taken very seriously. Bring a signed and dated doctor's note. Prescriptions must be in their correct bottles or original packaging.

QUICK TIPS TO HELP YOU MANAGE YOUR MONEY

CASH OR CARD Cash carries clout. Since the pandemic, paying by card is becoming more common in cities (eg in some nightclubs and cafes you can only swipe and tap to settle up). However, plenty of older pubs and restaurants just take cash. Keep some small notes for shops where a minimum purchase (usually €10) applies. American Express is not widely accepted.

TIPPING
Service and setting dictates tips. Most tip 5% to 10% (or round to the nearest euro). Say what you want to pay, or *'Stimmt so'* for no change back.

RECEIPTS
Receipts are mandatory. Save paper by saying *'Kein beleg'* (No receipt). Some bars only send receipts by email (sometimes the next day).

RESERVATION PREPAYMENTS
An increasing number of fine-dining restaurants require a prepayment (usually €50 to €100 a person) to confirm your reservation. You'll need to provide a credit-card number and a valid phone number (your reservation might be confirmed by phone on the same day). If you cancel before noon the same day, your prepayment might not be refunded.

CURRENCY
Euro

HOW MUCH FOR A...

Kiosk beer
€1.50

Toilet at train stations
€0.50

Public transport ticket
€3-4

DIGITAL WALLETS Set up Google/Apple Pay and tap instead of sticking cards into (and forgetting to remove them) transport ticket machines.

HAGGLING
Gentle haggling is common at flea markets, especially if you buy more than one thing or only want a few euros knocked off.

GLASS DEPOSIT
When ordering a drink at some establishments (usually concerts and nightclubs), you'll receive a *pfand* (deposit) token for the glass. Return the glass and token when finished to receive the deposit (usually €1) back.

DISCOUNTS & SAVINGS Discounts on transport, shopping, attractions and entertainment are widely available for seniors, children and students. You may be asked to show your passport or student ID to prove your age; driving licences aren't generally considered ID.

Additionally, many tourism boards sell official calls offering discounts (or extra goodies) on museums, sights and tours, usually with unlimited public transport.

RESPONSIBLE TRAVEL

Positive, sustainable and feel-good experiences around the city

ON THE ROAD

Calculate your carbon There are a number of online calculators. Try *resurgence.org/resources/carbon-calculator.html*.

Feeling the heat Summer heatwaves are steadily increasing in Germany. Most accommodation does not have air-con; book rooms in lower levels and pack accordingly.

Going electric Consider renting an EV; charging infrastructure is very accessible in Germany (especially in northern states, where renewables are predominantly generated).

Diesel bans Text If you're driving within Berlin's 'Inner Ring', your vehicle must have a green sticker (indicating that it meets emissions standards).

E-scooters Zip around cities on pay-per-use e-scooters, bikes and mopeds. Providers include Tier, Voi, Lime, Felyx and Bolt.

Organic supermarkets Organic food is *Bio* in German; *Bio* supermarket chains include Denn's and Biomarkt.

Organic food labels In addition to *Bio* and fair-trade labels, look for the 'Demeter' logo for sustainable agriculture.

ABOVE: MYRIAM KEOGH/SHUTTERSTOCK
RIGHT: MAKASANA PHOTO/SHUTTERSTOCK

GIVE BACK

Support deindustrialising communities Inactive mines in the Ore Mountains have become sightseeing attractions.

Eat at restaurants with meaningful employment policies These include Munich's Kuchentratsch (p158; a cake cafe with baking from local pensioners), Berlin's Kreuzberger Himmel (refugee-made, Middle Eastern cuisine via a social integration nonprofit) and Freiburg's Zuka Solicafe (vegetarian and often vegan restaurant supporting disability and refugee training).

Purchase sustainable souvenirs Favourites include wooden toys (the Ore Mountains is famous for them; pictured above), handcrafted ceramics and locally upcycled clothing brands.

Volunteer in Germany Websites include **Go Abroad** (*goabroad.com*) and **Transitions Abroad** (*transitionsabroad.com*).

Cultural Exchange Project (*culturalexchangeproject.org*) Offers opportunities to teach, au pair and tutor in Germany.

WWOOF (*wwoof.de*) Help out on small organic farms during harvest, tending animals etc.

SUPPORT LOCAL

Check out a weekly Bauernmarkt (farmers market; pictured below) – every German village has one (usually in the central square). It's a place to bag not only produce but also regional artisan goodies (cheese, sausage, schnapps etc) and handmade souvenirs.

The ultimate Black Forest souvenir is a handcrafted cuckoo clock. Many workshops remain small family businesses.

Flea markets are not just for secondhand goods – artists also sell here.

LEAVE A SMALL FOOTPRINT

Visit the car-free Hiddensee Island Emissions-free nature abounds, from hiking to fishing and bird-watching.

Shop preloved stuff Flea markets and secondhand shops are ubiquitous; find everything from antiques to clothes.

Buy eco cosmetics at German pharmacies There are plenty of highly affordable, everyday brands.

Consider snowshoeing over skiing The Black Forest has famous trails.

Take a cycling tour The 260km Lake Constance loop is a smooth, dreamy ride for reluctant bikers.

DOS & DON'TS

Do recycle using colour-coded bins Yellow for plastic, aluminium etc; blue for paper; brown for organic (food) waste; black/grey for non-recyclables.

Do recycle glass By bottle colour (white, green, brown) in designated bins.

Don't recycle on Sundays/after 8pm Avoid noise.

Do return glass Items with the word *Pfand* near the barcode can be returned at automated supermarket machines for a deposit refund.

CLIMATE CHANGE & TRAVEL

Lonely Planet urges all travellers to engage with their travel carbon footprint, which will mainly come from air travel. While there often isn't an alternative, travellers can look to minimise the number of flights they take, opt for newer aircraft or use cleaner ground transport, such as trains.

One proposed solution – purchasing carbon offsets – unfortunately does not cancel out the impact of individual flights. While most destinations will depend on air travel for the foreseeable future, for now, pursuing ground-based travel where possible is the best course of action.

The UN Carbon Offset Calculator shows how flying impacts a household's emissions:

The ICAO's carbon emissions calculator allows visitors to analyse the CO2 generated by point-to-point journeys:

RESOURCES
bundesumweltministerium.de
germany.travel/en/feel-good/sustainability
transition-pathways.europa.eu
tourcert.org

UNIQUE AND LOCAL WAYS TO STAY

Germany has all types of places to unpack your suitcase. Outside of high season, holidays and major trade shows, it's generally not necessary to book your accommodation too far in advance. You also may get a better rate if you're staying more than one night. Airbnbs are becoming more regulated and less available, but holiday rentals are still possible to find elsewhere.

HOW MUCH FOR A...

A hostel dorm
€25-40

A tent site
€15

A luxury seaside resort
€350

BUDGET STAYS vary considerably between regions, cities and rural areas. A romantic B&B suite in a countryside inn in the Bavarian forest may cost the same as a two-star room in Munich – always do your research before booking. Budget lodgings in Germany include hostels, *Gasthof* (inns with a traditional restaurant), *Ferienwohnung* (holiday apartments) and *Pensions*, the German equivalent of B&Bs or small hotels (independent, often family-owned). Most low-cost options are best perused at third-party-aggregator websites. Room sizes and decor vary; cheaper options have shared facilities. Lack of amenities is made up for in fair price and friendly service.

CAMPING SEASON generally runs from May to September. Campgrounds are well-kept, usually with great amenities, though in summer they get jam-packed – book ahead. Having your own wheels for remote locations is advised. Many campgrounds offer parked (non-drivable) RVs and permanent tents as 'glamping' options (check third-party websites). Camping on public land is forbidden.

DJH HOSTELS

Germany's 500-plus **Deutsches Jugendherbergswerk** *(DJH; jugendherberge.de)* hostels are for all ages. Beyond gender-segregated dorms, most have private rooms with bathrooms for families and couples. If space is tight, DJH hostels may prioritise families and under 27s. Special hostels include 30-odd remodelled castles and the world's longest hostel (a WWII site) on Rügen Island.

FARM STAYS

Family-friendly **farm holidays** (*Urlaub auf dem Bauernhof*) are a terrific (and inexpensive) back-to-the-roots experience. Kids get to run free and interact with barnyard animals; less-populated rural areas offer endless freedom to discover nature and enjoy quality family time.

Countryside accommodation (usually indicated with *Gutshaus* or *Landhaus* as part of the name name) ranges from bare-bones digs with shared facilities to manor estate rooms and fully furnished holiday apartments. Minimum stays are common, as is an *Endreinigungsgebühr* (final cleaning fee). Properties swing from organic, dairy and biodynamic to equestrian farms and even wine estates. Note that places advertising *Landurlaub* (country holiday) no longer actively work their farms.

Heuhotels *(hay hotels; heuhotels.de)* offer the option of literally sleeping in a barn on a bed of hay. These lodgings, unique to Germany, are typically found in Bavaria, the Black Forest and Lower Saxony. Some are on working farms, while others are run for seasonal tourism. Bring your own sleeping bag unless prior arrangements have been agreed upon.

If you're travelling in summer, book several months ahead. This is the most popular time to visit, though farm stays can be excellent in any season, whether in spring (new-born season, blooming fields, mild weather), autumn (mushroom foraging, harvest festivals and hay rides) or winter (cosy manors with fireplaces, sleigh rides, rural Christmas markets).

BOOKING

Local and regional tourism boards can be very helpful for finding accommodation; they might also make bookings on your behalf.

Book accommodation well in advance (at least two to three months) for weekends and school holidays (end of July to early September).

Bauernhof Urlaub *(bauernhofurlaub.de)* Family-focused stays on working farms.

Bed and Breakfast *(bedandbreakfast.de)* Find budget accommodation of all kinds (B&Bs, holiday apartments etc) and for all price points.

BVCD Camping Guide *(bvcd.de)* The Federal Association of the Camping Industry in Germany can help with camping questions and finding campgrounds.

German Youth Hostel Association (DJH) *(jugendherberge.de)* Germany's hostel network is Hostelling International–affiliated and has around 500 locations.

Germany Travel *(germany.travel)* Government official website for searching lodgings by region and type of travel.

Heu Hotel *(heu-hotel.de)* Sleep at a 'hay hotel' (literally, a barn with a hay bed).

Independent Hostels of Germany *(german-hostels.de)* Independently owned hostels.

Kindred *(livekindred.com)* Increasingly popular home-exchange platform.

Land Reise *(landreise.de)* Search rural stays around Germany, including mountain huts, farm stays and camping.

Romantik Hotels *(romantikhotels.com)* Network for high 'romance' independent hotels – heritage aesthetic, regional character and so on.

RENTAL RVS

Rent a candy-coloured VW campervan and hit the autobahn for the ultimate German road-tripping experience via **Roadsurfer** *(roadsurfer.com)*. The startup's fleet comprises 10,000 vehicles (from various car makers) across Germany.

ESSENTIAL NUTS-AND-BOLTS

SMALL TALK
Germans don't use 'How are you?' as a polite, casual greeting the way English speakers do. Just say 'Hello!' and ask staff your question right after.

LEGAL DRINKING AGE
Minors can drink beer or wine with supervision at 14, unsupervised at 16 and purchase alcohol at 18.

HOLOCAUST MEMORIALS
Look outside of apartment buildings for *Stolpersteine*: tiny brass plaques marking the former homes of Holocaust victims. There are more than 5000 in both Berlin and Hamburg.

FAST FACTS

Time Zone
GMT+1

Country Code
49

Electricity
220–230V/50Hz

SOCIAL ETIQUETTE

Being on time means being five minutes early. If you're running late for a reservation (even by five minutes), call ahead.

Men are expected to sit down when peeing.

Say *'Guten Appetit'* before eating. The proper toast with wine is *'Zum Wohl'* (to health); with beer it's *'Prost'* (cheers). Maintain eye contact when toasting or be 'cursed' with seven years of bad sex!

Respect 'textile-free' zones in saunas. Go naked, but have a towel to sit on.

ACCESSIBLE TRAVEL

Most public buildings have access ramps and/or lifts.

Historic villages with cobblestone streets present challenges; consider low-season sightseeing and accommodation not in the Altstadt (Old Town).

Accessible public transport includes grooved platform borders to assist visually impaired navigation, seeing-eye dogs being allowed everywhere and abundant electronic displays for the hearing impaired.

Reduced Mobility Rights (*reducedmobility.eu*) is a fabulous resource on accessible travel in the EU, detailing passengers' rights and air travel info, including a guide to Germany's largest and busiest airport, Frankfurt.

'Ground floor' is street level, with the 1st floor above.

Accessible hotels are wheelchair-friendly.

Some DJH hostels have access ramps and/or lifts.

Airbnbs/apartments are usually missing lifts/ramps.

Hand-controlled vehicles with wheelchair lifts are available from rental agencies at no extra cost.

Highway service stations usually have accessible toilets (no cost; just ask) and designated parking.

Wheelchair passenger assistance is provided by train operators.

The world's wheelchair-friendly capital for nightlife and clubbing is Berlin.

ALLERGIES & INTOLERANCES
Germany is quite accommodating. Menus are labelled with number/letter codes. Ask about hypoallergenic rooms and laundry.

HAY FEVER
The German Weather Service (DWD) provides pollen forecast. Northern Germany is renowned for its clean air.

SMOKING
Smoking is legislated differently in every state. Some bars, pubs and cafes allow smoking.

FAMILY TRAVEL
Playgrounds are everywhere – find and review them on the **Spielplatztreff** (spielplatztreff.de) app.

Water parks, splash parks, pools and Strandbaden (lidos) – indoor and outdoor – are popular in Germany and known for their great facilities.

Children under 15 travel free (accompanied) on local public transport and long-distance trains.

Long-distance trains have family carriages with extra space.

Rent a cargo bike with a front box in which kids can ride.

Beer gardens usually have play areas (a sandbox or jungle gym).

NATURAL REMEDIES
German physicians are big on naturopathy. Licensed *Heilpraktiker* (naturopathic healthcare professionals) can inform you about herbal treatments (typically organic and low-carbon sourced). You'll also find lots of options at many *Apotheken* (pharmacies). Antibiotics are often not prescribed on a first doctors' visit; you'll need to be insistent.

TOILETS
Marked 'WC' (said 'vee see' in German. Portable toilets are known as 'Dixies'. Look for 'pissoir' (public urinals) and female-friendly 'pussoir' at festivals and outdoor events. Restaurant and mall toilets usually cost €0.50 (sometimes only as a discretionary tip). Only flush toilet paper (old sewer systems are sensitive).

LGBTIQ+ TRAVELLERS
Pride parades and parties are July highlights.

Christopher Street Day (CSD) is the main event (named after the Stonewall Uprising).

Germany's largest Pride parades are in Cologne (over one million people attend), Berlin and Hamburg (pictured left).

LGBTIQ+ districts can be found in most cities; even smaller ones have at least one establishment.

Some door policies may allow only queer folks or certain genders.

Schöneberg in Berlin is the LGBTIQ+ scene's stronghold – find queer historic landmarks and lots of bars here.

LANGUAGE

German belongs to the West Germanic language family, with English and Dutch as close relatives.

In all but the most off-the-radar places, it is perfectly possible to travel in Germany without speaking a word of German, but life gets easier – and more enjoyable – if you master a few basic phrases. People are more likely to speak English in big cities, the western part of the country and in tourist hot-spots. Things get a little trickier in rural areas, especially in the former East Germany.

To enhance your trip with a phrasebook, visit **shop.lonelyplanet.com**.

BASICS

Hello.	Guten Tag.	goo·ten tahk
Goodbye.	Auf Wiedersehen.	owf vee·der·zay·en
Yes.	Ja.	yah
No.	Nein.	nain
Please.	Bitte.	bi·te
Thank you.	Danke.	dang·ke
Excuse me.	Entschuldigung.	ent·shul·di·gung
Sorry.	Entschuldigung.	ent·shul·di·gung

What's your name?
Wie ist Ihr Name? (pol) — vee ist eer nah·me
Wie heißt du? (inf) — vee haist doo

My name is ...
Mein Name ist... (pol) — main nah·me ist...
Ich heiße... (inf) — ikh hai·se...

Do you speak English?
Sprechen Sie Englisch? (pol) — shpre·khen zee eng·lish
Sprichst du Englisch? (inf) — shprikhst doo eng·lish

I don't understand.
Ich verstehe nicht. — ikh fer·shtay·e nikht

TIME & NUMBERS

What time is it?	Wie spät ist es?	vee shpayt ist es
It's (10) o'clock.	Es ist (zehn) Uhr.	es ist (tsayn) oor
morning	Morgen	mor·gen
afternoon	Nachmittag	nahkh·mi·tahk
evening	Abend	ah·bent
yesterday	gestern	ges·tern
today	heute	hoy·te
tomorrow	morgen	mor·gen

1	eins	ains	**6**	sechs	zeks
2	zwei	tsvai	**7**	sieben	zee·ben
3	drei	drai	**8**	acht	akht
4	vier	feer	**9**	neun	noyn
5	fünf	fünf	**10**	zehn	tsayn

EMERGENCIES

Help!	Hilfe!	hil·fe
Go away!	Gehen Sie weg!	gay·en zee vek

Call the police!
Rufen Sie die Polizei! — roo·fen zee dee po·li·tsai

Call a doctor!
Rufen Sie einen Arzt! — roo·fen zee ai·nen artst

Index

A
Aachen 224-5
accessible travel 248
accommodation 246-7, see also individual locations
activities 15, 18-25, see also individual activities
airport 238
Alsfeld 117
Annaberg-Buchholz 136, 137
Arbon 205
architecture 10-11, 74-5, 118-19, 126-9, 138, 166-7, 168-9, 223, 229
art 48-9, 96-7, 132-3, 152-5, 223, 230, see also museums & galleries, street art
ATMs 238
Augsburg 180
autobahn 37, 240

B
Baltic Coast & Islands, the 70-85, **72**
  accommodation 73
  drinking 73
  food 73, 84-5
  itineraries 32-3, 83, **32-3**, **83**
  money 73
  navigation 73
  planning 72
  travel seasons 73
  travel to/within 73
Bamberg 168-9
bathrooms 249
Bauhaus 118-19, 229
Bautzen 138
Bavaria 160-85, **162-3**
  accommodation 165
  drinking 165, 169, 183, 185
  food 165, 182, 183, 185
  icons 182-3
  internet access 165
  itineraries 28-9, 34-5, 179, 180, **28-9**, **34-5**, **179**, **180**
  money 165
  navigation 165
  planning 162-3
  travel seasons 164
  travel to/within 164
beer 20, 21, 36, 146-9, 169, 185, 220, 222-3, 230, 232-3
Berlin 40-65, **42-3**
  accommodation 45
  drinking 45, 64, 65
  entertainment 47, 65
  food 45, 62, 63, 64, 65
  icons 62-3
  internet access 45
  itineraries 57, 58, **57**, **58**
  money 45
  navigation 45
  nightlife 50-1, 62
  planning 42-3
  shopping 64
  tours 46, 47, 49, 65
  travel seasons 44
  travel to/within 44
Berlin Wall, the 58-9
Berlinale Film Festival 23
bicycle travel 67, 78, 170, 204-5
Binz 78
bird-watching 81
Black Forest, the 186-209, **188-9**
  accommodation 191
  drinking 191, 208
  food 191, 196-7, 209
  internet access 191
  itineraries 34, 205, **205**
  money 191
  navigation 191
  planning 188-9
  travel seasons 190
  travel to/within 190
boat trips 8, 55, 92, 98, 131, 212-13, 226-7
books 38
boxing 91
Bregenz 205
bridges 114, 173, 199, 211
Brothers Grimm, the 116-17
budgeting 239, 240, 243, 246
bus travel 241

C
cable cars 183, 184
camping 246
car travel 37, 240, 241, 247
Carnival 23, 231, 235
castles, fortresses & palaces
  Albrechtsburg 131
  Augustusburg 137, 234
  Benrath 234
  Charlottenburg 64
  Colditz 140
  Drachenburg 226-7
  Felsenburg Neurathen 133
  Festung Königstein 133
  Friedenstein 120
  Giebichenstein 111, 120
  Grüne Zitadelle 120
  Harburg 180
  Heidelberg 211-12
  Herrenchiemsee 184
  Hohenschwangau 174-5
  Jagdschloss Granitz 84
  Kaiserburg 167
  Kaiserpfalz Goslar 120
  Landgrafenschloss 120
  Linderhof 177
  Meersburg 205
  Moritzburg 131
  Neues Palais 68-9

000 Map pages

castles, fortresses & palaces, continued
  Neuschwanstein 173-4, 182
  Nymphenburg 150-1
  Pillnitz 131
  Putbusser Schlosspark 84
  Quedlinburg 111
  Residenz (Munich) 150
  Residenz (Würzburg) 184
  Residenzschloss 127-8
  Sanssouci 67-8
  Schwarzenberg 137
  Thurn und Taxis 171
  Vogelsang International Place 234
  Wackerbarth 131
  Wartburg 120
  Weikersheim 179
  Wernigerode 120
  Wittumspalais 109
  Zitadelle Petersberg 114
  Zwinger 128
cathedrals, *see* churches & cathedrals
Central Germany 102-21, **104-5**
  accommodation 107
  drinking 107, 121
  food 107, 120-1
  internet access 107
  itineraries 30-1, 117, **30-1**
  money 107
  navigation 107
  planning 104-5
  travel to/within 106
Charlemagne 224-5
Chemnitz 137
children, travel with 249
Christmas markets 22, 167
churches & cathedrals
  Aachener Dom 224-5
  Ägidienkirche 114
  Alte Kapelle 171
  Dom St Nikolai 76
  Dom St Peter 171
  Dom St Stephan 184

000 Map pages

  Eichstätt Dom 184
  Erfurter Dom 113
  Frauenkirche (Dresden) 128-9
  Frauenkirche (Munich) 158
  Katholische Hofkirche 127
  Kirche St Jacobi 76
  Kölner Dom 219
  Magdeburger Dom 111, 121
  Marienkirche (Greifswald) 76
  Marienkirche (Stralsund) 75
  Marienkirche (Zwickau) 137
  Marktkirche St Benediktii 111
  Münster St Georg 179
  Naumburger Dom 121
  Nikolaikirche 75-6
  Ost-West Friedenskirche 157
  Schottenkirche St Jakob 171
  Severikirche 113
  Schlosskirche 121
  St Andreaskirche 223
  St Coloman 174
  St Georgskirche 180
  St Martin Church 184
  St Michaelis Kirche 100
  St Nikolai Church 93
  St Peterskirche 158
  St Wiperti 111
  Stadtkirche Wittenberg 121
  Stiftskirche St Servatius 111
  Thomaskirche 135
  Wieskirche 175
climate 18-25
Colditz 140
Cologne 214-35, **216**
  accommodation 217
  drinking 217, 220, 230, 234
  entertainment 231
  food 217, 234
  money 217
  navigation 217
  nightlife 234
  planning 216
  travel seasons 217
  travel to/within 217
concentration camps 53, 120, 159
costs 239, 240, 243, 246
cruises, *see* boat trips

  cuckoo clocks 206-7
  customs regulations 238
  Cuvilliés, François de 151
  cycling 67, 78, 170, 204-5

D
Dinkelsbühl 179
disabilities, travellers with 248
Donauwörth 180
Dresden 126-9
drinking 14, 248, *see also individual locations*, nightlife
drinks, *see* beer, water, wine
driving 37, 240, 241, 247
Duisburg 229
Düsseldorf 222-3, 230-1

E
Easter 24
electricity 248
emergencies 242, 250
Erfurt 112-15
etiquette 37, 52, 248
events, *see* festivals & events

F
fairy tales 6-7, 116-17, 227
family travel 249
farms 61, 247
festivals & events 18-25, 114, 117, 131, 135, 193, 235
films 39
Flensburg 76
food 14, 36, *see also individual locations*
forests 60-1
fortresses, *see* castles, fortresses & palaces
Freiberg 140
Freiburg 186-209, **188-9**
  accommodation 191
  drinking 191, 208
  food 191, 193, 209
  internet access 191
  itineraries 34
  money 191
  navigation 191
  planning 188-9

shopping 192-3
travel seasons 190
travel to/within 190
Füssen 172-5

G

galleries, see museums & galleries
gardens, see parks & gardens
gay travellers 18, 51, 249
Gengenbach 208
Goethe, Johann Wolfgang
   von 108-9
gorges 171, 200-3
Görlitz 138
Göttingen 117
Greifswald 76-7
Grimma 140

H

haggling 243
Hamburg 86-101, **88**
   accommodation 89
   drinking 89, 92, 101
   entertainment 92, 99, 100
   food 89, 101
   internet access 89
   itineraries 99, **99**
   money 89
   nightlife 94-5, 100-1
   planning 88
   tours 91
   travel seasons 89
   travel to/within 89
Hanau 117
Harburg 180
health 242
Heidelberg 210-13
Heiligendamm 81
Herrnhut 138
hiking, see walking & hiking
historical buildings, see also
   castles, fortresses & palaces
   Albrecht-Dürer-Haus 167
   Alter Klopstock 111
   Alter Schwede 77
   Altes Rathaus 169, 182
   A-ROSA Altes Kurhaus 79

Bachhaus 120
Bauhausgebäude 119
Beethoven-Haus 235
Brandenburg Gate 57, 62
Chilehaus 100
Chinesisches Haus 68
Dokumentationsstätte
   Regierungsbunker 235
Fernsehturm 57, 62
Gildehaus zur Rose 111
Goethe Gartenhaus 108-9
Granusturm 224
Händel-Haus 120
Haus Muche/Schlemmer 119
Heiligen-Geist-Hospital 75
Historisches Rathaus 235
Liszt-Haus 109
Luther's Geburtshaus &
   Sterbehaus 121
Masters' Houses 119
Mendelssohn-Haus 135
Nietzsche Archiv 109
Rathaus (Aachen) 224
Rathaus (Hamburg) 92-3
Rathaus (Quedlinburg) 111
Reichstag 57, 62
Rote Flora 97
Siedlung Törten 119
Tränenpalast 58
Wohnhaus 108
Zeche Zollverein 229
history 9, 12-13, 52-53, 56-9,
   74-9, 108-15, 206-7, 224-5
holocaust memorials 52-3, 248
hostels 246

I

internet access 238, see
   also individual locations
internet resources 39
islands 64, 81, 83, 205
itineraries 26-35, **26-7**, **28-9**,
   30-1, **32-3**, **34-5**, see
   also individual locations

K

Kassel 117
kayaking 213

L

lakes 60-1, 184, 204-5
Landsberg am Lech 180
language 250
Leipzig 134-5
LGBTIQ+ travellers 18, 51, 249
literature 38
Lübeck 75
Ludwig II, King 176-7

M

markets 91, 97, 159, 192-3, 223,
   245, see also Christmas markets
medications 242, 249
Meissen 131
mines 136, 229
monasteries 111, 115, 171
money 37, 238, 243, see
   also individual locations
Munich 142-59, **144**
   accommodation 145
   drinking 145, 146-9, 158-9
   food 145, 158-9
   money 145
   navigation 145
   planning 144
   shopping 159
   travel seasons 145
   travel to/within 145
museums & galleries
   Adolf Hitler's bunker 53
   Albertinum 129
   Alte Nationalgalerie 54
   Alte Pinakothek 154
   Altes Museum 55
   Antikensammlungen 153
   Archäologischer Park &
      Römermuseum 235
   Audi Factory 184
   Augustinermuseum 209
   Auswanderermuseum
      BallinStadt 97
   Bach-Museum Leipzig 135
   Bauhaus Dessau Museum 119
   Black Forest Museum 207, 209
   BMW Museum 158
   Centre Charlemagne 224

museums & galleries, continued
- Checkpoint Charlie 58
- C/O Berlin 49
- Dachau Concentration Camp 159
- Dark Matter 47
- DenkStätte Weisse Rose 159
- Deutche Raumfahrtausstelung 140-1
- Deutsche Bahn Museum 184
- Deutsches Museum 158
- Deutsches Zusatzstoffmuseum 92
- Dialoghaus Hamburg 97
- Dokumentationszentrum Prora 79
- East Side Gallery 49, 58, 63
- Erlebniswelt Haus Meissen 131
- Europäisches Hansemuseum 76
- Fabrik den Fäden 141
- Fachwerkmuseum im Ständerbau 111
- Feuerle Collection 47
- Fränkisches Brauereimuseum 169
- Friedensmuseum 235
- Galerie Commeter 97
- Galerie der Gegenwart 97
- Galerie Eigen + Art 49
- Galerie Neue Meister 129
- Gasometer 235
- Gedenkstätte Berliner Mauer 58
- Gedenkstätte Berlin-Hohenschönhausen 46-7
- Gedenkstätte Buchenwald 120
- Gedenkstätte Deutscher Widerstand 53
- Gedenkstätte Haus der Wannsee-Konferenz 53
- Gemäldegalerie 49
- German Football Museum 229
- German Pharmacy Museum 212
- Glyptothek 153
- Goethe-Nationalmuseum 108
- Goethe-Schiller Archive 109
- Hamburg Bunker 93
- Hamburger Bahnhof 49
- Hamburger Kunsthalle 97
- Harry's Hamburger Hafenbasar & Museum 99
- Haus der Kulturen der Welt 65
- Haus Schwarzenberg 49
- Herzogin Anna Amalia Bibliothek 109
- Hijack 97
- Historisches Grünes Gewölbe 127-8
- Historisch-Technisches Museum 79
- Holocaust Memorial 52-3
- Humboldt Forum 57
- Industriemuseum Chemnitz 140
- James-Simon-Galerie 55
- Jüdisches Museum 65
- Jüdisches Museum Franken 184
- K20 223
- K21 223
- Kaffeemuseum 99
- Karl May Museum 140
- Kulturforum 49
- Kulturhistorisches Museum Rostock 76
- Kunstareal 153
- Kunstmeile 96
- Kunstpalast 223
- KW Institute for Contemporary Art 49
- Landesmuseum für Vorgeschichte 121
- Lenbachhaus 158
- Ludwig Forum Aachen 225
- Medizinhistorisches Museum 92
- Mercator Höfe 49
- Militärhistorisches Museum Dresden 140
- Miniatur Wunderland 99
- Monsterkabinett 47
- Museum Berlin-Karlshorst 53
- Museum Brandhorst 155
- Museum der Bayerischen Könige 175
- Museum der Bildenden Künste 140
- Museum Folkwang 229
- Museum Frieder Burda 209
- Museum für Kunst und Gewerbe 97
- Museum für Völkerkunde 140
- Museum Ludwig 221
- Musikinstrumenten-Museum 135
- Neanderthal Museum 235
- Neue Nationalgalerie 49
- Neue Pinakothek 154
- Neues Grünes Gewölbe 128
- Neues Museum 54, 62
- New Collection 155
- NRW-Forum Düsseldorf 223
- NS Dokuzentrum 159
- Odonien 220
- Ozeaneum 84
- Passat 84
- Pergamonmuseum - Das Panorama 54-5
- Pinakothek der Moderne 155
- Pommersches Landesmuseum 84
- Propyläen 153
- RAW Gelände 49
- Reichsparteitagsgelände 184
- Richard Wagner Museum 184
- Rombach & Haas 207
- Römisch-Germanisches Museum 221
- Sachsenhausen concentration camp 53
- Sammlung Boros 46
- Schiller Museum 109
- Schleswig-Holsteinisches Freilichtmuseum 84
- Schlossmuseum 111
- Schokoladenmuseum 220-1
- Schwarzwälder Freilichtmuseum 209
- SMAC 140
- Soul of Africa Museum 235
- State Gallery of Modern Art 155
- Sudetendeutsches Museum 158
- Suermondt Ludwig Museum 225
- Tankstelle Galerie 49
- Terra Mineralia 140

Teufelsberg 47, 49
Topography of Terror 52
Urban Nation 49
Verkehrsmuseum 129
Zeppelin Museum 205
music 19, 20, 25, 38, 114, 120, 129, 134-5, 185, 234-5, 235

N
national parks 8, 79, 81, 121
navigation 239, 240
Nazis 52-3, 56, 79, 159, 184-5, *see also* concentration camps
Neuendorf 82
newspapers 39
nightlife 50-1, *see also individual locations*
Nördlingen 180
Nuremberg 166-7

O
observation points, *see* viewpoints
Oktoberfest 20, 148-9

P
palaces, *see* castles, fortresses & palaces
parking 241
parks & gardens 46, 58, 60-1, 64-5, 93, 84, 141, 156-7, 158, 199
Pillnitz 131
Plauen 140
podcasts 38
Pöhla 136
Potsdam 66-9
Prora 79

Q
Quedlinburg 110-11

R
Regensburg 170-1
reservations 243, 247
responsible travel 241, 244-5
Rhineland, the 214-35, **216**
 accommodation 217
 drinking 217, 222-3, 230, 234
 entertainment 231
 food 217, 225, 234
 itineraries 229, **229**
 money 217
 navigation 217
 nightlife 234
 planning 216
 travel seasons 217
 travel to/within 217
rideshares 239
Romantic Road 178-81
Rothenburg ob der Tauber 179, 182
Ruhr 228-9

S
safe travel 242
Saxon Switzerland 132-3
Saxony 122-41, **124**
 accommodation 125
 drinking 125, 141
 food 125
 internet access 125
 itineraries 137, 138, **137**, **138**
 money 125
 navigation 125
 planning 124
 travel seasons 125
 travel to/within 125
Schiltach 208
Schonach 207
Schwarzenberg 137
ships 79, 84, 99, 131
Siebengebirge 226-7
SIM cards 238
skiing 141, 183
smoking 36, 50, 249
snowshoeing 194-5
social media 39
spas 133, 140, 208, 225
Steinau an der Strasse 117
Stralsund 75-6
street art 49, 219
swimming 208
Świnoujście 83
synagogues 114-15

T
Tauberbischofsheim 179
taxis 239
telephone 238, 248
theatres 129, 135, 185, 234, 235
time 248, 250
tipping 243
tobogganing 198-9
Todtnau 198-9
toilets 249
Torgau 140
train travel 239, 240
trains, tourist 131, 226, 235
travel seasons 18-25, 36, *see also individual locations*
travel to/from Germany 238-9
travel within Germany 240-1
Travemünde 78, 83
trekking, *see* walking & hiking
Triberg 207
Tubingen 208-9

U
Usedom 83

V
viewpoints 81, 92, 93, 99, 156-7, 173, 227, 235, *see also churches & cathedrals*

W
Walhalla 171
walking & hiking 61, 80-1, 132-3, 136-7, 141, 194-5, 200-3, 207, 224
Walpurgisnacht 25
Warnemünde 83
water 242
waterfalls 133, 199
weather 18-25
websites 39
Weikersheim 179
Weimar 108-9
wildlife 202
wine 21, 183, 185, 222-3
Wismar 77
Würzburg 179

Z
Zittau 138
zoos 141
Zwickau 137

GERMANY NOTES

'The first time I went on the Hasenhorn toboggan I remember thinking, why would I want to go on a kids ride? How wrong I was!'

KAT BARBER

'As a runner, I love pulling on my trainers and hitting the fresh, morning expanses of the English Garden before Munich awakes.'

MARC DI DUCA

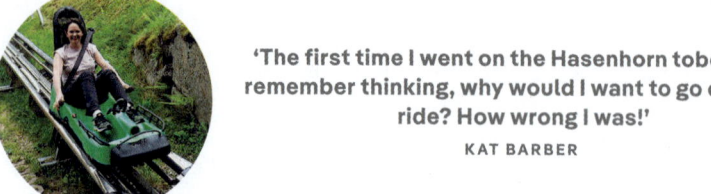

'Soaking in the radon waters of Bad Brambach was so pleasant...that I nearly missed the last train to Plauen.'

LEONID RAGOZIN

'No matter how often I visit, stepping into the Kölner Dom still gives me goose bumps.'

ANDREA SCHULTE-PEEVERS

'Northern nature is a perfect playground for little ones – my one-year-old and I played with acorns and pine cones, and picked berries and tasted them.'

BARBARA WOOLSEY

Although the authors and Lonely Planet have taken all reasonable care in preparing this book, we make no warranty about the accuracy or completeness of its content and, to the maximum extent permitted, disclaim all liability arising from its use.

All rights reserved. No part of this publication may be copied, stored in a retrieval system, or transmitted in any form by any means, electronic, mechanical, recording or otherwise, except brief extracts for the purpose of review, and no part of this publication may be sold or hired, without the written permission of the publisher. Lonely Planet and the Lonely Planet logo are trademarks of Lonely Planet and are registered in the US Patent and Trademark Office and in other countries. Lonely Planet does not allow its name or logo to be appropriated by commercial establishments, such as retailers, restaurants or hotels. Please let us know of any misuses: lonelyplanet.com/legal/intellectual-property.

THIS BOOK

The 1st edition of Lonely Planet's Experience Germany guidebook was written and researched by Kat Barber, Marc Di Duca, Anthony Ham, Leonid Ragozin, Andrea Schulte-Peevers and Barbara Woolsey.

This guidebook was produced by the following:

Destination editor
Sandie Kestell

Production editor
Will Allen

Cartographer
Valentina Kremenchutskaya

Image Editor
Jo-anne Riddell

Coordinating editor
Andrew Bain

Assisting editors
Pete Cruttenden, Kate Mathews, Charlotte Orr

Cover researcher
Valeria Suasnavas

Thanks
Wayne Murphy, Darren O'Connell

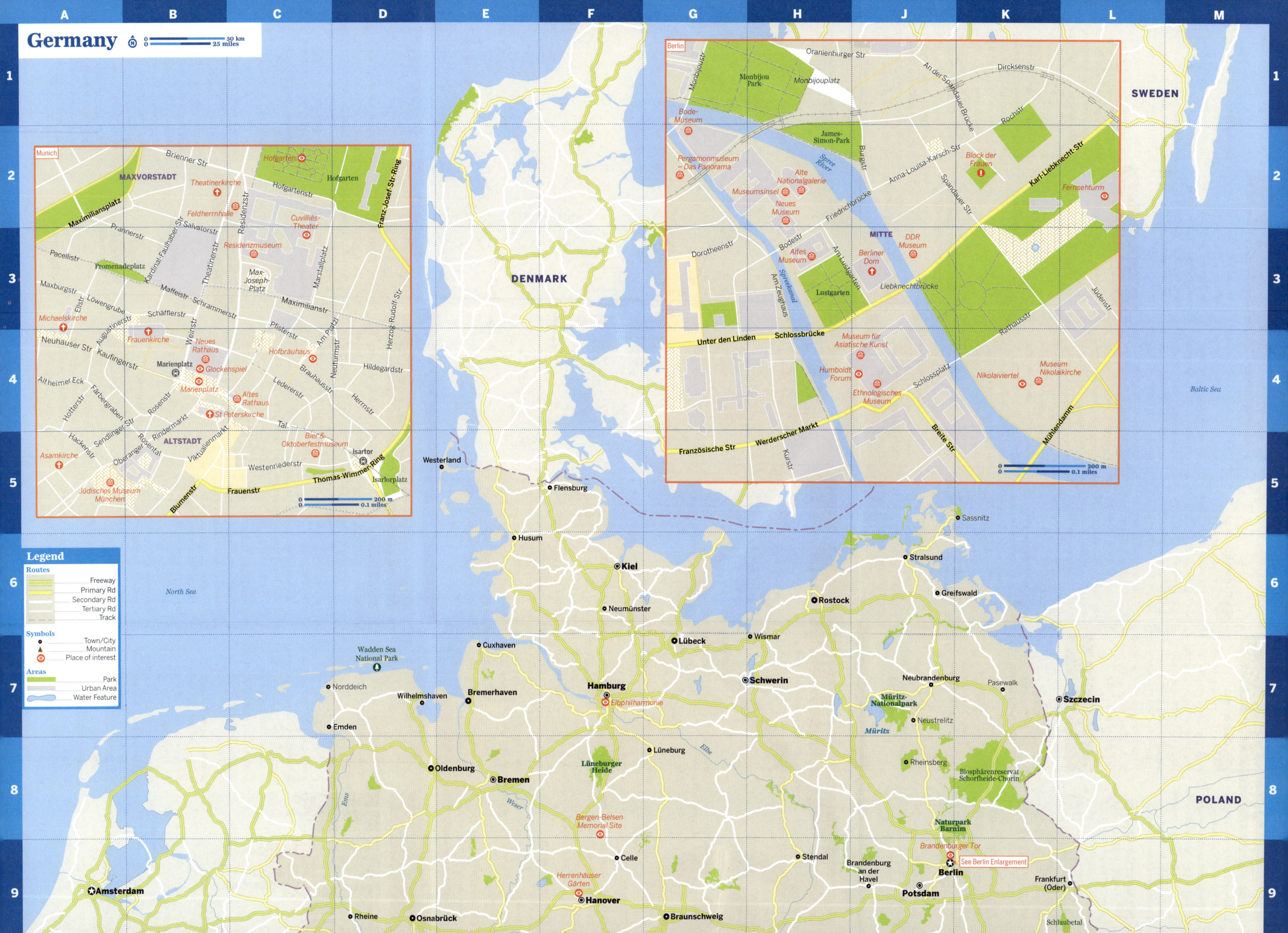

GETTING AROUND

Driving on autobahns can be satisfying for speedsters, although not as climate-friendly as trains. Germany's trains are frequent but pricey for last-minute bookings and busy periods.

Road Conditions German roads are excellent and no tolls are charged on any public roads. The country's pride and joy is its 13,000km network of autobahn motorways. Every 40km to 60km, you'll find elaborate service areas with 24-hour petrol stations, toilets and restaurants.

Speeding Fines Speed cameras are commonplace and pop up without warning. While you won't lose points on your home licence, the faster you're driving over the limit, the higher the fine. Rental companies process fines and automatically charge credit cards.

Car Rental An economy-size vehicle could cost anything from about €50 to €60 per day, plus insurance and taxes. Pay-per-use car sharing offers more convenience and flexibility, and these days you can pick a vehicle up right from the airport in a designated parking lot.

Ridesharing Carshare apps like Miles (miles-mobility.com) and Share Now (share-now.com) offer more flexible payment schemes (by ride duration or distance) than rentals. Sign up well before your trip as the approval process (ID and international driver's licence verification) can take time. Online carpooling providers like Bla Bla Car (blablacar.com) and Mitfahrzentrale (mifaz.de) connect drivers with passengers for long-distance rides.

Car Ferries Ferries connect Germany's two seas and provide convenient transport in its lakeland river-filled interior. Except when travelling to vehicle-free islands, car ferries are common and easy to take. Frequent ferries connect popular North and Baltic Sea islands; short-distance ferries shuttle passengers and vehicles along the Rhine and Elbe Rivers.

HOW MUCH FOR

EV Charging
€0.45–0.75/KWh

Standard rental car
from €50/day

Train ticket Frankfurt–Berlin
around €50

MONEY

Cash Cash is king in Germany. Always carry some and plan to pay cash at places like cafes and pubs. Since the pandemic, e-payments are catching on, but setting aside smaller bills for tips and emergencies is always a good idea. Barkeepers and kiosks may gripe about big notes.

Credit Cards A piece of plastic is essential for booking hotels and sometimes for reserving tables at high-end restaurants. In Berlin, a small yet rising number of coffee and nightlife joints only take electronic payments, too. Usually Visa and Mastercard are accepted (not American Express, Diners Club). At kiosks, a minimum purchase of €10 usually applies.

Tipping Hotels: €1–2 per bag/cleaning day. **Restaurants:** Most Germans will tip 5–10%. **Cafes, bars and clubs:** Simply round up to the nearest euro in

cafes and bars. Quality of service and setting definitely dictate how Germans tip. Say either the amount you want to pay or 'Stimmt so' if you don't want change returned.

Glass Deposit System In higher-capacity venues (think concerts, beer gardens, Christmas markets and nightclubs), you'll encounter Germany's Pfand (deposit/return) system. Ordering a drink in a glass, you'll pay a deposit (usually €1/glass) and get a plastic token. Upon finishing, return the glass back to the bar with the token for your deposit. At Christmas markets, people keep their Glühwein (mulled wine) mug as a souvenir.

Discounts Reductions on transport, shopping, attractions and entertainment are widely available for seniors, children and students. In some cases, you may be asked to show your passport or student ID to prove your age; driver's licences aren't generally considered ID. Many tourist offices sell **Welcome Cards**, offering discounts on museums, sights, tours and public transport.

HOW MUCH FOR

Kiosk beer €1.50

Toilet at train stations €0.50–1

Second-class train from Berlin–Munich €40

Train seat reservation €5.50

BERLIN WALL: THE BIKE EDITION

This easy Berlin bike ride retraces the echoes of Berlin Wall history between Prenzlauer Berg and the East Side Gallery.

Start Bösebrücke
End East Side Gallery
Length 13km; 2–3 hrs

1 Bösebrücke
Start at Bösebrücke, where the Grenzübergang Bornholmer Strasse became the first border crossing to open on 9 November 1989.

2 Mauerpark
Pedal onward to Mauerpark, now a buzzing hangout built on the former death strip and flanked by a 300m-long section of graffiti-covered Wall.

3 Gedenkstätte Berliner Mauer
Continue along Bernauer Strasse, where fragments of border installations and escape tunnels line the path through the Gedenkstätte Berliner Mauer.

4 Tränenpalast
Take a left on Chausseestrasse to arrive at the border-crossing pavilion nicknamed Tränenpalast ('Palace of Tears') because of the tearful farewells that took place here.

5 Brandenburger Tor
Minutes away is the Brandenburger Tor, the epicentre of jubilation and celebration following the Wall's fall.

6 Potsdamer Platz
Follow Ebertstrasse to Potsdamer Platz, where a few Wall segments evoke memories of when the city's widest death strip was here.

7 Niederkirchner Strasse
Head south on Stresemannstrasse, then turn left on Niederkirchner Strasse to cycle past a 200m-long Wall section.

8 Checkpoint Charlie
Keep going via Zimmerstrasse, past the legendary Checkpoint Charlie border crossing

9 Peter Fechter Memorial
Next you'll pass the Peter Fechter Memorial, paying tribute to the 18-year-old Wall victim.

10 Heinrich-Heine-Strasse crossing
Near the corner of Prinzenstrasse and Sebastianstrasse, you'll pedal past the site of the former Heinrich-Heine-Strasse border crossing, where mail and merchandise were processed.

11 Peter Fechter Memorial
Cross the Spree River at Schillingsbrücke and wrap up at the East Side Gallery.

FOOD & DRINK

Table Etiquette
Say Guten Appetit or Mahlzeit before digging in. To signal that you have finished eating, lay your knife and fork parallel across your plate.

If drinking wine, the proper toast is Zum Wohl (to health); with beer it's Prost (cheers).

Dine like a local
Table reservations If dining at trendy restaurants, especially at weekends, book a week in advance. Some fine-dining spots reduce their menu prices on weekdays.

Gasthöfe and Gaststätten (inns), cafes and beer halls can usually squeeze you in at a moment's notice.

Self-service Quite common in beer gardens.

Settling up Request the bill by saying Rechnung, bitte.

Splitting the tab Sometimes the person who invites will pay, but generally bills are split. To make sure, servers will ask, zusammen oder getrennt (together or separate)?

Tipping Gratuity is usually not included on bills and is a reflection of customer satisfaction. In restaurants, 5% to 10% is standard; cafes and bars, round to the nearest euro. Don't name the tip amount, specify the total amount you wish to pay (tip included) or the total change you want back. Stimmt so means keep the change.

Pubbing Around
Social drinking is deeply engrained in German culture, so much so that beer's known as liquid bread. In Germany, consuming alcohol in public is common, so a Friday Feierabend (what Germans call their time when a day's work is done) usually starts with bottle of Pils in a park or square – or even on the train home (though technically not allowed, it's normal).

Takeaway A beer-on-the-go is playfully called a Wegbier or Fusspils (pilsner on foot, but the word also means athlete's foot).

Convenience stores (known as spätis in Berlin and kiosks elsewhere) are popular hangouts for everyone (not just students) and sometimes even host DJs, dancing and football viewings.

Kneipen are old-school pubs with cheap beer, wooden furniture, darts and billiards, sometimes slot machines or a jukebox and very friendly locals. Diverse crowds whoop it up here too – in Berlin, some Kneipen even stay open around the clock.

Locals first A table marked Stammtisch is for regulars only. Buying rounds in bars is not usually a thing, though Germans might buy each other the odd drink or shooter.

Last call To end the evening, an Absacker (last drink) is customary. Leaving without saying goodbye is often considered rude.

HOW MUCH FOR A

Lunch special €10

Pint of craft beer from €5

Glass of wine €6

Words

Guten Tag (goo-ten tahk) Say 'good day' between 10am and 6pm.

Guten Abend (goo-ten ah-bent) Start saying 'good evening' after 6pm.

Auf Wiedersehen (owf vee-der-zay-en) 'Goodbye', but among friends Tschüss (bye) will do.

Sprechen Sie Englisch? (spreh-khen zee eng-lish?) 'Do you speak English?'

Könnten Sie mir helfen? (kern-ten zee meer hel-fen) Don't be shy to ask for help with a smile and this phrase.

Guten Appetit (goo-ten a-pay-teet) Even if you're starving, wait for everyone to be served and then say 'good appetite' before digging in.

Prost! (prawst) Use as a toast with beer. When drinking wine, the proper term is 'Zum Wohl' (tsoom voal).

Guten Morgen (goo-ten mor-gan) 'Good morning' is the proper formal greeting before 10am or 11am. **Hallo** can be used any time of day.

Winter travel Stay toasty with gloves, scarves, a hat, thermal underwear, warm and waterproof boots, plus a cosy coat.

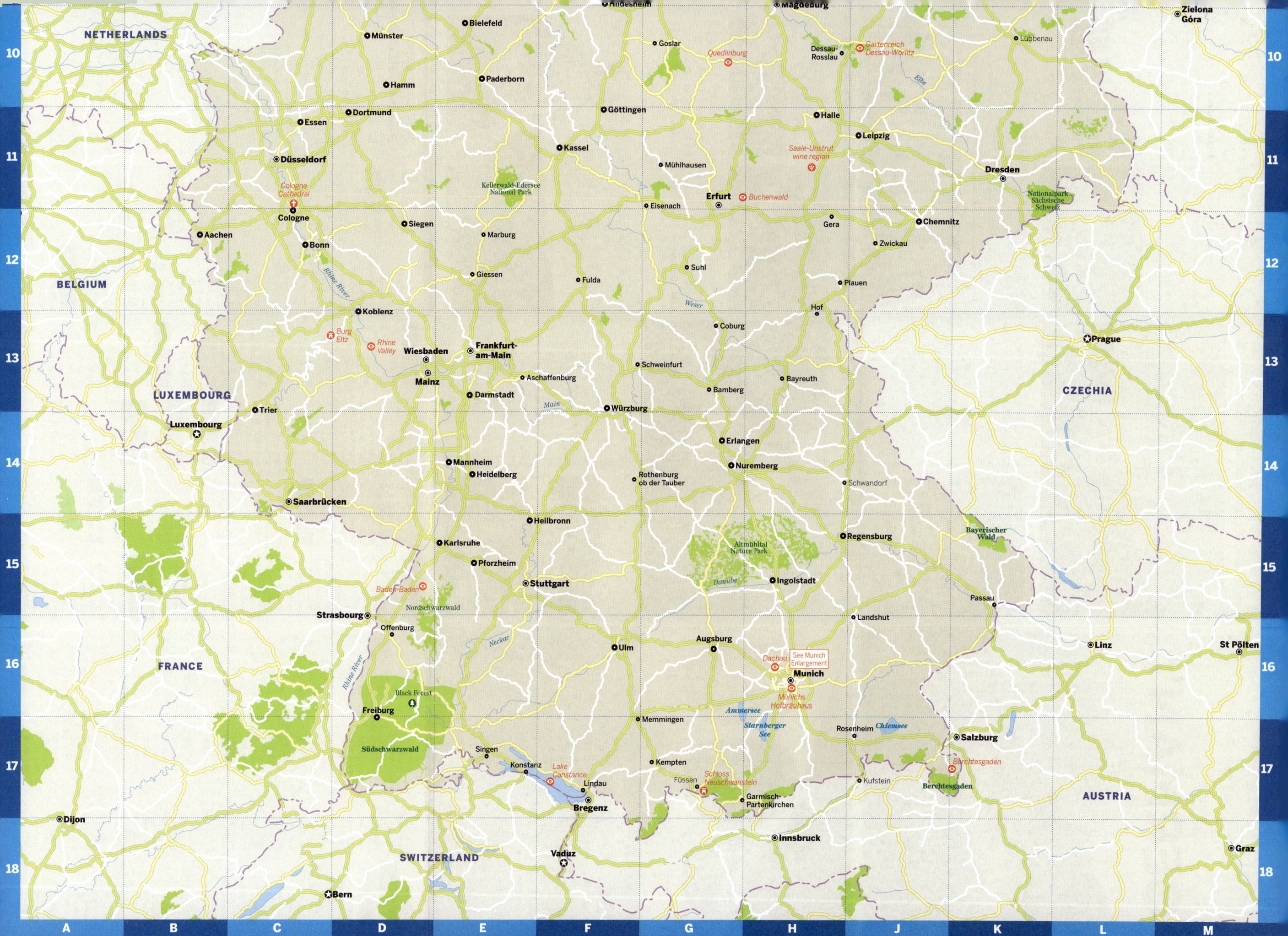

GERMANY MAP

Lonely Planet

- Must-see Highlights
- Travel Tips
- Cycling Tour

NEED TO KNOW

Opening Hours
Opening hours can vary seasonally and between cities and villages.
Shops 10am–6pm Mon–Sat.
Supermarkets 8am–8pm Mon–Sat (earlier in rural areas)
Cafes 10am–6pm
Bars 8pm–2am
Clubs midnight to morning
Restaurants 11am–10pm
Banks 9am–4pm weekdays
Post offices 8am–7pm Mon–Sat

lonelyplanet.com

OUR PICKS

▶ Soak up the magic of **Schloss Neuschwanstein**, a fairy-tale vision in stone that is cradled by Alpine foothills and inspired Disney's Sleeping Beauty castle. **G17**

▶ Escape the cities and drift around **Quedlinburg**, a medieval warren of crooked lanes and half-timbered buildings. **G10**

▶ Berlin's famous landmark, the **Brandenburger Tor** was trapped behind the Berlin Wall during the Cold War, before becoming an emblem of reunification today. **J9**

▶ Explore the striking **Elbphilharmonie**, the crown jewel of Hamburg's HafenCity, an old port turned vibrant urban quarter. **F7**

▶ Feel and bathe like royalty in **Baden-Baden** as you unwind in traditional Friedrichsbad or in one of its modern Caracalla thermal spas. **D15**

▶ Honour the souls of those tortured and murdered in concentration camps like **Buchenwald**, **Dachau** and **Bergen-Belsen**. **G11, H16, F8**

▶ Frolic around Hanover's sprawling **Herrenhäuser Gärten**, home to synchronised fountains and its whimsical grotto. **F9**

▶ 'Walk on water' during low tide in the **Wadden Sea National Park**, a mosaic of salt marshes, beaches and dunes. **D7**

▶ Quench your thirst while getting tipsy on the dry sparkling wine that is the hallmark of the wonderful **Saale-Unstrut** wine region. **H11**

▶ Walk, cycle or cruise through the romantic **Rhine Valley**, past vineyards, castles, wine villages and mythical Lorelei Rock. **D13**

GET PREPARED

Clothes

Layer like a pro Germany's weather loves to keep you guessing. Pack versatile layers, a waterproof coat and sturdy shoes for allweather sightseeing.

Comfy shoes Cobblestones and uneven pavements are everywhere. Opt for closed-toe flats with good grip to keep your feet happy and your steps steady.

Going out Smart casual usually does the trick, but for upmarket venues ditch the jeans and sneakers. Jackets and ties are typically only required in the most formal scenes.

City style Anything goes in cities, but if you want to blend in, remember that Hamburg, Stuttgart, Frankfurt and Munich tend to be more fashion conscious than, say, Berlin, Cologne or Leipzig.

GERMANY

Towns/Cities

A
Aachen B12
Aschaffenburg E13
Augsburg G16

B
Bamberg G13
Bayreuth H13
Berchtesgaden J17
BERLIN J9
Bielefeld E10
Bonn C12
Brandenburg an der Havel J9
Braunschweig G9
Bremen E8
Bremerhaven E7

C
Celle F9
Chemnitz J12
Coburg G13
Cologne C12
Cuxhaven E7

D
Darmstadt E13
Dessau-Rosslau H10
Dortmund D11
Dresden K11
Düsseldorf C11

E
Eisenach G11
Erfurt G11
Erlangen G14
Essen C11

F
Flensburg F5
Frankfurt (Oder) L9
Frankfurt-am-Main E13
Freiburg D17
Fulda F12
Füssen G17

G
Garmisch-Partenkirchen G17
Gera H12
Giessen E12
Goslar G10
Göttingen F11
Greifswald J6

H
Halle H11
Hamburg F7
Hanover F9
Heidelberg E14
Heilbronn E15
Hildesheim F9
Hof H13
Husum E6

I
Ingolstadt H15

K
Karlsruhe E15
Kassel F11
Kiel F6

Koblenz D13
Konstanz E17
Kufstein J17

L
Landshut J16
Leipzig J11
Lindau F17
Linz L16
Lübbenau K10
Lübeck G7
Lüneburg G8

M
Magdeburg H9
Mainz D13
Mannheim E14
Marburg E12
Memmingen F17
Mühlhausen G11
Munich H6
Münster D10

N
Neubrandenburg J7
Neumünster F6
Neustrelitz J7
Nordeich C7
Nuremberg G14

O
Offenburg D16
Oldenburg D8
Osnabrück D9

P
Paderborn E10
Passau K7
Passau J17
Pforzheim E15

Plauen H12
Potsdam J9

R
Regensburg H15
Rheine D9
Rheinsberg J8
Rosenheim J17
Rostock H6
Rothenburg ob der Tauber F14

S
Saarbrücken C14
Sassnitz K5
Schwandorf H14
Schweinfurt F13
Schwerin G7
Siegen D12
Singen E17
Stendal H9
Stralsund J6
Stuttgart E15
Suhl G12

T
Tier C13

U
Ulm F16

W
Westerland E5
Wiesbaden D13
Wilhelmshaven D7
Wismar H7
Würzburg F13

Z
Zwickau J12

Sights

Baden-Baden D15
Berchtesgaden K17
Bergen-Belsen Memorial Site F8
Brandenburger Tor J9
Buchenwald G11
Burg Eltz C13
Cologne Cathedral C11
Dachau Concentration Camp H16
Elbphilharmonie F7
Gartenreich Dessau-Wörlitz J10
Herrenhäuser Gärten F9
Lake Constance F17
Munich
Hofbräuhaus H16
Quedlinburg G10
Rhine Valley D13
Saale-Unstrut wine region H11
Schloss Neuschwanstein G17
Wadden Sea National Park D7

National Parks & Gardens

Altmühltal Nature Park G15
Bayerischer Wald K15
Berchtesgaden H16
Biosphärenreservat Schorfheide-Chorin K8
Black Forest D16
Kellerwald-Edersee National Park E11
Lüneburger Heide F8

Müritz-Nationalpark J7
Nationalpark Sächsische Schweiz K11
Naturpark Barnim J8
Nordschwarzwald D15
Schluchseital K9
Südschwarzwald D17
Wadden Sea National Park D7

Water Features

SEAS
Ammersee G16
Baltic Sea M4
Chiemsee J17
Müritz J7
North Sea B6
Starnberger See H17

RIVERS
Danube G15
Elbe J10, G8
Ems D8
Main F13
Neckar E16
Rhine River D12, D16
Weser G12

BERLIN

Streets
Am Lustgarten H5
Am Zeughaus H3
An der Spandauer Brücke J3
Anne-Louisa-Karsch-Str J4

Bodestr H3
Breite Str J4
Burgstr J2
Dircksenstr K11
Dorotheenstr G3
Französische Str J8
Friedrichbrücke H2
Jüdenstr L3
Karl-Liebknecht-Str K2
Kurstr H5
Monbijoustr G1
Mühlendamm K5
Oranienburger Str H1
Rathausstr K4
Rochstr K1
Schlossbrücke H4
Schlossplatz J4
Spandauer Str J2
Unter den Linden G4
Werderscher Markt H5

Plazas
Monbijouplatz H1

Neighborhoods
MITTE J3

Parks & Gardens
James-Simon-Park H2
Lustgarten H3
Monbijou Park H1
Wadden Sea National Park E4

RIVERS
Spree River H2
Spreekanal H3

MUNICH

Streets
Altheimer Eck A4
Am Platzl C4
Augustinerstr A4
Blumenstr B5
Brauhausstr C4
Briennerstr B2
Elisstr A3
Färbergraben A4
Franz-Josef-Str-Ring D3
Frauenstr B5
Hackenstr J4
Herrnstr D4

Herzog-Rudolf-Str D4
Hildegardstr D3
Hofgartenstr C2
Hotterstr A4
Kardinal-Faulhaber-Str B3
Kaufingerstr A4
Lederererstr C4
Löwengrube A3
Maffeistr B3
Marstallplatz C3
Maxburgstr A3
Maximilianstr C3
Maximilianstr C3
Neuhauser Str A4
Neuturmstr D4
Oberanger A5
Pacellistr A3
Pfisterstr C3
Prannerstr A3
Residenzstr C3
Rindermarkt B5
Rosenstr B4
Rosental B5
Salvatorstr B2
Schrammerstr B3
Sendlinger Str A5
Tal C4
Theatinerstr B3
Thomas-Wimmer-Ring C5
Viktualienmarkt B5
Weinstr B4
Westenriederstr C5

Plazas
Max-Joseph-Platz C3

Sights
Altes Rathaus B4
Asamkirche A5
Bier & Oktoberfest-museum C5
Cuvilliés-Theater C3
Feldherrnhalle C2
Frauenkirche B4
Glockenspiel B4
Hofbräuhaus C4
Hofgarten C2
Jüdisches Museum B4
Marienplatz B4
Michaelskirche A3
München A5
Neues Rathaus B4
Residenzmuseum C3
St Peterskirche B4
Theatinerkirche B2

Promenades
Promenadeplatz B3
Hofgarten C2
Isartorplatz D5

Railway Stations
Isartor D5
Marienplatz B4

Neighborhoods
ALTSTADT B5
MAXVORSTADT A2

Images by: Cecelia Kortscher/Getty Images, Aidin Kamber, Andrea Rohne, Buycrayola, Canadastock, Chris Rhoades, CMG_Q, foto-select, Glimpse of Sweden, Kittyfly, LianeM, Roman Babakin/Shutterstock

Meet our writers

Kat Barber
@katbarberwriter

Kat is an Australian travel writer who loves finding the best coffee, best views and best swimming spots wherever she goes.

Marc Di Duca
@marcdiduca

Marc has been a travel guide author for over two decades, covering destinations as diverse as Siberia and the Caribbean for Lonely Planet.

Anthony Ham
@AnthonyHamWrite

Anthony has been visiting Germany since he was a child, speaks the language, and has travelled the world to research and write nearly 200 guidebooks for Lonely Planet. He has also written two books of narrative non-fiction, including *The Last Lions of Africa*.

Leonid Ragozin

Leonid Ragozin is a travel author and a freelance journalist with long experience in the BBC and other Western media. His book about Russia and its war against Ukraine, *En Europeisk Tragedie*, was published in Norway in 2022.

Previous spread Königssee (p184), Bavaria
MARCO BOTTIGELLI/GETTY IMAGES

GERMANY

Kat Barber, Marc Di Duca, Anthony Ham, Leonid Ragozin,
Andrea Schulte-Peevers, Barbara Woolsey

▬ Explore villages unchanged in centuries. Visit storybook castles that leap from the pages of fairy tales. Become a child again in a Christmas market. Immerse yourself in urban German life, dynamic and contemporary. Follow in the footsteps of European cultural giants, from architects and writers to Bach, Handel and Brahms. Climb to the summit of storied cathedrals. Drift down rivers and hike through forests. Sample German beer in a humming beer garden. Try the marvellous best in regional German cooking.

This is Germany.

TURN THE PAGE AND START PLANNING
YOUR NEXT BEST TRIP →